Pug – Churchill's Chief of Staff

Pug – Churchill's Chief of Staff

The Life of General Hastings Ismay KG GCB CH DSO PC, 1887–1965

Andrew Sangster

Pen & Sword
MILITARY

First published in Great Britain in 2023 by
Pen & Sword Military
An imprint of
Pen & Sword Books Ltd
Yorkshire – Philadelphia

Copyright © Andrew Sangster 2023

ISBN 978 1 39904 577 3

The right of Andrew Sangster to be identified as Author of this work has been asserted by him in accordance with the Copyright, Designs and Patents Act 1988.

A CIP catalogue record for this book is available from the British Library.

All rights reserved. No part of this book may be reproduced or transmitted in any form or by any means, electronic or mechanical including photocopying, recording or by any information storage and retrieval system, without permission from the Publisher in writing.

Typeset by Mac Style
Printed in the UK by CPI Group (UK) Ltd, Croydon, CR0 4YY.

Pen & Sword Books Limited incorporates the imprints of Atlas, Archaeology, Aviation, Discovery, Family History, Fiction, History, Maritime, Military, Military Classics, Politics, Select, Transport, True Crime, Air World, Frontline Publishing, Leo Cooper, Remember When, Seaforth Publishing, The Praetorian Press, Wharncliffe Local History, Wharncliffe Transport, Wharncliffe True Crime, White Owl and After the Battle.

For a complete list of Pen & Sword titles please contact

PEN & SWORD BOOKS LIMITED
47 Church Street, Barnsley, South Yorkshire, S70 2AS, England
E-mail: enquiries@pen-and-sword.co.uk
Website: www.pen-and-sword.co.uk

Or

PEN AND SWORD BOOKS
1950 Lawrence Rd, Havertown, PA 19083, USA
E-mail: Uspen-and-sword@casematepublishers.com
Website: www.penandswordbooks.com

Contents

Preface vii
Introduction ix

Part I: India to the War Office 1

Chapter 1	From Cradle to the North-West Frontier	3
Chapter 2	The Somaliland Camel Corps	7
Chapter 3	1920–1925, Staff Training and Marriage	12
Chapter 4	1925–1930, The Seats of Power	16
Chapter 5	1930–36, To India and Back to War Office	19
Chapter 6	1936–9, How Serious?	23

Part II: Second World War 29

Chapter 1	September 1939–May 1940, Chamberlain Years	31
Chapter 2	May 1940 to May 1941, Disaster to Hope	39
Chapter 3	June, 1941–1942, Three Problem Areas	60
Chapter 4	1943, The Year of Conferences	72
Chapter 5	1944, Overlord and More Conferences	90
Chapter 6	1945, Yalta and the End of the Road	102

Part III: India, Nato, and Other Posts 111

Chapter 1	1947, Post War and India	113
Chapter 2	1948–1952, Some Minor Roles	135
Chapter 3	1952–7, Secretary General to NATO,	142

Chapter 4	Retirement	157
Chapter 5	Churchill and Pug	163
Chapter 6	Contemporaries and their Insights	170
Chapter 7	Final Words on Pug Ismay	190

Notes   199
Bibliography   211
Abbreviations   213
Index   215

Preface

General Hastings Ismay seldom emerges in popular history books, always hovering somewhere in the background and for many he remains an unknown person. Everyone who knew him called him by his nickname 'Pug' in an affectionate way. The name 'Pug' was not cynical or demeaning, and as such this writer has chosen to use his nickname throughout the text because it proved impossible not to appreciate his character. Having written about Goebbels, Himmler, Göring, Franco, and even the head of the Soviet secret police Beria, it felt like a pleasant holiday researching this enigmatic military bureaucrat. Pug has left his memoirs, although he barely mentions his last post with NATO, and there was one biography written about him over half a century ago. It was possible to find out more about him in the archives of King's College London, and even in the *Foreign Relations of the United States* files in America than in any published material.

Pug started life fighting tribesmen on the Northwest frontier of India and never saw combat in the Great War as he was fighting Somali Dervishes from the back of a camel. He worked his way through an army college in India, became a minor bureaucrat in the War Office, and assisted a Viceroy in India. However, from 1939 his position changed from these minor roles to those of significant importance, raising the question as to how and why this seemingly insignificant beginning should lead him so close to the top of the national leadership, which concluded with him having an international reputation. It was in business terms the same as asking how the caretaker was suddenly elevated to the board of management, or in church terms how did an assistant curate become a suffragan bishop overnight. Pug managed a close friendship with Britain's most famous Prime Minister, Winston Churchill, as well as with Eisenhower even when President of the United States of America. The question of his rise from insignificance was not truly resolved in this writer's mind until the closing moments of research, when it became apparent it all had to do with personality.

From 1939 Pug held three highly significant posts which cast him onto the international stage, though seldom were the floodlights focused on him. First, he was one of the very few men who held the same post for the duration of the Second World War as Churchill's Chief of Staff, where only those at the top really understood his importance. He was regarded by many as a mere backroom bureaucrat who wore an army uniform, but he proved indispensable to Churchill and many others as this book will explore. After the war he remained a close friend of Churchill, helped him write his six-volume history, served on his cabinet when he returned to power, and was consulted constantly by Churchill as well as Clement Attlee. For a time he was considered for the post of Viceroy to India preparing the way to independence, but Mountbatten was selected, and Pug in his second significant post, travelled with him as his Chief of Staff and witnessed the devastating process of the partitioning of India and Pakistan, and his insights were curious and perceptive. On his return Attlee asked him to be chairman of the Council for the Festival of Britain, then Churchill made him Secretary of State for Commonwealth Relations. However, in 1952 he took on his third significant task when he was appointed Secretary-General of NATO helping to forge the Western defence during the early Cold War years, which was a vital time for the foundations of NATO.

All this from a soldier who started life as a mere subaltern battling tribesmen from his horse, missing the Great War because he was fighting Dervishes from the back of a camel. This book will explore not only his life, what others thought about him, but why he was always selected to major posts. It was not just his hard work, his ability to communicate, his loyalty and trustworthiness, but an aspect of his character which this exploration will unfold as an insight into human nature.

Introduction

The Introduction has three sub-sections. The first explains the layout of the book including the chronology of Pug Ismay's life, the second part provides an explanation as to why he is barely mentioned in popular history, and the various sources, including major archives, where the information was gleaned. The final sub-section gives a brief sketch of Pug to cast some light on him and explain why he was worth exploring.

Layout of Book

In writing about a significant figure in history who is not a household name, it is often difficult to work out the approach and the most suitable angle to take. The book is in three distinctive sections, with Part One dealing with a brief look at Pug's background, school, and Sandhurst and next his life as a young soldier in India and then Somaliland fighting with the Camel Corps. He missed the Great War in Europe which was from a cynical point of view probably safer for him, attended a staff college for those with potential, and started to walk the corridors of the War Office in Whitehall, and after a brief stint working for the Viceroy Willingdon in India returning to Whitehall as the dangers of Nazi Germany were becoming evident.

Part Two explores his work during the Second World War, first with Neville Chamberlain and then with Churchill whose Chief of Staff he became. King George VI later said to Pug that only three people held the same post for the entire duration of the war, himself, Pug and Edward Bridges (head of the Civil Service and Cabinet Secretary) and given the strain of these years it was a remarkable achievement working alongside the often-tempestuous Churchill who frequently clashed with his Chiefs of Staff and their American counterparts. It was during these years that Pug was recognised and referred to as the 'oil-can' who soothed the way at fraught meetings, attended nearly all the major international conferences, met the world leaders, and somehow kept his stability and was so appreciated that he had hardly any critics following his years of service, which was remarkable, if not unique. He was often regarded as the 'bridge' across the stormy waters of Churchill's administration at home and abroad. He developed a close relationship with Churchill which lasted until death, always at his side even at the personal level. Pug all but venerated Churchill who in return trusted him, used him on many occasions, treating him as a confidante and friend.

Part Three of the book examines his post-war activities which continued until he was 70 years of age. He held some voluntary posts, but in 1947 he was asked to be Chief of Staff to Mountbatten overseeing India's independence. This led to the partitioning of India and Pakistan which proved to be an unmitigated disaster costing literally countless lives. When he returned, he held some minor posts, not least being Secretary of State for Commonwealth Relations. His hopes for retirement were dashed when in 1952 he was appointed Secretary-General of NATO, helping bring West Germany into the Western defence system during the early years of the infamous Cold War era, and made the work of NATO more publicly known and acceptable. In his memoirs he barely mentions this work for NATO for reasons which can only be speculative, but archival research in Britain and America revealed his role was significant. The next chapter concludes with his 'end-days' which were inundated with lengthy correspondence from others seeking information and his views. He was fortunate that his wife Darry (Laura Kathleen) was as committed and had the same sense of duty, because for years of their marriage he was often thousands of miles away and yet she always supported and encouraged him in every aspect of his work.

Part Three then explores his unique relationship with Churchill, one of business, occasionally difficult, but more often sheer pleasure if not fun, and which eventually transpired to be one of deep friendship and trust. This final part of the book explores how Pug was regarded by some of his contemporaries, selecting those who worked alongside him or observed him in action. In life when we hear a person's opinion, we often weigh the value of their views by who they are, begging the question of trustworthiness and therefore the value of their thoughts. If we want to hear about a leading politician or soldier, it is best to avoid a person who relies on second-hand hearsay or is bigoted, but someone who had met the person in question and has sound reasons to have an opinion in the first place, and whose words can be trusted. As an historian it is always tempting and necessary to find the denunciations of the subject being explored, not least to avoid the criticism of writing a hagiography, and Pug undoubtedly had his weaknesses which are noted. Eight people were eventually selected. Only one person (Lord Moran) was cynical about Pug but finding the views of politicians proved difficult for reasons ranging from them not understanding Pug's role, to their propensity to want to concentrate on themselves, a classical example was chosen in Harold Macmillan.

However, from reading the views of leading Americans such as Eisenhower, George Marshall, and even the Anglophobic General Mark Clark it becomes clear Pug was highly respected and appreciated. His British colleague General John Kennedy described Pug 'as one of the most remarkable men of the war', and Field Marshal Lord Alanbrooke with whom Pug frequently argued during and after the war remained on good friendly terms with mutual admiration. Two critical civil servants, John (Jock) Colville, Churchill's secretary, and Alan Lascelles (King George VI's Secretary) kept open and honest diaries, and their reflections proved to be both interesting and incisive.

The final part of the book takes a sweeping look at Pug, his weaknesses, his strengths, and attempts to answer the question concerning his historic value, and the very human question as to why such a person living through the years of turmoil of the Second World War, its aftermath including the start of the Cold War, could have survived as a person who was so widely liked and loved, making him 'one of the few'.

Historians and Sources

Twelve popular histories of these years were explored to discover the number of references to Pug. Together they amounted to nearly 10,000 pages, but Pug was only mentioned twenty times, a mere 0.21 per cent, but nine of these twenty references only noted his presence making it a more realistic 0.11 per cent. History books naturally take different perspectives and concentrate their efforts in varying areas. The more military inclined historian concentrates on field commanders and battles, others on strategy and tactics, some on international politics, some are more focused on one nation, while others can be nationalistically inclined. The historians Norman Davis, Liddell Hart, Max Hastings (in his second book), William Shirer, and Gordon Corrigan never mention his name at all.[1] Martin Gilbert in his huge volume mentions Pug three times but in passing, Andrew Roberts once, referring to when Churchill first commented to Pug that 'never in the field of human conflict was so much owed by so many to so few'.[2] Michel Henri refers to Pug once, describing him as Churchill's 'Military Adviser', and Gerhard Weinberg refers three times to Pug, twice just listing his presence, but one time quoting Pug from his letter to Wavell as he speculated on various people's thinking about Operation Overlord.[3]

Antony Beevor mentions Pug five times, twice because he was accompanying Churchill, twice making phone calls, one of which was to check that the Americans were correct when telling Churchill Tobruk had fallen, and the interesting time Pug communicated with his assistant over the phone in Hindustani in case the line had been tapped.[4] Max Hastings in his second major history of these years quotes Pug's reaction to 'the cringing subservience of Russian generals when he first visited the Kremlin in 1941'.[5] Unlike most historians Michael Burleigh has six references to Pug, and they refer to him for a purpose and not just listing his attendance at meetings. He relates Pug's account of a British soldier released by the Russians, quotes Pug's words describing Stalin, the way Churchill sought his views, how Pug advised him, outlined his role and explained the American Admiral Leahy's post with Roosevelt as being best described as that of Pug's relationship with Churchill.[6] Later, when helping Churchill with his memoirs in 1951, Pug acknowledged the same similarity comparing Leahy's relationship with Roosevelt as similar to his own work with Churchill.[7]

Burleigh is unusual, but with the enormity of events it is not surprising that Pug has so few references amongst most historians, despite the fact he was close to Churchill, known to Roosevelt and Stalin. He was not a field commander, did not make major decisions, did not appear to influence major events which begs the question as to why he is worth any attention. Historians of the war years 1939–45 understandably tend to dwell on the main events, and not those behind the stage curtains. In the early years of the war Churchill was a key figure on the world stage, becoming a junior partner to Roosevelt and Stalin for logistical reasons near the end of the war, but he was still deemed a critical man during this period of world history. As is generally known, Churchill was impulsive, often quarrelled with his Chiefs of Staff, never suffered fools, caused many of the tensions within the Anglo-American coalition, and while accepting Stalin as an ally he despised him and his form of communism. He often made himself ill through overwork, but not even his most hardened critics could deny his determination to win one way or the other. Churchill needed a man like Pug, not just as a 'whipping boy', but as a trusted and loyal confidant who frequently acted as a bridge, an intermediary between Churchill and his own military staff, a person of information, advice, often described as the 'oil-can' who smoothed the way, prepared the explanations, the arguments, the presentations, checked the speeches and reports, and through his staff could activate necessary decisions. Given Churchill's character, Pug was a critical cog in the machinery of war, but generally hidden from public and wider historical consideration.

The published sources for some understanding of Pug and his role arise from his own memoirs, his 1970 biographer who had the benefit of knowing Pug, and most importantly from the views of some of his contemporaries which will conclude the exploration of this unusual and generally unknown backroom general, this genial bureaucrat who was Churchill's bridge to resolve so many issues.

Another major source were his thousands of papers held in the Liddell Hart Centre, King's College, London. These invaluable archives reveal the family man, the sort of person he was, and to a degree explain how a man who had fought tribesmen on the Northwest frontier, and missed the Great War by fighting with the Camel Corps in Somaliland, could become Churchill's Chief of Staff during the whole of the Second World War, assist Mountbatten in the independence and partitioning of India, become Secretary General to NATO and hold many other posts when he really wanted to retire. The NATO years were further enlightened by the American archives checking their papers relating to their foreign policy in Western Europe. However, by all accounts he was an unusual person, significant in the parts he played, but generally unknown to the public and underplayed in popular history.

A Brief Oversight of Pug

During the Second World War he was Churchill's number one military bureaucrat and his personal Chief of Staff, remaining close friends to the end of Churchill's life. As noted in the Preface he was a member of the Camel Corps fighting in Somaliland and better acquainted with India and North-East Africa than Britain, and yet his critical years were alongside Churchill during the most dangerous times in British history. His journey to the Second World War makes Part One of this book more like a subplot, but it shaped the man who would mix with the main personalities of 1939–1957, and he proved to be a man committed to duty and service, from assisting Mountbatten in the independence and partitioning of the Indian subcontinent, to a minor role as a Secretary of State, then becoming Secretary-General of NATO during the early stages of the Cold War.

Pug was a sociable and amenable person, and he often regaled his friends during the trauma of the Second World War with stories and anecdotes from his unusual exploits in India and Africa. He loved talking of polo, horses, playing backgammon and described his dream of keeping his ideal cattle, Jersey cows. He was a born soldier but one whom civilians liked, with such men as Churchill's secretary John Colville, King George VI's Private Secretary Alan Lascelles, and many others, even including politicians even if, like Attlee they were of the opposite party to Pug's natural political inclinations, although this must be speculative because he always remained neutral in party politics. This determination to remain impartial added to his reputation of trying to be fair when he stood apart from the bitter Hindu-Muslim conflict. He was known for his hard work, his dedicated loyalty, especially to Churchill whom he almost venerated. He had a reputation for telling the truth, he dealt with many minor issues as a matter of honour and with major issues which historically have often passed unnoticed. As far as can be ascertained, Pug seemed to have no enemies, unlike many of his contemporaries, and this was undoubtedly because of his pleasant personality and charitable disposition. Colville recorded that the only person he ever heard 'speak ill of Ismay', was Moran, but then Churchill's doctor was well-known for being critical not only of many people but even of military operations.[8] Pug, on the other hand, could be critical of a person's performance but he was not known for speaking badly of another person.

Unlike General Brooke and many others Pug never kept personal diaries, his letters to his wife Darry tended to be personal but they offered occasional insights into his thinking. He was intensely security-minded, and during the Second World War and in the postwar period when he assisted Mountbatten in giving India and Pakistan independence, he kept no diary, and his memoirs provide only broad sweeps of the brush, avoiding personal criticism of others enjoyed by most people. In these memoirs he barely mentions his time in NATO. Much of his work must be gleaned from those who worked with him, from their inferences or an overview of his involvement in major events. Even in his memoirs it soon becomes evident that he was self-deprecating, humble in the best sense of the word, and apart from the enemy very rarely spoke or wrote unkindly about anyone. Most of the time he was full of praise for military commanders, the administrative civilians and even politicians on both sides. He was critical of Field Marshal Brooke for allowing his forthright diaries to be published after the war, but instantly balanced this criticism by adding that he was the best of all the CIGS (Chief of the Imperial General Staff) ever appointed.

Pug describes himself as a cog in the machine, he was Churchill's personal Chief of Staff and his top military bureaucrat who often acted as a bridge between the Chiefs of Staff (COS) and Churchill who frequently clashed. He must have been good in his work to survive the duration of the war and continued serving until he had turned 70. He was Churchill's source of information, his personal textbook for military details, often advice, and one of his tasks was checking Churchill's speeches on military matters for mistakes or omissions. He worked very hard and for long hours and was known for his gentlemanly disposition, for being kind and friendly, and this undoubtedly accounted for Churchill's affection for him. It raises an issue occasionally addressed in this study, that he tended to look at the past through rose-coloured glasses, and people and events as seen by Pug are not the same as viewed by many historians. Nevertheless, Pug produced some interesting insights into major and relatively minor events with some amusing anecdotes on the way, and which to one degree or another challenge some better-known historical insights, or he managed to paint the other side of a person or an event to give it a different perspective.

He was often known as Churchill's favourite 'Pug' and there is no doubt that he was intensely loyal to Churchill from the start of their relationship to the very end. According to one of Churchill's severest critics, after the war Churchill tried to cover up mistakes, one being his refusal to acknowledge the fiasco of Dieppe. While it is certain that the disaster resulted from Mountbatten's poor planning and over-enthusiasm, it is less certain as to how far Churchill was aware of the operation which had previously been cancelled. This critic, Nigel Knight, suggested that Churchill during the writing of his book had been told by Pug that he had recalled Churchill's knowing about the raid, but he was ignored and Churchill drafted his own version.[9] Whether this was true or not is difficult to ascertain, but either way it is certain that Pug would have stood by Churchill whom he virtually adored. There is no question that the failure at Dieppe pre-occupied Churchill's mind and following a difficult episode at Chequers with a bitter argument between Brooke and Mountbatten, it was Pug who tried to mollify the anger, then and later. Even in other people's bitter contentions Pug tried to smooth the way.[10] When after the war Pug had hoped to retire to his Jersey cows and live the 'good life', he continued to serve his country, and when Churchill was again elected to the premiership, he called back the reluctant Pug, who promptly came at his bidding.

As this exploration will reveal Pug's role was a technical desk job, or on the surface a minor one, heading a critical and efficient war administrative structure, and arranging the necessary secretariats for the famous war conferences and for many other important occasions. He was assisted by two deputies, Joe Hollis from the Royal Marines, and Ian Jacob a major-general, who were both loyal to Pug and efficient. However, the gift of Pug Ismay was in acting as a bridge between the one-time soldier and now politician Churchill and the military leaders in COS, and later the combined British and American COS, which elevated him, most agree, including Churchill, to a person of substance and historical interest. He was one of the few men who understood and respected Churchill's petulant nature in demanding his way even with the top military experts. He understood Churchill well enough to pick the right moment or mood to present a COS decision to the prime minister, which if given at the wrong moment could have explosive consequences. He was also capable as a fellow military man of being able to convey Churchill's views to the

COS in such a fashion they did not all resign. He was often the only man who could calm the unsettled moments in times of crisis, not just within the British camp, where he smoothed 'rocky relations between Brooke and Churchill'…as 'Dill managed for relations between Brooke and Marshall', but Pug always did his best to ensure the Anglo-American coalition worked.[11] He was such a mediator that later, when John Dill, the British military representative died in post in Washington, Lord Halifax, off the record, informed Churchill that Marshall had suggested Pug should be the replacement; Halifax warned Marshall that Churchill would not want to lose Pug and he was right.[12]

This book is about Pug the man, it explores his role as far as possible, the way he regarded matters, and reminds us that he was the archetype of the legendary English gentleman.

Part One

India to the War Office

Part One traces Pug Ismay's life from his family background, through school to Sandhurst and out to fight on the North-West Frontier. He reluctantly missed the Great War by fighting with the Camel Corps in Somaliland, after which he married, returned to India and attended Staff College. He had a brief spell in the Indian equivalent of the War Office (Simla), then to the London Whitehall War Office, hoping for a military command but was sent in a ceremonial military role back to India to assist Viceroy Willingdon. He was invited back to London under the guidance of Maurice Hankey, where slowly but surely his character and aptitudes were noticed, and by 1939 he became a key component in the war administration. From fighting tribesmen in North-West India and Somaliland, he had suddenly risen to be close to the centre of administrative power during the whole of the Second World War.

Chapter One

From Cradle to the North-West Frontier

Pug's father Stanley Ismay (1848–1914) whose family seat was near Sittingbourne in Kent, lost his family fortune through gambling, escaping the embarrassment by joining the Indian Civil Service where he could earn a living to the standards which he thought fit for his class as a gentleman. He was a distant cousin of the shipowner Thomas Henry Ismay, but despite his early problems Stanley rose through the ranks with a distinguished career and after his retirement became the Chief Judge of the Mysore Court and knighted. He had married Beatrice Eileen in 1875, daughter of Hastings Read of the East India Company, (she died in 1932) they had four children, thus Ismay's Christian name of Hastings, who was born 21 June 1887.

Unlike many of the typical British residents Stanley Ismay preferred India to England, and rather than return to his home country in old age as most did, he retired into the comfort of the India he now regarded as his home. Following their social class tradition, Pug was sent home to England for his education at the age of eight. There he stayed with his aunt Lady Mullaly at Stratford-on-Avon where he became part of her family with her four children, spending years away before seeing his parents again. He started his education at a private preparatory school, then went to Charterhouse in 1900 where pupils to this day are known as Carthusians. He did not present as overly academically gifted at school, and by his own admission being a sportsman was valued more highly, not that he played the traditional school games. He failed two scholarships which would have brought financial benefits, though he recalled that his housemaster thought it was an error, claiming he should have passed, saying that it was an 'exasperating miscarriage of examinations which happens often enough'.[1] Later, probably out of curiosity because he had started to write his memoirs, Pug wrote in 1956 to Mr Young the Charterhouse Headmaster asking for information about the so-called 'near miss' in the 1902 scholarship efforts, for which he received a reply.[2] It was probably mere curiosity as to why he had failed. His life at Charterhouse appeared, as with many other children, as 'an up and down life', somewhat like Churchill at Harrow, good in parts like the curate's egg, and a report on Pug's progress was written by a Gerald Davies detailing his character and progress taking up some fourteen pages.[3]

According to his memoirs his parents had wanted him to enter Cambridge and serve in the Indian Civil Service, but Pug had always wanted to join the cavalry because of the influence of the Boer War, which was typical of many young men. The boarding schools, especially during this era, were breeding grounds for military officers, politicians, the legal profession, and if necessary, the Church. According to Pug his father was upset that he could not enter Cambridge, but he passed in 1904 into Sandhurst with high marks. At school he had always been seen as a 'small boy', but at Sandhurst he filled out in size and his physical structure indicated the signs that he would become as hefty as his later photographs illustrated. According to his memoirs Pug grew another six inches in the two years after Charterhouse. He never found Sandhurst as much fun as Charterhouse, soon realising that it was not the easiest place to form friendships, as much of their time was spent training on the parade ground and learning to shoot. While there he met the future Field Marshal Gort and many others he would know later in life, but many of his Sandhurst associates were killed in the Great War. The remuneration for a soldier was not substantial, and Pug was desperate to join the Indian Army where it was possible to live off the limited income. To achieve this hope, he had to pass out in the top thirty and came fourth, clearly indicating he had improved in examination techniques since failing the scholarship at Charterhouse.

At the end of 1905, aged 18, Pug returned to India, spending a year with the Gloucestershire Regiment, nine months with the 33rd Punjabis then the 6th Dragoons. He was finally posted to the 21st Prince Albert's Own Cavalry (known as the PAVOs) at Risalpur in the North-West Frontier Province, raised before the Mutiny to protect the Punjab-Afghanistan border.* This frontier area was established on 9 November 1901 and later became part of Pakistan. Pug described himself as a 'bird of passage' as he was transferred one way and another before finding his home with the

---

* More popularly known as Daly's Horse raised by Daly in 1849.

21st Cavalry, Frontier Force at Jhelum, including his later appointment to Captain Oswald Dyke on 31 March, 1911.[4] This initial start of being shunted around from post to post he had found 'depressing as belonging to nobody'.[5]

Pug was still very much a young man but found his new home in the old Indian Army, which formed part of the Punjab Frontier Force (sometimes known as the Piffers) who were often active on the well-known North-West Frontier. Like others he had to pay £50 to equip himself, but with the promise it would be re-paid on discharge. He discovered that it was an old-fashioned family type regiment where it paid to have family connections in the past, and the colonel was more like the father of the family. There were some Indian officers who often acted as the link between the senior white officers and the soldiers. The Europeans held the highest ranks, and the rest were a mixture of Muslims and Hindus, but in those days the army unity held the adherents of these two religions together as they both respected the perceived warrior status. Whereas in the civil service there could be divisive moments between these two main religious bodies it was not the case in the army, as being a soldier was regarded as an honourable profession. Nearly forty years later Pug would watch horrified as the Indian Army was carved up on religious lines in the partition of 1947, and his memories of these early days in the traditional and religiously united Indian Army never left him.

It could be at times an active commitment, hunting down gangs of raiders and controlling tribesmen, both of which involved considerable danger. At one time Pug collapsed with sunstroke and spent time in hospital to recuperate, others died in the skirmishes. One danger which terrified Pug was his awareness of the common illness of cholera, writing that 'I am ashamed to say that I went cold with fear' as he would rather die in battle than waste away in bed.[6] Nevertheless, he loved India, especially the polo and social life, the hunting, pigsticking, spending his annual two months of leave visiting the sociable areas, and his parents who were now living in luxury at Ootacamund (often called Ooty, Madras). He met all classes of people, attended dances at Government House and played golf, but his love was focused on horses. In his memoirs he amusingly recalled his horse called *Drummer Boy* who was virtually uncontrollable until he came to the parade ground when he fell into line and performed precisely what was required at the right moment, behaving like some soldiers.

6 Pug – Churchill's Chief of Staff

Many officers in his position tended to join the Indian Civil Service as a career opportunity because their chances of army advancement were minimal, but Pug loved army life and was determined to stay. He began to look ahead to finding a place in the Staff College and started to read; later his breadth of reading astonished his friends and acquaintances. There were more movements for the 21st Cavalry but they tended to operate along the North-West Frontier, and at the age of 23 he became adjutant. This had been designated for an older officer who had been killed, nevertheless it was a curious promotion for a young man and indicated the esteem others felt for him. He learnt to speak the language common to the frontier known as Pushtu and spent four years as adjutant.* He was now thinking of his next step, uncertain of the future, blissfully unaware that the Great War was on the horizon, when he heard of a war brewing in Somaliland against the Mad Mullah where the British were fighting on camels and ponies. He was told by a friend that they were short of an officer in the Indian contingent, so he applied successfully for the post and paid off his debts before he left. He was a man who enjoyed action like many others of his age.

---

* Better known as Pashto, still common in north Pakistan and the official language of Afghanistan.

Chapter Two

The Somaliland Camel Corps

In January 1914 he received a letter from an adjutant called 'Tommy' which referred to Ismay's acceptance for the post, and in July 1914 Pug set sail for Somaliland in North-Eastern Africa, sad at leaving his comrades, but happy to be heading towards action.[1] However, on his arrival on 9 August he was dismayed to hear that a major war had broken out with Germany. He was not alone in feeling that he was missing a major opportunity as other officers applied to be returned to their regiments but were ordered otherwise. They were typically young men seeing war as a noble adventure, but although fighting tribesmen on the North-West Frontier or Dervishes in Somaliland was dangerous, they regarded this as a secondary role compared to the industrialised war and carnage developing in Flanders. In the same month he gathered from the regimental orders of the 21st Cavalry that he had been promoted to captain.[2] While in his new post he had many letters from old friends outlining the war in Europe, one from an Eric Dobs explaining what life was like in the Western Front trenches, and another from a Cecil Allanson in the Gurkha Rifles with an account of fighting in the Dardanelles, later describing its failure and his being wounded.[3]

Pug may have thought he was missing a great opportunity, which was hardly the case, but in his memoirs he tried to explain why the orders to fight in Somaliland were necessary, pointing out that the European powers enlarging their colonial assets had seized what was called British Somaliland following the Egyptian evacuation. Many men would die there upholding this assumed British territory, which ceased to exist in 1956, making it tempting to reflect on the loss of life in Afghanistan as the Western powers withdrew in 2021. Somaliland had not been a violent occupation and was peacefully managed by a British Vice-Consul from the coastal towns of Berbera and Bulhar, controlling a massive area of scrubland which was malaria ridden and largely unproductive.

Nevertheless, the British occupancy was contested by Sayyid Mohammed Abdullah Hassan, known to the British as the Mad Mullah, supported by a Muslim poet known as Salihiyya Sufi. He led groups of determined Dervishes, following the same pattern as those who had wreaked havoc in Sudan in 1885 (fighting General Gordon) under the Mahdi. Many perceived in this Mohammed Abdullah Hassan, another Mad Mullah. The Dervishes may have been mere tribesmen in British eyes, but Pug admitted in his memoirs they were good soldiers, and while others denigrated them as fanatics, the fact remains they were a committed and determined body of fighters who had decided the British were the enemy by occupying their homeland. It will be long debated by historians as to whether the Dervishes were driven by religious or nationalistic motives, or even the economic crisis triggered by European occupation and the colonial ramifications for their nomadic lifestyle.

The British decided to fight the Mad Mullah with a Camel Corps (and ponies) using a mixture of British and Indian officers and troops. Pug's many papers contained his messages detailing his pursuit and keeping track of the Dervishes, one from a remote area called the Dudub Pass passing on information and his intended actions.[4] He was an acting intelligence officer, and reported on descriptions of forts, maps, Dervish organisation, tactics, the leading figures, and even a genealogical background of the Mullah; it was a considerable document over 100 pages long.[5] The conditions were uncomfortable and dangerous, with long exhausting scrubland campaigns and food and water at a minimum, fighting against men who knew their land better than the occupiers.

Pug's immediate commander was Lieutenant Colonel Thomas Cubitt, and these years were marked by lengthy expeditions and patrols, trying to track down the various caves and fortresses where the Dervishes had made camp. Pug described an action in attempting to take a fortress at a place called Shimberberris in which he and fellow officers attacked the main gates under gunfire in which some of his colleagues lost their lives, with Pug noting that the Somalis were better soldiers than they had anticipated.[6] After this they were told by the government to put more offensive activities on hold because the war was going badly in France. Mullah's forces were weakening so Pug and his colleagues simply went on patrols to keep an eye on their whereabouts and what was happening. Pug kept copies of his many orders and observations which are retained in the archives, one from 'Major H.L. Ismay, Commanding the Mounted Column, to The Officer Commanding Troops, Somaliland, Burao, 26 April 1919', stating:

> In view of the very distressed condition of the ponies, I decided to retain only one troop, and the Lewis Gun section of 'C' Company, and to send back the remainder to BURAO. I also sent back all camels which had shown signs of distress on the morning's march.[7]

This is an interesting report showing Pug's sensitivity towards the animals in his care.

On 1 April 1919 in the *London Gazette* Pug was appointed as Lieutenant Colonel for his services with the Camel Corps.[8] After the Great War and with the armistice signed, it was decided to utilise the new RAF to finish the Mullah problem, who had already decided to move and in Pug's opinion probably trying to hide in Italian Somaliland. The resistant but now fleeing Dervishes were concentrating around an area known as Tale from where various reconnaissance reports were studied, including information that it was believed the Mullah was heading in that direction.[9]

The RAF were all too happy to demonstrate the power that planes could play following their actions in the Great War. There is a sense of annoyance in Pug's writing that the directions and orders came from the Air Ministry, which was an embryonic indicator of interservice tensions. Pug thought the plans were simple enough but not sensible as the Camel Corps had to wait until the planes had finished their task; he protested to no avail, and the Air Ministry remained adamant.[10] There were six aircraft, only one performed accurate bombing, one had a forced landing, and four failed to locate the target. The Dervishes took refuge in caves and the Camel Corps followed looking for information.* They chased some groups of Dervishes, but it was not easy and they suffered from lack of food.

The RFC (Royal Flying Corps which had become the RAF on 1 April 1918) decided it was a success, and despite Pug's reservations about using aircraft against tribesmen, it could be successful but brutal as Mussolini

---

* Hassan, the Mad Mullah, died on 21 December 1920 from smallpox aged 64; his grave is unknown but supposed to be near Imi in the Somali Region of Ethiopia.

was to prove when he took Ethiopia in 1936. The role of the RAF in Somaliland became in time something of a contentious issue, and the scrubland warfare was beginning to attract more public attention after the Great War. An article appeared in *Blackwood's Magazine* written by Sir Douglas Jardine, (Secretary Somaliland 1916–1923) drawing attention to this almost forgotten area.[11] This was followed by a book on the entire Somaliland war by the same author.[12] The debate over the role of the RAF became somewhat controversial in the early 1930s, often referring to the role of Hugh Trenchard, with disputes over the value of bombing compared to the more useful incursions by the Camel Corps.[13] As late as 1960 the debate raged on concerning the RAF contribution, in which Pug became involved with letters to the press.[14] He also wrote to the press with some criticism of the accuracy of a book written on the subject by Andrew Boyle.[15]

On 29 November 1920 a report in *The Times* mentioned promotions and rewards including a DSO for Pug which was further noted in the *London Gazette* the same day.[16] The Colonial Secretary Leo Amery also wrote a report commending the Camel Corps 'led by Colonel Ismay' and acknowledging the worthiness of the DSO.[17] The Dervish rebellion eventually collapsed and according to a report the Mullah died from smallpox either on 23 November 1920 or 10 January 1921, no one could be certain.[18]

It had not been a happy time for Pug who felt he had missed out on the Great War, which with the benefit of hindsight many modern readers may question. He may have felt cut off from major events while in the Camel Corps, and as early as April 1917 he expressed some unhappiness in which he described the feeling of no man's land and the possibility he might leave the army.[19] He had times of leave from Somaliland and stayed in England, visited his mother in India (his father having died in 1914), and was in continual correspondence with her during her lifetime. He tended in these letters to address her as 'My dearest little Mother', and usually with homely information, writing on 18 March 1917 'the mail eventually rolled up last Wednesday and brought news telling me of your safe return to the old home. I'd give a great deal to have servants like yours out here.'[20] He also wrote to her about the conditions in Somaliland with a frank honesty, referring to the Royal Flying Corps, the possibility of peace, the conditions for the soldiers, his eight-day trek, the problem of deserters, and by 1917 was explaining that his work was dominated by politicians and was unsatisfactory.[21]

Pug had also travelled to see Gallipoli to experience what he called 'modern war', but it was banned as a holiday venture as was France. He had attempted to join his old regiment fighting in Mesopotamia and they had tried to draw him back but to no avail. He had three leave periods, but he had no choice but to return to the Somaliland scrubland and deserts. It might be that Pug was disappointed in not being involved in the Great War, because he had become an expert on colonial tribal warfare but lacked experience in the new industrialised modern warfare of 1914–18, and he never held a command position under these conditions, and later would acknowledge that this was a serious disadvantage. As a typical young soldier he enjoyed excitement from the polo matches to the battlefield, but Somaliland had given him experience in organisation, administration, intelligence, planning and reporting, and although he probably did not realise it at the time this was to be part of his future. The experience of Somaliland never left him and years later in 1958 he gave a speech on the subject to the Royal Geographical Society.[22]

He eventually set sail for England in April 1920 feeling unhappy and somewhat frustrated at the last few years, mainly because he felt he had missed out in the main action of the German war, which were the feelings of a typical young officer seeking action. Today he could have been considered lucky because although he had faced death in Somaliland, his chances of being killed or seriously wounded would have been more likely on the Western Front or Gallipoli. Reading between the lines it seems that he was on the verge of depression, which was later confirmed by the London Medical Board who diagnosed him as suffering from extreme war-weariness, and he was given leave for a year.

While waiting at Aden he was offered a place at the Staff College at Quetta, and even considered resigning and responded with a polite refusal. Following a few months recuperating in the quietness of England he changed his mind about staff college and asked if he could be reconsidered; he had to wait but was given another nomination and permitted to sit the next examination in February 1922, and if successful he might be accepted.

Chapter Three

1920–1925, Staff Training and Marriage

Pug spent most of his time during his stay in England with his aunt, Lady Mullaly at Stratford-on-Avon socialising with her friends, and there he began his recovery from the years of strain and frustration. He became involved with her local social contacts and playing tennis, and especially with the Spencer Flower family who enjoyed the game at a higher level than socially. They were well off and backed by American family wealth, and Pug fell in love with their daughter Darry (Laura Kathleen) after a tennis match. It was reminiscent of John Betjeman's 1940 poem *A Subaltern's Love Song*:

> Miss J Hunter Dunn, Miss J Hunter Dunn,
> Furnish'd and burnish'd by Aldershot sun,
> What strenuous singles was played after tea,
> We in the tournament – you against me!

Within three weeks they were engaged, and while Henry Clegg her father approved, he was concerned about the Indian climate for his daughter, and the general impression that India was a dangerous place with disease, snakes and tigers. Nor did Pug have any substantial financial resources, but Henry Clegg's concerns about Darry's health were all too true because when eventually arriving in India she soon suffered from various fevers and developed hearing problems.

   The day after their engagement, four months into his one-year leave period he decided to report to the medical board again and informed the board that he was back to normal. He pointed out that he had another eight months of leave left, but they sent him back to India to join his regiment at Bannu on the North-West Frontier. His marriage would have to wait for his return in August 1921.

When he arrived at Bannu to join his regiment he described the mess as full of 'ghosts' as all his old friends were dead or wounded, and he was the only member of the 1914 polo team who could still sit on a horse.[1] The people and times had changed, there was now mechanical transport, no serious fighting, but he was free to indulge his love of playing polo and prepared himself for the anticipated examinations. These were held in Rawalpindi in February 1921, and it was the time when he first became aware of Gandhi and the subsequent riots as he travelled to the college. After the next war Pug would meet Gandhi and admire him as a person, but at that time he was regarded as a potential enemy.

He sat the papers finding the questions relating to the European war difficult to answer, but he was better prepared for questions on the nature of frontier wars and, as it transpired, he was successful. In April his regiment was moved to Rawalpindi, and he applied for the rest of his leave, and returned to England to marry Darry. It proved to be a happy marriage and Pug was especially fortunate in his wife as Darry proved an excellent companion in the years to come, always supporting him, often giving him advice, prepared to live with a man who spent months away at a time, and together they produced a supportive family of three daughters. He returned to India in the autumn where he continued to do little else but play polo.

In February he joined the Staff College at Quetta, enjoying his time and talking to other students in attendance. From his retained collection of notes and lectures it is almost possible to follow the main ingredients of the course. Various study conferences were called, one being about improving the discipline in the army.[2] Amongst his notes Pug took special interest in the attitude of the British public to soldiers, which until the Great War many had viewed as a bunch 'of swearing blackguards', with Pug concluding that the ranks needed more education, the necessity of providing entertainment, stimulating competition and officers taking the men into their confidence.[3] These were sound innovative ideas and although in the 1920s few believed there could be another world war, when it eventually came social class lost much of its significance as talent, intelligence and courage were all to be found in the ranks which had hitherto been regarded as 'gun-fodder', and a Public School background was no longer an essential requirement for officer class material.

The course offered a total survey of military history, building up to the Great War and studying strategy and tactics from the past and how they developed, with the need to look ahead. Pug made a collection of all the lecture notes adding his own comments in the margins or at the end of the paper. There were extensive lectures on the problems of the North-West frontier, with which Pug had some experience, and these notes were often covered by his own comments.[4] Famous historical battles such as Waterloo came under extensive study, but culminating in lectures on the Great War with the Commandant of the Staff College (Major General Sir Louis Vaughan) giving a talk on 'how to overcome the stopping power of the machine gun'.[5] Pug kept an extensive scrapbook of the course; the subjects of study were vast and wide-ranging and his 'memory-book' covered nearly 100 pages.[6] Most of the treasured papers he retained were the lectures, the plans and leaders of the Great War, which he had missed, indicating his awareness that he had a significant gap in recent military history.

Pug wrote a dissertation and in his memoirs admitted that his predictions on air warfare and armour were both wrong, as was his protest at abolishing cavalry, much of this intimating his absence from the Great War in Europe. He did however predict the possibility of total war which would involve military and civilians which was prescient. The Staff College Commander General Vaughan said it was 'a remarkable document. He was graded A, an officer of exceptional merit. I consider this officer one of the two best, if not the best of the students who have passed through my hands.'[7] This was a remarkable report for a man whose only experience had been fighting tribesmen and clearly indicated there was more to this man than his limited experiences.

Having been successful he wanted to do some duty in England, as he did not appreciate being separated from his young wife. He knew the opportunity was unlikely, and he stayed in India and was posted to the Quartermaster General's Branch (known as Q Branch) at Simla (Shimla) at the start of 1923. Here he had to come to terms with bulks of files, memos, administration, and sometimes wondering about their purposes, but he started to learn the process of understanding how a large headquarters worked. He found a small house at Jakko and met Darry at Bombay, and while working there he met two future Field Marshals, Claude Auchinleck and Bill Slim. The Ismays were invited by the Viceroy of India (now Lord Reading) and they had social contact with the upper echelons of Europeans and Indian society, but by now Pug knew his wife, as predicted by her father, was suffering from the Indian climate and developing hearing problems. Fortunately, he made an extremely useful connection with Air Vice-Marshal Sir Philip Game, who told him of a vacancy at a Staff College course in Andover for an Indian Army officer. In his memoirs he joyfully wrote 'Homeward bound'.[8] After all the years in India and Africa, England remained home for him. At Andover he did not become a pilot but learnt a great deal about air power theories, and later realised how important the Andover training was in appreciating the value of the air force.

Once again Air Vice-Marshal Sir Philip Game became a useful contact, informing Pug that his brother-in-law (Colonel Walker) was vacating his seat as Assistant Secretary of the Committee of Imperial Defence. Pug took the train to London, met the chief, Sir Maurice Hankey, was vetted and told any appointment depended on the Prime Minister. He then spent the next six months at Simla, before being summoned home in December 1925. He had left Darry at home and later with the help of Mrs Clegg they had purchased a small house.

Chapter Four

1925–1930, The Seats of Power

In December 1925 Pug reported for duty at the offices of the Cabinet and Committee of Imperial Defence. He described in his memoirs how he felt like a 'new boy at school', and it was different from his previous experiences, even in Simla.[1] He was to learn all he needed to do from Maurice Hankey (Secretary to the Cabinet) which pleased Pug who knew his mentor had an excellent reputation. He was not only entering a strange world for him, but for many today which demands some explanation.

Pug's new world focused on the work of the Committee of Imperial Defence (CID) which was still in its infancy. It was a small group of the top military leaders who offered advice to politicians about defence and possible military problems, connecting in a viable way these two essential elements for any democracy. In this role Hankey, as the Secretary, was the first to be allowed to join the political cabinet, and it was the first-time official records were kept. The Boer War had taught that there had to be a connection between the Cabinet, the War Office and Admiralty, with the need for the CID to advise the Cabinet. The Prime Minister was in charge and therefore free to invite others. For too long there had been an ongoing clash between the politicians known as *frocks* and the military called the *brass hats*. It was deemed critical that politicians and military worked together, and as Pug later noted, a house divided against itself cannot stand. The concept was tampered with during the Great War by enlarging the structure, but it was soon decided that the committee had to be small to make headway, and as such the new CID emerged from 1924 as an essential part of the national defence mechanism.

It was not always a band of brothers because of interservice rivalries, with the RAF becoming the third component along with the army and admiralty. Later during the critical war years General Alan Brooke would be the chief of the military committee (known as CIGS, Chief of Imperial General Staff) and his diaries exposed much of the interservice friction, but it tended to work well and was an essential component during the war years, though hardly known by the public. It was in this fraught area of easing interservice and military-political tensions that Pug would one day play a significant role.

Pug admitted his title of Assistant Secretary to the Committee of Imperial Defence had little meaning to his friends, even amongst his military circles. The work centred around Hankey who had four assistant secretaries, and they were all involved in the normal day-to-day business, or if a problem arose Hankey would give it to one of his assistants to follow the latest issue through. In addition to this work there were secretarial duties especially relating to the many sub-committees, increasing in number as various responses were needed for the ever-occurring latest crisis.

Pug had barely arrived when the 1926 General Strike emergency occurred, and various sub-committees sprang into life to work on the problems of keeping the country running. This emergency caught Pug's attention and amongst his collected papers in the archives are many of his collected press-cuttings relating to the strike.[2] Significantly, one of these committees was chaired by the Chancellor of the Exchequer, Winston Churchill with Pug appointed as the secretary making this the first time Pug encountered Churchill. He noted in his memoirs Churchill's powerful personality and direct approach writing that 'it had been a thrilling experience to see him in action'.[3] Pug wrote this in his memoirs and it would have been more interesting had he kept a diary, but later he would be averse to diaries if they became public. The issues which arose were varied for the committee, ranging from the perceived threat that Russia may be looking towards Afghanistan threatening the British Indian Empire, to the possibility of a channel tunnel between Britain and France which was quickly dismissed.

It was a five-year appointment which drew to a close during the final months of 1930, and it proved to be a busy and exhausting time, but looking back Pug realised it had 'broadened his horizons', he met many new friends and acquaintances and had 'grown in confidence' but was now looking forward to his 'horse rather than a desk'.[4] It was evident that Pug was generally liked as a person and had proved efficient, and he had even been invited to the exclusive gentlemen's club Brooks to lunch with Lord Esher, who had initiated the structure and work of the CID after the Boer War. Hankey told Pug he might be asked to serve again, neither of the two men believing that one day he would return as Chief Staff Officer to the Prime Minister. This meeting with Lord Esher and his relationship with Hankey clearly indicated that Pug was already being noted for his efficiency in administration, his general aptitudes and hard work. In Pug's own memory he recorded that at least during this year of 1930 the international sky was cloudless, but very soon the more astute would notice the upheavals in Germany.

He was due to return to India but after these busy and different five years he was given leave for six months. His contribution had been valued and he was gazetted in the Birthday Honours with the Companionship of the Bath, Civil Division. There was some confusing embarrassment because at the same time Pug was awarded the CIE which was an Indian Empire award for chivalry founded by Queen Victoria in 1879 (and last awarded in 1947). Hankey telegrammed him (1 January 1931) on the issue of two awards, and this was rapidly followed by a letter explaining there had been an error because these awards had been given for the same reasons.[5] It was evidently a cause of considerable confusion and embarrassment. Over a week later Pug received a letter from Hankey, referring to the award of both the honours of CIE and CB to Ismay, with a copy of a letter to Hankey informing him that it had been 'formally agreed by the King that Ismay's CIE should lapse'.[6]

It would be interesting to know Pug's reaction, but speculatively he would have taken this bureaucratic nightmare with a gracious smile. Nor had it been easy on the domestic front as Darry's much-loved father had died in 1927 and then two years later her brother Peter had died unexpectedly. Pug and Darry had three daughters, (Susan, Sarah, Mary) and during this time Pug had to spend considerable time at his desk and often working in the evenings. He and Darry planned a well-deserved break and had hoped to take a holiday in Florida.

Chapter Five

1930–36, To India and Back to War Office

Pug was hoping that he could take a military command but was warned that it was not the time for a few years, and that he would be transferred to the 12th Cavalry known as the Sam Browne's. As they were preparing for the Florida holiday Hankey suddenly called informing Pug that the India Office wanted to start their own CID, and the newly nominated Viceroy Lord Willingdon wanted him as his Military Secretary. Neither Pug nor his wife welcomed this idea, and Darry insisted he had to pass the medical board. Pug took this as a personal set back as he thought it might deny him the chance of a higher military command. He obviously raised this concern but was reassured that it was only for two years, and his promotional chances were safe. Like many aspiring army officers Pug wanted an active field command, but it appeared that his superiors during these interbellum years had discerned his organisational abilities and his friendly charming personality, and as such they wanted him in administration, or as in this case in a more diplomatic setting.

He left for India with Darry leaving the children with Mrs Clegg, travelling with Lord Willingdon and his wife, both of whom Pug liked very much. He rarely spoke ill of anyone because, like his contemporary Field Marshal Alexander, they were sincere gentlemen. It did not take him long to realise that his role was very different from any other post he had held, it was he wrote 'my first introduction to pomp and circumstance'.[1] He must have reflected whether Hankey had the wrong reading about the post or was putting him in a place from which he could be retrieved for future use, but naturally Pug never mentioned this in his memoirs.

A major aspect Pug appreciated about the new Viceroy Lord Willingdon was that he did not appreciate the social exclusiveness between Europeans and Indians, which had dominated British rule in India for far too long.

When the Viceroy was informed that Indians were not permitted to join or even enter the yacht club, he started a new one. Pug soon realised that his new role was a personal and ceremonial appointment, heading the various ADCs, and organising social functions with due ceremony. His military ambitions as suggested by Hankey never occurred, and even his title of Military Secretary was misleading. He only had to attend the Viceroy's executive committee when military subjects came under discussion, and technically he was the official link between the Viceroy and Commander-in-Chief. This aspect of his post was the embryonic link for his future, linking the leading politicians with the military command. However, the bulk of his work in India was simply overseeing the entire staff, all dressed in magnificent uniforms, organising official functions, and accompanying the Viceroy around India on his various visits.

The title Military Secretary had probably been dangled before Pug to encourage him to take on this purely ceremonial high-ranking post. He was responsible for the Viceroy's safety, but during his time there were no attempted assassinations. The potential threat of violence was an area of concern which could not be ignored, it was a time when, to use Pug's language, Gandhi was 'a thorn in the side' especially over his well-publicised hunger strikes. Despite Gandhi's pacifist demands there were fanatical would-be assassins who were waiting for an opportunity to strike, as Gandhi himself would later suffer, and Congress had made it abundantly clear that the British should leave the country. In later years Pug would be totally immersed in the sub-continent's political turmoil of independence and partition.

He had some consolation during this brief time in so far that he experienced more of India and met many people at all levels, and not just military figures. He continued with his love of polo, but fell off his horse and was unconscious and lost his hearing on his left side. He had several accidents playing polo, and the newspaper the *Calcutta Statesman* mentioned both his skill at the game and the accidents.[2] The day after this mishap they heard that Mrs Clegg had broken her thigh which transpired to be serious. In the days before frequent jet aircraft passenger carriers the sea-passage to Britain was long and sometimes arduous, and Pug's wife must have felt the anxiety of her divided family. Later she would suffer the same in her relationship with Pug on his endless global trips, but she was a wife of great fortitude and common sense.

The authorities kept to their word, and after two years in 1932 he was offered a first-grade appointment in the Intelligence Directorate of the War Office with promotion to full colonel, which he quickly accepted and left India to travel back to England. In May 1933 he reported for duty at the War Office as GSOI (General Staff Officer – Intelligence). They had not been back in England long when Mrs Clegg died because of her fall. With her father and brother dead Darry inherited everything, and they were able to buy a house in London and were freed from financial worries. Money was never part of Pug's life, and this sudden wealth made no difference to his lifestyle or his longing to be in the military. He had a solid and pleasant domestic background with Darry and his three daughters but was again steeped in the work of the War Office.

He found the War Office a very different experience from his work with Maurice Hankey in CID, discovering in his opinion that it felt rather overcrowded. When he mentioned this to his friends, they said he was too used to CID, and being a gentleman, Pug added that all the people who worked there did a good job and at times it was interesting. In this Intelligence department he had to collect, analyse, evaluate, and pass on information to the right people, especially in military matters. Technically Eastern Europe was his remit, but he was also involved in the Middle East, America and the Baltic States. This wide-ranging task given to Pug demonstrated at this time a weakness in the intelligence field. Even the Secret Intelligence Service, often known as MI6, did not have a series of paid trained agents but rather mere associates who could be contacted. The SIS was given no substantial financial support by the government and this 'was not remedied until 1938, when it was almost too late. The SIS was all but neglected and was expected to run quietly on a shoestring. The Foreign Office and the Treasury were not forthcoming in the interwar years, and the organisation had to work on minimal support.'[3] Until the mid-thirties their main concern had been Communism abroad and at home, and this had been reflected in the War Office which by later standards would appear almost amateur. Despite his massive responsibility Pug only made one trip abroad to Poland which he found uncomfortably nationalistic, hating the Germans, loathing the Russians, preferring the Austrians, which was understandable as Poland had a history of being partitioned, especially by the Russians. These were not his best years in the War Office, where the Intelligence work was somewhat archaic, but he did sensibly suggest a Middle East command in Cairo.[4]

On 8 January 1935 Major General William Twiss, the Military Secretary India, wrote proposing Pug's nomination as Director of Military Operations India; his gifts were being noted and he was sought after.[5] However, Pug was aware he was being considered in London and in April 1936 Hankey sent for him offering him the post of Deputy Secretary to the CID to assist him. The work was now intensifying because at long last people were waking up to the Nazi-German threat. Hankey explained that the Prime Minister had authorised the offer which meant the green light was immediate. However, Pug knew this meant the final break from active soldiering, and just at the last moment he received an offer from India for the command of the First Cavalry Brigade at Risalpur on the North-West Frontier. By now Pug and others knew the world was changing with the rise of fascism and war in Europe was becoming a distinct possibility. He felt he had little choice but to turn down the offer from India writing 'as I signed the letter, I felt a pang at the thought that my days of real soldiering were over. It was like saying good-bye to the dreams of my youth'.[6]

He would retain his military career, no longer from a saddle but as a backroom officer with a key to a mechanism which would grow in relevance and importance. During this time, he would become professionally close to Hankey and started to develop a deep understanding of the complex organisation in the central hubs of the War Office and Whitehall in general. He was trusted to give a lecture to the Royal United Service Institute on the organisation and functions of the Committee of Imperial Defence, which would have been checked by Hankey or even written by him, and later repeated this task prior to the next world war.[7] He was evidently accomplished at public speaking which would in later years prove advantageous to him and his superiors. The archives holding Pug's papers contain many of his speeches and lectures on a wide variety of important subjects, and indicated that he was totally trusted, that he could prepare his papers well and deliver them with aplomb and assurance.

Chapter Six

1936–9, How Serious?

In August, Pug returned to the office of the CID, which he wrote was like returning home, but he was returning as an older man, knowing that he had physically slowed down. Approaching 50 and still suffering from his polo accident, he admitted he 'preferred the lift to the stairs'.[1] The years 1936–39 gave a distinct appearance of uncertainty and instability. King Edward VIII had abdicated over his relationship with Mrs Simpson, but more pertinently the German re-occupation of the Rhineland had occurred and was barely noticed, Mussolini had invaded Abyssinia (Ethiopia) which had caused irritation and sanctions from the League of Nations, the Spanish Civil War had drawn protests from the left-wing and caused further destabilisation, there was more concern over the German *Anschluss* in Austria, and this was followed by the drawn-out Czech crisis in 1938.

In the Western democracies everyone was hoping for appeasement and always seeking for some form of escapism. It was not until Hitler defied the Munich promises and took the rest of Czechoslovakia and started looking towards the Danzig Corridor in Poland, that the rest of the world started to wake up to the imminent dangers. In September 1938 the head of the SIS (Secret Intelligence Service), Hugh Sinclair had sent Pug, then a colonel, 'a summary of certain naval indications which showed that Germany is preparing for a world-wide war', and hinting at Germany's plans regarding Czechoslovakia.[2] Because of his position Pug was privy to information making him aware of future international dangers.

Many people recognised the dangers of the Nazi threat, but few realised how serious the potential disaster was becoming. Sinclair also sent him suggestions about defence against enemy sabotage, with projected possibilities of action against power stations and transmission lines, as well as briefs on bacteriological warfare, the possible use of anthrax, foot and mouth, and the contamination of water and milk supplies.³ Downing Street like everyone else had the milk delivered on the doorstep, and Pug's attention was focused on these hazards. In his memoirs he noted that England had not re-armed as fast as others, calling England's previous stance a form of unilateral disarmament, which had been well-intentioned in trying to lead the world towards a general disarmament. There is a distinct hint that he was wearing rose-coloured glasses when he looked back, as many would point out that weak economics following the financial ramifications from the Great War and a victor's confidence had taken the focus off a possible renewal of international problems. This was why both the British and American armies were small with the forlorn hope that humanity would not repeat the industrial carnage of 1914–18. In many ways Sinclair's memos were a wake-up call.

During 1936 there had been growing suspicion by some on administration, and in Pug's world it had been decided that a new Minister of Co-ordination of Defence should be appointed to take the weight off the prime minister. Some anticipated Churchill would be brought in because of his military and political experience, but Stanley Baldwin felt it would damage the chances of peace; these were, of course, Churchill's wilderness years. The post was given to Sir Thomas Inskip who was a sound parliamentarian and a good lawyer, but he had no experience of national defence, prompting Pug to reflect on the then current rumour that this nomination was 'the most remarkable appointment since the Emperor Caligula made his horse a consul, which was a comment overheard in a certain club'.⁴ Pug later pondered whether with Churchill in this role he would have built up the national defences more quickly. He admitted it was not an easy task noting that when Lord Chatfield replaced Inskip in 1939 he also found it difficult. The men in this position needed a mandate from the government instructing that the defence of the nation was the top priority above all things, and to be given the authority and necessary money. As a body, politicians were too divided to reach such a decision and this also reflected the public who understandably wanted peace. Inskip's task, Pug noted, was not made easier by the service chiefs who were more concerned about their own departments than joint planning.

Pug was sensitive enough to note that when he re-joined the CID, the times were changing and referring to his previous imagery noted that there were now 'clouds in the sky'. However, in his new position he felt more at the centre of things, noting that Churchill was good regarding the shortcomings of defence and pondered whether he was trying to frighten the government to take more decisive action. Pug wrote that everyone regarded the Royal Navy as first class, and the French Army was the most powerful in Europe, but he personally 'felt an impending calamity'. He knew that the general feeling amongst the politicians was that unrest should not be stoked, and to avoid creating despondency and upsetting industry. Pug questioned whether Britain was now safe as 'Hitler had stolen a march on us'. He wrote this in his memoirs and whether he felt this at the time, or with the benefit of hindsight is impossible to fathom, except he was an unusually honest man.

The CID was concerned over many matters, ranging from anti-aircraft guns, balloons, RDF (radar), shelters and evacuation and looking back Pug was struck by the inadequacy and moderation of their approach. He was now at the centre of thinking and planning, and as chairman he had to produce reports to the Home Defence Committee in which he admitted that he was 'groping in the dark'.[5] He noted that dictators did not have to concern themselves about public opinion, whereas he had to contend with a variety of divided democratic politicians. He regarded the Air Defence Committee as important, and Churchill as one of the most vocal and imaginative members, (which was the first time he had serious contact with the future war leader), especially in the Research Committee for Air Defence where they had two major successes in their pursuit of radar and an eight-gun fighter plane.

Baldwin had once made the famous statement that 'the bomber will always get through' and although Anderson shelters and evacuation for children were planned, there was a fear that aircraft now made the English Channel less of a defence than it had been in times past. Much of this fear was based on the Great War experience and the work of the Italian theorist Giulio Douhet who wrote on the future theories of air power.[6] Douhet differed from other prominent early theorists by proposing that civilian populations should be directly targeted as part of the air campaign. It is widely believed the Germans had read his work and had built up their Luftwaffe based on Douhet's theory, that by bombing war-industries and the homes of the civilian workers this action would damage a country's military. Douhet claimed that it was a way of avoiding the 1914–18 war of attrition, but it created a genuine and understandable fear.

It was, as Pug admitted, difficult preparing plans for the unknown at this stage, not having firm evidence of the enemy, their intentions or when they might strike. It was carefully considered by the CID who concluded that they thought it would be Germany possibly backed by Italy and Japan, and they projected the date for the autumn of 1939. The first part was easy to understand because diplomatic circles were aware of the early machinations of the proposed Axis alliance, but their dating for the outbreak of war indicated remarkable prescience. Pug was equally aware that in the climate of the day the politicians did not want the public frightened, believing politicians were not living in the real world, but also admitting that there was nothing concrete as they tried to see into the future. Nevertheless, steps had to be taken for the defence of the British Islands, which included sufficient reserves of resources, the build-up of bomber strength, following Douhet's theories, and preparing a military force to go to France (BEF). Pug at the time was concerned that he had underestimated the issues, but he was relieved that his paper never left Hankey's desk.

It was also discussed whether there should be necessary accommodation for the CID and Cabinet in the event of a bombing war, projected accommodation was discussed and set in hand. In the event of war, it was decided to follow Lloyd George's idea of a small war cabinet. Pug proposed an Anglo-French Supreme War Council, and this was agreed with him being sent to France to talk to Gamelin who agreed with the policy. However 1937 ended with Pug feeling that Parliament and the public had little idea of the depth of the emergency. His thinking reflected today's problems that climate scientists know the world is on a self-destructive tangent, and the politicians and public pay lip service and little else, more concerned about the issues of the day rather than tomorrow.

As Hitler moved into Austria (*Anschluss*) Hankey told Pug he was intending to retire in July 1938 having been the secretary to the cabinet for twenty years; Hankey believed that the Cabinet and CID should have the same secretary. At first Pug was concerned he might not be considered as Hankey's successor, mainly because he knew the military personnel but not the politicians who held the power of decision. He even threatened to resign, but he was answered as to what else he could do because he was too late for the army, so he threatened to enter politics.[7] The decision was made in his favour and he emerged as one of the top bureaucrats in London.

Pug thought that the concept that the Cabinet and CID should have the same secretary might be a misjudgement, as they needed a soldier for the CID and a civilian for the Cabinet, even though they were supposed to have a common purpose if not identity. As it transpired, to Pug's relief the Prime Minster decided to separate the two appointments, with Pug to be Secretary to the CID, and Sir Edward Bridges to be head of the Combined Office and Secretary to Cabinet. On looking back Pug recalled that when Hankey moved out he 'felt lonely'.

It was during these months that the Sudetenland situation was beginning to boil. To Pug's astonishment Chamberlain decided to meet Hitler, with Pug at first thinking it was like going cap in hand to a gangster, but he accepted that Chamberlain was doing his best to avoid war. As is well-known Chamberlain had three encounters with Hitler and Pug, concerned about a possible failure, called up territorial antiaircraft units for the defence of London. He regarded these as elementary demands because if the enemy attacked 'I might be hung up from a lamp post'.[8] When Chamberlain returned with his well-known 'Peace in our times', there was a sense of overpowering relief. Pug's wife Darry was less happy and told Pug she was critical that Czechoslovakia had been sacrificed. This later caused Pug to ruminate that perhaps the West should have fought earlier, over which he would later talk to friends like Alan Lascelles and Jock Colville, but they pointed out that it raised the question as to whether the Commonwealth would have been supportive at such an early juncture, as it would have appeared much more like an aggressive attack rather than defence.

When a few months later Hitler occupied the rest of Czechoslovakia, Chamberlain realised 'Hitler was a consummate liar', and he gave a guarantee to Poland as Hitler turned his irredentist nationalistic plans towards Poland and the Danzig corridor. Chamberlain promptly doubled the size of the Territorial Army (from thirteen to twenty-six Divisions) without consulting the CID. Pug knew that during the interbellum years the army had existed on a hand to mouth basis and the land forces were too often regarded as garrison support for the navy, air force and colonies. It had taken to the year 1937 to change this view, which Pug 'hoped would show the world we were in earnest'. The army in Britain and America had been impoverished and reduced and a rapid build-up was essential, as would be seen in the coming years when the navy and air force had to protect amphibious landings because it would be 'army boots' on the ground which were essential for victory.

When Italy attacked Albania, Chamberlain also guaranteed Greece and Romania, which like Poland was impossible, and which Pug described using a later expression that 'the Cold War was on us.'[9] Time would show that Britain survived the war because of Allies, but these early promises have sometimes been described as immoral on the grounds that they were worthless, but many like Pug, perhaps rightly, believed them to be a matter of principle and integrity. He underlined this thinking when he recalled meeting an old German friend who asked what Britain could do to save Poland, Pug replied 'little, but as with Belgium in 1914, it showed England would go to war as a matter of integrity'.

In August 1939 Parliament was on its annual holidays when Pug then heard of the Molotov-Ribbentrop agreement (Russo-German pact), and he was as astonished as everyone else asking who would ever have believed these 'two gangsters could join!' The Secretariats of the Cabinet and CID were merged into a single body known as the War Cabinet, but Pug had a sense of guilt as he walked by the Cenotaph remembering the dead of 1914–18 'because we had allowed the Germans back at our throats'.[10]

These pre-war years had been so busy for Pug he had even stopped playing or watching polo, often working at home in the evenings on his various papers. They were difficult and delicate times as various experts tried to predict the future. On 2 September Pug wrote a personal letter to his wife admitting he had no idea what was happening in Poland, that if the French and British stand firm it will be a short war, and 'I am quite certain that whatever may happen at first, we'll come out on top in the end'.[11] Pug was not always right in his predictions, few are, but he was obviously a man who always looked forward with hope which was so necessary in those days, he was always a man of considerable optimism.

Part Two

Second World War

Part Three explores the war years 1939–1945 with Pug Ismay first serving Chamberlain, then as Chief of Staff for Churchill. Pug was at the centre of the war administration for the whole duration and was always close to Churchill. In this role he provides many insights not only into the events of the day, but also Churchill and many other people. His observations on Munich are interesting as were his views on the French during the Battle for France. His insights and anecdotes in walking beside Churchill during the Battle of Britain and the Blitz are enlightening, as were his meetings with other critical people both in terms of his observations and anecdotes.

His main role emerges as the intermediary bridge between the political leadership of Churchill and the military leaders, earning the sobriquet of the 'oil-can' as he smoothed the way forward, not least during the international conferences he attended, often helping ease the cantankerous Anglo-American debates and calming the personal friction. Pug's observations on Churchill concerning D-Day in Normandy provide further insights into Churchill and his activities, also Churchill's incursion into Greece because of his fear of Communism spreading which Pug also experienced in a trip to Moscow regarding the future of Poland.

It was Pug's personal commitment to hold the war administration structure together which prompted him to offer Churchill his resignation on a trip to Canada for the Octagon Conference, which was refused, but which Pug did to avoid a mass resignation of the COS. This characteristic feature of Churchill at odds with his COS continued even after Germany's surrender over the vexed question of the Far Eastern strategy. Pug attended the conferences at Yalta and Potsdam reflecting Churchill's growing concern of Stalin and his expansion in Europe. Following the election, he found himself serving Attlee, his third Prime Minister in the war years. Immediately after the war Pug and his wife took a holiday in America and in his memoirs offered some interesting insights on public opinions during this visit.

Chapter One

September 1939–May 1940, Chamberlain Years

On 3 September 1939 it was Pug who informed the Chiefs-of-Staff that no news had been received from Germany, indicating Britain was at war, and which was received without comment. Then, following instructions, Pug went to the designated air-shelter as the first air raid warning sounded, where he tried to comfort some of the young secretaries, whom, he noted in his memoirs, would soon be taking air raids in their stride. He noted the immediate news was appalling, the Polish Army was not as strong as anticipated, and the French remained in a defensive position saying they were not yet prepared. Pug was somewhat critical of them while admitting there were no British troops in France yet. The Royal Navy was active but of no help to Poland, and on 4 September Pug went to the Air Ministry to hear the result of an RAF raid on naval units at Brunsbüttel and Wilhelmshaven, where little damage was done for the loss of seven bombers and their crews. It was all very disheartening.

The first meeting of the Supreme War Council (France and Britain) was held at Abbeville in the same month. Pug attended and found there was no agenda, but it was decided on Gamelin's policy of marching together into Belgium if the Germans used that country in an attack, (known as the D-Plan), and further agreed that the two Allies would not make separate agreements with Germany; this was of course, all advisory. It was not long before Pug had doubts about the French strategies, reporting back that they were keen to take a part in the Finnish-Soviet war and be involved in Scandinavia, expressing the opinion that 'the French plan is political, sponsored by Daladier, etc., because of the ill effect of this continued inactivity on French morale' but pointing out that the French General Staff were not much in favour.[1] Pug preferred the idea of sticking 'to our original thesis that we can win a long-drawn out siege by outstaying Germany'.² The French, looking back were basically unprepared and Pug's solution would not work either. The French concept of operating in the northern climes of Europe has since been regarded by some historians as an effort to keep the war away from French soil. Pug's views on France would emerge again, but in other peoples' reported conversations and not in his memoirs.

Typically, Pug enjoyed the meetings as they provided a welcome break in his normal routine, and he enjoyed watching from a destroyer a mine being blown up by rifle-fire. He rarely found the Anglo-French meetings productive, not least he noted because no records were kept. Pug always believed record keeping was the safest and best form of security and he was correct in this thinking.

He later accompanied Chamberlain to Field Marshal Gort's HQ in France, inspected the defence lines and feeling grateful that a German attack in winter was unlikely. He met General Dill whom he found concerned about the lack of armour, and like Dill's successor General Brooke (CIGS) held a high opinion of the German military. It was at this stage on meeting Air Marshal Barratt that Pug came upon a problem which would surface again and again, namely the RAF was independent of Gort, operating as far as Pug could see as two almost antagonistic forces.

He toured the famous Maginot Line where he described the inhabitants as 'troglodytes' and wondered whether their environment 'would sap the offensive spirit from the bravest soldier'.³ It was a very different atmosphere from his days on camels fighting in the scrubland of Somaliland. The only piece of good news came from the Royal Navy when the *Graf Spee* was bamboozled into scuttling itself, but the French were more interested in ground support rather than naval news from across the Atlantic Ocean. After the war John Colville noted that Pug was 'the only man I personally heard say, well before the cataclysmic events of May and June 1940, that he believed the quality and morale of the French army to be lower than was generally supposed'.⁴ Pug often came up with strategy ideas which he soon realised were not sound, but he was a reliable observer of all around him, especially troops.

At home food rationing and conscription were slowly increasing and becoming part of the national scene, yet life seemed normal. On looking back Pug admitted that Chamberlain's statement that *Hitler had missed the bus* seemed right, and like many others had hoped the impending storm would blow over. In his memoirs he admitted he had been mistaken to be so optimistic. As noted above, in the various meetings he attended in France he picked up the sense of French despondency, later telling his wife he was 'not sure the French would fight well'.

On the social side Pug was harried by old friends looking for a useful post and by individuals who came up with ideas of winning the war with tanks which could fly, pilotless aircraft, and burning down German forests. Pug was always polite to what he considered as probably madcap ideas, but later in the war there were radio-directed bombs used by the Luftwaffe at Salerno (1943) and today weaponised drones can be operated from thousands of miles away with devastating impact. He may have been a top military bureaucrat but all he could do during these dramatic months was take notes and observe while others made the decisions which at this time were mainly reactive to the incoming events and news. There was no basic strategy apart from defence and the hope that the Germans, if they fought, would lose as in the Great War. Pug was concerned at what he had seen with the RAF Commander Barratt mentioned above, that the three services each thought they were the most essential with a degree of competition, which Pug forecast had to cease, because such was the imminent threat that they had to work together. The Germans had already demonstrated this with their mobile form of attack which they used in the Spanish Civil War with their Luftwaffe, and then in Poland where their troops and armour were assisted from the air, especially by the recently-built Stuka bomber.

However, the attitudes of the force commanders occupied Pug's thinking, and with some justification. In the Great War there had only been two Chiefs of Staff, the navy and army each giving their own viewpoint. During the Phoney War now three Chiefs of Staff would discuss issues and send their findings or disagreements to the Ministerial Co-ordination Committee where it would all be aired again; greater speed was needed. It was not helped by the chairman of this committee having no executive powers, like Pug he simply reported back.

The Chairman, Lord Chatfield was asked to resign by Chamberlain in April 1940. Churchill as First Lord of the Admiralty took his place, and even though Pug admired the man he had some early doubts. Just before the German attacks had started Churchill had informed Chamberlain that the meetings were too acrimonious and it needed a Prime Minister's authority. Even during the debacle of the German invasion of Norway the lack of inter-service co-operation surfaced; as Pug noted in his memoirs 'is that all we learned, at not too prohibitive a cost, was how things should not be done'.[5] He then offered an amusing anecdote prevalent at the time, that when a confused junior officer looked up and down Whitehall and asked which side the War Office was on, he received the reply 'I'm afraid I don't know for certain, at the beginning of the war we thought they were on ours, but now we are not sure at all.'[6]

Chamberlain told Pug that Churchill was to have full authority, and he would be assisted by a suitable Central Staff Officer who would join the Chiefs of Staff and that would be Pug. It was evidently a good choice because 'he knew Whitehall forwards, backwards and sideways'.[7] According to one of Churchill's biographers Pug, who was described as 'soon to be one of Churchill's invaluable props', and Edward Bridges thought the Prime Minister and not the First Lord should preside, giving it stronger executive bite.[8] Pug was also wary that the service chiefs would not appreciate the new system and voiced his misgivings, but the decision was final. A letter from Chamberlain written to Churchill on 1 May 1940, informed Churchill that:

> With the approval of the First Lord of the Admiralty [Churchill's post at the time], Major-General H. L. Ismay C.B., D.S.O., has been appointed to the post of Senior Staff Officer in charge of the Central which, as indicated in the memorandum, is to be placed at the disposal of the First Lord. Major-General Ismay has been nominated, while serving in this capacity, an additional member of the Chiefs of Staff Committee.[9]

Pug was convinced that Churchill, whom he already admired, would have responsibility without authority, but as Churchill noted 'my personal and official connection with General Ismay was preserved unbroken and unweakened from May 1, 1940, to July 17, 1945, when I laid down my charge'.[10] Churchill wrote this in 1947–8 and would later resume this relationship with Pug when he was returned to political power. Later in 1946, Pug wrote a personal letter to Churchill stating that 'one of the first things that you said to me after you assumed the office of Minister of Defence was "we must be very careful not to define our powers too precisely". In point of fact, they were, as you know, never defined, but the system worked admirably.'[11]

The administration by strict democratic political standards remained ill-defined, but under the exigencies of a major war Churchill would assume an overall power, almost like that of a dictator, but unlike Germany it was accepted by the British from major military leaders down to the vast majority of the population. It was, Churchill stated, Pug's job to keep him informed on all matters, to convey Churchill's instructions, and to ensure the links between the various departments worked.[12] Although Pug's main task was the bridge of communication between Churchill and the COS and *vice versa*, in this task he was the persistent and essential go-between, though he never signed any of the reports. His job was manifold, and 'with this collection of posts emphasised how much of a hybrid he was, while always being Churchill's faithful "Pug"'.[13] One of Churchill's biographers noted:

> The new high command structure, with the good-natured 'eminence khaki' General Pug Ismay mediating between the Prime Minister and his service chiefs, harnessed Churchill's drive and prevented him from going off the rails…Desmond Morton, for example, later asserted that without a curb on his actions Winston would have been a Caligula or worse, and quite properly had his throat cut.[14]

This was somewhat exaggerated, but it underlined Pug's tenacity at keeping the ship of war balanced and steady. The new war machinery was complex but seemingly efficient, and during a debate in the House of Commons on the war situation, the outline of the Chiefs of Staff Structure was defined, including Pug's role.[15]

When Pug had met Churchill, he suggested his office should remain in the War Office, but Churchill typically brushed this aside, instructing him that his staff should be Oliver Lyttelton (for supplies), Desmond Morton (the political man) and Professor Lindemann (scientific work). Pug remained unconvinced and prepared a paper of his views, but such were the pressures the paper was all but ignored. By being immersed in his own bureaucratic military world Pug was not so aware of the parliamentary dissent over the conduct of the war. Contrary to much opinion, Churchill stood loyally by Chamberlain, but when on 10 May Germany invaded the Low Countries, Chamberlain resigned. When Churchill became Prime Minister and assumed the post of Minister of Defence Pug was surprised but delighted; he wrote that he was sure Britain would not lose the war, but he could not see how they could win it; he found in Churchill some hope to this dilemma. Pug knew that Churchill preferred men who were imaginative and unorthodox, qualities which he did not possess. He was probably kept in post by Churchill because he was robust, friendly by nature and he could be trusted, and by a similar token Churchill later chose General Brooke as Chief of Staff (CIGS) because he needed strong men and not yes men, even if it meant disagreement; this was Churchill's strength of character. This period of transition was both refreshing and disturbing as Pug had hopes in Churchill but being somewhat conservative by nature was concerned about some of his changes. Churchill was undoubtedly pleased that in Pug, he had a man who had 'an almost uncanny skill in presenting succinctly in writing a complicated case' and could in the best sense of the word be 'diplomatic'.[16]

In his later history of the war when presenting the case for the Norwegian Narvik attack, Churchill included Pug's report writing that it 'cannot be better stated than in a paper written by General Ismay on 21 April'.[17] His presentation of reports and evaluations were excellent as far as Churchill was concerned, not least because it was widely known that Churchill had a sharp eye for grammatical errors, faulty syntax, and liked a sentence to flow, with the added danger that he would explode over American spelling. More to the point Churchill, before the days of computers, needed and demanded everything in writing. He sent a memo to Pug and Edward Bridges (Secretary to the War Cabinet) stating:

> Let it be clearly understood that all directions emanating from me are made in writing or should immediately afterwards be confirmed in writing...I do not accept any responsibility for matters relating to national defence on which I am alleged to have given decisions unless they are recorded in writing.[18]

Churchill was fastidious in his demands instructing he should not be expected to proof-read messages, which he often did. However, it was a delicate position for Pug as he had to steer his way between the military and the politicians, possibly open to suspicion by both sides of the great divide. Pug was not in the position of making the major decisions, but he carried all the dangers of ensuring the communications between these two sectors were carried through efficiently, with speed and accuracy being uppermost. The machinery of the War Office was well-known for its overwhelming complexity, Churchill 'relied on a tight office under General Hastings Pug Ismay' who was also Churchill's 'eyes and ears'.[19] Pug was the man behind the scenes who could organise the major stage settings with alacrity and precision, essential but often unobserved.

When Pug had heard about the German attack on Norway he felt almost shattered by the unexpected news, because he had been certain the war would start in the Low Countries, and he promptly called for a Chiefs of Staff meeting at 6.30 in the morning. Pug referred to Hitler's action as 'laying hands on an innocent country', ignoring the fact that the British had already shown an interest in Norwegian ports and waters. The Norwegians had been justifiably concerned about German intentions, 'but they were equally concerned that Britain's interference in their dilemma might provoke the very war they feared. When the German invasion eventually happened in April, the King of Norway when told asked who was invading?'[20]

More to the point, Pug noted there were no constructive ideas arising from the Chiefs of Staff, but Churchill demanded the British fleet to clear Bergen and Trondheim of the enemy preparing for our own forces. This would demand interservice co-operation as troops needed to be landed from the sea by the navy, and when possible, the navy also needed air cover. It was a question of resources, lack of time for planning and although it started to take place the Chiefs of Staff argued that a full assault was impossible. Pug later wondered whether they were right and later Brooke would try and stop Churchill invading Norway again, and he was probably correct in the light of hindsight. Pug was, according to John Colville, forthright in expressing his views in the Cabinet stating, 'that as far as he could see the Cabinet were proposing to do the only thing that could lose the war: namely *not* to take vigorous action'.[21] In this line of thinking Pug was either supporting Churchill or possibly thinking along Churchillian lines of aggressive action.

When the Germans broke into the Low Countries it was another early call for Pug who later expressed surprise that the Dutch and Belgians had refused military staff discussions, less so the Dutch because they had managed to stay neutral in the Great War. It was perhaps foolish, but as two small countries they could only hope to remain outside the possible conflict. The Dutch called for help, but it was simply impossible and Pug in his memoirs reflected the sadness of the situation as the gathering information came to light from those who had managed to flee the onslaught.

It was at this stage of events (10 May) that Churchill became Prime Minister and formed a five-man war cabinet comprising himself, Chamberlain, Clement Attlee, Halifax, and Labour's Arthur Greenwood. This group was augmented by the service chiefs (COS); all these positionings and personnel changed as the war continued. There was much criticism of Churchill becoming Minister of Defence alongside his primary role as Prime Minster. Pug was the one man standing alongside Churchill as his intermediary between politician and the military and who remained alongside Churchill as a permanent fixture for the duration.

Chapter Two

May 1940 to May 1941, Disaster to Hope

The initial hope of any success on the battlefield was dashed within days when the Germans broke through at Sedan on a wide front. They used the mobility of their armour with air support which would later be dubbed the Blitzkrieg war. Churchill flew to France with Dill and Pug and from the minute they had arrived Pug detected a sense of depression. The French had hoped with the Norwegian war and the Soviet-Finnish war that the focus of the combat would not be on French soil, but this proved to be a futile hope. Pug was shocked to hear that the French thought the Germans might be in Paris very soon. At the British Embassy there was a sense of gloom and in a meeting at the Quai d'Orsay they met Paul Reynaud, Édouard Daladier and General Gamelin, the latter telling Churchill there were no reserves for a counter-attack which astonished him, who had like many others thought France had the largest and most efficient army in Europe. Pug was privately dismayed at the French reaction and military performance. Colville wrote in his diary that 'Pug Ismay is not too happy about the military situation. He says the French are not fighting properly: they are, he points out, a volatile race and it may take them some time to get into a warlike mood. Pray Heavens not too long!'[1]

The French asked for fighter-planes and Pug, using his skill in Hindustani, spoke to his assistant in London by phone as he also spoke this language, which was noted with pleasure by Churchill.[2] On their return the news became even more unpleasant as the Germans pressed forward and the BEF was in immediate danger of annihilation. The lack of news from the French was frustrating and Churchill decided to return to France only five days following his last visit. He was late back having told Pug and two others to be waiting for him hours before he returned showing, as Colville noted, a degree of lack of consideration for his staff.[3]

On hearing Churchill's news Pug felt pessimistic, feeling the French were not only retreating but were being routed. However, they discovered Gamelin had been replaced by General Weygand, which for a time offered some hope. Pug felt Weygand was just the right man to turn the Germans back, but his colleague General Kennedy described Weygand as a 'romantic and remarkable figure…but he looked old, and yellow and unhappy', which by other accounts was more accurate, characterising Pug's optimism and belief in other people.[4] However, despite Pug's hopefulness, the news became even more disastrous as it was soon realised that the BEF was in danger and the evacuation of Dunkirk became the next unpalatable task.

Churchill and Pug flew once again to France on 31 May in which every aspect of the war was discussed, including Churchill insisting that French troops would be evacuated to Britain through Dunkirk. By 4 June some 350,000 British and French troops had been evacuated. The navy had saved the day for the army, the RAF was often denigrated for not being there, which was untrue because they were fighting high in the skies thwarting German planes accessing the beaches, and it underlined Pug's belief that the services could co-operate successfully. From Colville's diary it was apparent that Pug was distraught by the French, wondering whether having soaked up British resources the French would then accept a generous armistice offer by the Germans, but Colville, who reported this conversation thought Pug was being alarmist, and the next day he found Pug dismal and depressing.[5] Pug was closer to what eventually happened than Colville, and the armistice was signed with the southern half of France free, known as Vichy, which was to have an unbalanced relationship with Britain, often in armed conflict, and later, under Admiral Darlan's influence sought a closer relationship with the Germans.

When Italy declared war on 10 June Churchill was back in France with Pug, this time uninvited but still travelling with him. Pug gave the interesting insight that Churchill, who was never known to let a friend down, simply did not want 'to default on the French', it was more the emotional and political rather than military factors which dominated Churchill's mind and these factors would be repeated again during the war years.[6] Churchill was first class at understanding the enemy, was imaginative in military ideas (although too much for some) but he was not so good at administration and needed to surround himself with civil administrators for his political work. As such, it was Pug who became his personal Chief of Staff along with his secretariat, and he provided Churchill with the necessary links with the leading military figures both in the COS and those in the field of combat. He must have been regarded as good at this work, as Churchill was not averse to sacking those whom he felt lacked reliability. It appeared to be a warm relationship with Pug dining at No 10 Downing Street and frequently at Chequers, having family meals with other guests. It was often over the dining-table that Churchill would throw out ideas and demand opinions, and on one occasion Pug declared the Chiefs of Staff were too old and slow, and that they needed a chairman who could enforce decisions, and 'then thought the P.M. would end by being appointed Commander in Chief of all three forces', which explained why Churchill liked his company so much.[7]

Churchill often spoke to Pug about highly sensitive matters, such as reorganising the War Office, the Air Ministry, and the tensions between such key-characters as Archibald Sinclair, (Secretary of State for Air), Hugh Dowding and Max Beaverbrook. Not everyone enjoyed the meals at Chequers where social chatter was constantly inundated with Churchill's sudden ideas on how to conduct the war. He was known, as portrayed by Brooke in his diary, with coming up with 'madcap' ideas, on one occasion suddenly unrolling a map of the Red Sea asking whether it would be possible to occupy the port of Massawa, but General Marshall-Cornwall indicated all the problems to 'the obvious relief of Dill and Ismay who knew Churchill might well have' set the orders in motion.[8] David Lloyd George had once said that Churchill could come up with ten ideas at the same time, and he was something of an anachronism, but Pug and others recognised that he was fundamentally in touch with the realities of the day.

On this next trip to France Pug met General de Gaulle for the first time finding him courageous and efficient, but somewhat frigid, prickly and humourless.[9] On reflection Pug may have recalled that here was a proud French soldier devastated by the defeat of his country who had no time for humour and any social interchange. Plans were set for bombing Italy's cities of Turin and Genoa and although agreed, the plan demanded a refuel stop in France, which was stopped by some local French personnel who blocked the aircraft with agricultural equipment, once again indicating the strain of the days for the French command and nation. They were ominous times for both France and Britain, and Pug noticed the pain for Churchill who felt obliged to listen to Air Chief Marshal Dowding that no fighter aircraft could be spared for France, because they would be essential for the defence of Britain. All Churchill felt able to offer was a redoubt in Brittany which transpired to be a dangerous gesture, described by Pug as a 'castle in the air'.[10]

Later Pug felt somewhat repentant at the way he had regarded the French, as he reflected that this was another battering from the Germans with losses far greater than Britain. In terms of the Brittany redoubt, General Brooke was sent to organise it, realising at once that it was not only futile but would unnecessarily lose British lives. He phoned General Dill and in his forthright fashion demanded it should be stopped, not realising that Churchill was listening in. There ensued a heated argument, Brooke stuck to his guns and Churchill acquiesced. Brooke's strength of character was noted by Churchill who soon put him in charge of the Home Defence, then later made him Chief of the Imperial General Staff (CIGS). As noted above Churchill needed strong men to support and challenge him, not mere minions.

On the way back from France in a light plane called the Flamingo (de Havilland DH.95) they spotted a German fighter below, it was fortunate the pilot did not look up, because as Pug noted 'the course of history might have been changed'.[11] The return to France was almost made immediately to meet Reynaud, but they landed at a bombed airfield, had to find a small car (with Churchill according to Pug taking up 'more than his fair share of room') eventually finding an exhausted Reynaud who explained the situation was so bad that an armistice was a political necessity. Churchill was unhappy but had no choice, and Pug pointed out that the French had in their prison camps some 400 German pilots shot down by the RAF and French air force. There was a chance of removing them to Britain, but it was put aside, probably with immense ramifications. It had been their fifth visit to France which had exhausted all of them.

One of de Gaulle's advisers came to discuss the possibility of an 'indissoluble union between France and Britain' which Pug thought extremely unlikely. The next request was again that fighter planes be sent to France, which Pug reported to Churchill and which he reluctantly had to refuse on RAF advice. The next day the Cabinet debated and approved a draft Declaration of Union, which the French did not accept, but it had been an effort to keep their allies fighting. They were about to set out for France when the news of the armistice arrived. Just prior to this Churchill had asked the COS to study the various possibilities of defence and continuing the war, and as Pug noted 'we are on our own now'. It was not an easy report because it was acknowledged that the enemy tended to have the 'whip-hand' in every sphere of activity, but they concluded that while Germany had most of the cards, the morale of citizens and troops would prevail.

It was ironic as Pug noted, that the first offensive was to sink the French fleet at Mers-el-Kébir which shook the French, convinced the Americans that the British were serious about fighting the Germans, and dismayed many others by killing French allies. It will long be debated, ranging from those who argued that it was essential the French fleet could not fall into German hands, and others who claimed it would have been scuttled as happened later in the war with some of their other ships. Pug, being a gentleman, was at first appalled but later decided there was no choice in the matter. The debate continues and this writer in 1970 once experienced in a French bistro a heated argument between Frenchmen on this very subject. It was not an easy time for de Gaulle struggling alone, and although some colonies such as Chad, the Cameroons, and the French Congo opted for de Gaulle, the French attempt to take Dakar with Royal Navy support failed, probably it was rumoured, through French leaks which gave Vichy a boost in its North African colonies and made the Americans even more distrustful of de Gaulle and the Free French.

These leaks were disturbing as no one could ascertain how they happened, but it was clear that Vichy France had been aware of the British and French plans. The Secret Intelligence Service (SIS often referred to as MI6) were sensitive about this issue, and Pug as Churchill's Chief of Staff was consulted as the Prime Minister was looking for scapegoats. Pug at this time reacted somewhat heatedly at the various accusations being murmured by the SIS, and effectively accused Menzies, head of that body, of being disingenuous.[12] It was the task of the head of the SIS to keep the door shut on major secrets, and there is an indication in this episode that Pug was supporting Churchill, but making the point that important information should only be made to the correct sources.

In 1940 there was an atmosphere of gloom, a conviction that the Germans would start their attack by bombing and the country was under resourced, in addition to this Eire was denying the British the use of their ports. On the other hand, after Dunkirk Britain still had an army and the people appeared united, leading Pug to tell his wife that their chances were 'three to one on, and he believed it'.[13] He noted that Britain was not alone, having the backing of the self-governing Dominions and Churchill had surfaced as the dedicated leader, warning parliament that Dunkirk was a brilliant retreat but not a victory. Pug rightly noted that Churchill's speeches helped unite the nation and he was already bringing his influence to bear on America.

After the fall of France, it was now a matter of strategy and how to organise it at the highest level. In his memoirs Pug goes into considerable details about the bureaucratic changes, mainly implemented by Churchill, and through which the new prime minister tended to centralise power and authority around himself. It was not always well received by his parliamentary critics, especially the combination of being prime minister as well as minister of defence, but such were the growing issues of the day he gradually received support even from some of his more intransigent critics. Pug summarised this by writing that 'henceforth the Prime Minister himself, with all the powers and authority which attach to that office, exercised a personal, direct, ubiquitous and continuous supervision, not only over the formulation of military policy at every stage, but also over the general conduct of military operations'.[14] Later it led to some critics claiming Churchill was forming his own style of dictatorship, but all knew he was still answerable to parliament, a body which found any form of dictatorship abhorrent. It did mean, given the emergency, that henceforth the prime minister was in direct contact with the COS.

This concentration of power around himself enabled Churchill to seek advice from whom he felt was worth listening to, and he implemented his own ideas with an immediacy which his predecessors could never have achieved. It often led to internal conflict, especially with the service chiefs, and this naturally enveloped Pug in many ways. A classic example was when he established the Combined Operations under Admiral Sir Roger Keyes which suited Churchill's belligerent approach to the enemy, as it was a force intended to harry the Germans along the coast with commando attacks, which he later described as 'punching the enemy on the snout'. As Colville was to note in his diary observations, Keyes was not acceptable to many, including some who sat at the COS meetings. There was debate over his role and his title, with Pug, as the intermediary, having to write to Keyes (11 October 1941) suggesting his title should be Director of Combined Training and not Operations.[15] 'As an admiral of the fleet, accountable only to Churchill, Keyes believed himself immortal', and in February 1941 Pug had been instructed by an 'impatient Churchill to stop Keyes bombarding him with letters by redefining the Director's relationship'.[16] This led to some acrimony about Keyes defending himself on his supposed 'bluffing over his discontent with his position'.[17]

The following month the contentious debate continued with Keyes writing to Pug relating to his disagreement with the Chiefs of Staff, that his departure from the post of Director of Combined Operations was due to false rumours, suggesting he was responsible for unduly influencing Churchill in Naval matters.[18] Pug had to write to Keyes refuting claims that he had any knowledge of allegations regarding Keyes nor had he passed on such rumours to Churchill.[19] It was so contentious that Keyes raised the issue in parliament with a speech on his position as Director of Combined Operations and the circumstances of his departure from this post, the importance of amphibious operations, and his lack of faith in the Chiefs of Staff system and the war machine in Whitehall.[20] This episode typified much of the cantankerous dialogue with which Pug had to be involved, and yet he never lost his balance and gentlemanly approach, and a few months later (5 January 1942) Keyes wrote to Pug thanking him for a letter of condolence sent by Ismay after the death of Keyes's son on a Commando raid.[21]

The Planning and Intelligence Staffs were increased and worked together, with committees established once a problem had been identified as needing special consideration, and then made redundant once the problem was resolved, a typical example being the Battle of the Atlantic Committee to deal with the dangers of the U-boats. The nature of war was changing rapidly, innovative responses were essential, and Churchill was forever conscious of the need for science and new ideas, bringing men with such capacity into the forward-thinking committees. Among these various men were now famous people such as Professor Lindemann and Major Jefferies who were capable of innovative ideas, inventions and evaluation of an emerging problem. The Planning and Intelligence departments mentioned above also travelled into a sophisticated phase on how to deceive and mislead the enemy.

Naturally it led to clashes as the Service Chiefs often disagreed with their political master, but although it led to heated moments with Churchill arguing his case he never went against their joint decision or advice, even though he would frequently raise the same issue again and again. Suggestions were made, especially by *The Times* that this major committee needed an independent chairman, but Churchill ignored this and he remained in control appointing one of the COS to be chairman whenever they met without him. In doing this Churchill managed to meld the political and military powers into a cohesive body. What is critical from these insights into the complexities of the war command was that Pug was the common thread, later stating that he 'did not have a finger in every pie' but he was present at all levels, be it political or with any of the three military services. He was Chief of Staff to Churchill, a member of the COS, and Head of the Office of the Minister of Defence. In his own words he was a 'cog' in this rapidly changing world of command. Churchill later described him as the 'head of the handling machine', but Pug preferred the title 'agent'.[22]

He was a two-way channel of communication between the political and military bodies, obviously often under suspicion by the two worlds he worked for, but because of his personality it never reached a crisis point or led to distrust. It was an unprecedented role which raised a few eyebrows, but Pug managed this suspicion by acting more as a mediator between the conflicting elements. His strength was in his ability to take lengthy reports and present them in a direct and succinct fashion which was pleasing to most, especially Churchill who always preferred brevity and making the point. He also, with his team, often had to read any speeches or reports Churchill was preparing on military matters, ensuring they were correct and not conveying blunders. Pug was therefore close to Churchill, often reporting for his first duty to his bedroom for when Churchill woke up, to brief him on the next COS meeting, then back at lunchtime, and all too aware of Churchill's habits of catnapping, his very late nights and other personal idiosyncrasies.

Churchill demanded from Pug necessary information, issued him instructions, and often Pug would encourage him to tone down any harsh minutes or memos. Churchill recognised he needed this type of support because of his own 'thrusting' type of personality, not just relying on Pug, but men like Brendan Bracken, and later Brooke to challenge his more outlandish military ideas, and even his wife who reminded him from time to time that he needed to guard his reputation. Pug was always deep in this colourful kaleidoscope, not just at the official level of meetings, but in the dinner-time discussions at Chequers where the future was explored and the past pondered over. On one occasion Pug and Eden agreed that because of the fall of France 'her shame had been so great that she could never rise again' with Churchill disagreeing.[23]

In the meantime, the Battle of Britain raged in the skies with Pug occasionally keeping Churchill company as he travelled to see the fighting. Churchill enjoyed the experience, Pug was less certain; after a visit to No. 11 Group Fighter command, he later recalled 'there had been heavy fighting throughout the afternoon and at one moment every single squadron in the group was engaged; there was nothing in reserve, and the map table showed new waves of attackers crossing the coast. I felt sick with fear.'[24] It was understood the Germans appeared to be planning an invasion, but Pug remained under the impression that it would not happen soon, which was not a view shared by others. On looking back Pug was convinced that the Air Arm had better insight than the other two services and had prepared reasonably well, and proved that even the navy needed air support to stay safe and assist in any attack. The only continuous argument was the number of fighters compared to the production of bombers for a counter-offensive.

As the Battle of Britain continued, Pug reflected on Dowding's insistence that no more fighters should be sent to France, which proved to be the right decision. He visited with Churchill the various airfields, where the pilots waiting for action and possible death 'were delighted to see Churchill and gave Pug a kindly welcome'. Churchill's favourite place was the operations room of No 11 Group, Fighter Command as it was the overall nerve centre of what was happening thousands of feet above. Pug was the first to hear Churchill's famous words on a trip back from this centre, 'Never in the field of human conflict has so much been owed by so many to so few', which he composed during that car journey. Pug only went on a few of these trips as most of his time was spent in Whitehall where with everyone else, they waited to hear news of the battle. It can be speculated that Churchill would often take him because he enjoyed his company.

Enemy aircraft were being destroyed but the RAF were also losing planes, their only consolation was that pilots parachuting down arrived mainly on home soil, whereas Luftwaffe pilots were sent to prison camps. To Pug's delight Churchill created a Ministry of Air Production under Lord Beaverbrook whom Pug thought was ideal. On the other hand, when General Brooke was CIGS, his diary indicated a deep distaste for Beaverbrook. It is worth noting at this time in this study that Pug tended to like people or if otherwise kept it to himself. Brooke in his published diaries never held back on his personal feelings about Beaverbrook or Churchill, which in his memoirs Pug criticised Brooke about publishing his diaries, but again without mentioning his name.[25] It is also clear that Pug admired Churchill, was loyal at the time and thereafter, and it must be remembered when reading Pug's views when describing Churchill and many of his colleagues, he had a propensity of looking back with rose-coloured glasses; sometimes it may be necessary to draw attention to this tendency.

The Battle of Britain appeared to be going the British way and Pug felt, probably correctly, that this ensured Operation *Sea Lion* would become unlikely. Later Churchill would describe El Alamein as the first great victory, but for many the initial success was fought in the skies of 1940 and more deserving of this accolade, which Pug felt as he described it as one of the most decisive battles in world history. Following the battle of fighter planes, it was promptly followed by the Blitz and for fifty days London was bombed before the Luftwaffe turned their attention to other cities and ports. Again, Pug accompanied Churchill to visit the bomb sites where he was staggered by the amount of damage, the loss of life, and the positive reaction of the local people who greeted Churchill with joy and wanted retaliation against the Germans.

Pug was equally amazed at Churchill's compassion, and for a man who never took exercise, he was surprised to see how fast Churchill walked to cover as much ground as possible. Pug later recalled a time to Churchill when he had visited a rest centre, where there 'was a poor woman who had lost all her belongings sobbing her heart out. But as you entered, she took her handkerchief from her eyes and waved it madly shouting "Hooray, hooray"'.[26] Pug was always surprised at people's reactions to

Churchill when he appeared in public, even during the days when the future looked less than hopeful. On one trip back incendiaries were dropped around Churchill's car which were aimed as markers for the bombers, but Churchill returned safely to be met by a nervous staff, with Pug being 'rebuked' by some officials for putting the prime minister in danger. Churchill was especially angry about the use of aerial mines dropped by parachute, they could land anywhere, were difficult to defuse and created considerable damage and death, and Churchill expostulated in an outburst that he would have all Germans castrated, but in a 'more considered memo to Pug Ismay, he ordered preparations to be made for "equal and proportionate" retaliation with similar devices'.[27]

The threat of invasion remained at the top of the priority list and Churchill often chose Dover as a place to visit as he thought it would be a potential German landing area, and always hoped to see some action in the skies above. He never lacked physical courage, always wanting to be near the front line, and later pressure had to be applied to stop him crossing to France on D-Day Normandy in 1944. Later still, Brooke in his diaries sketched a time when Churchill had to be withdrawn from near the front line looking like an upset schoolboy. In Ramsgate Churchill had to enter a public air raid shelter where seeing no-smoking he extinguished a new cigar, something he would never normally do; it was, Pug noted, his respect for the public. He noted that during these long car trips Churchill had time to ponder and often worked on his famous terminology, such as changing the title of LDV (Local Defence Volunteer) to Home Guard which changed their image overnight. He was constantly attentive to the codenames for military operations, not wanting 'silly' names for events during which men would be killed. It was Churchill who changed the name Communal Feeding Centres which sounded like a mix between a farm and a charity shop, to British Restaurants. Pug illuminated some of Churchill's character by frequently walking alongside him. The inside information was frequent in his memoirs, often making sense when reading minutes of meetings. When, for example, at a COS meeting the Naval Chief explained that battleships could not travel south of the Wash in the event of a German invasion attempt because of limited manoeuvring, Churchill appeared unusually accepting. He told Pug that he understood the Royal Navy well enough that in an emergency he knew they would respond, which was a good point which had been proved before and would happen again during the war.

As the difficult year of 1940 progressed and Italy, once Mussolini had decided it was safe, had entered the war late, the War Cabinet's attention was drawn to the Middle East. Following his 1936 invasion of Abyssinia (Ethiopia) everyone recognised that Mussolini had ambitions of a resurrected Roman Empire with his eyes on North Africa and the Mediterranean which gives the impression that the phrase was his creation, but it had in fact been used much earlier by the Romans and, most dangerously, Egypt. The British commander in this region was General Wavell whom, despite reservations from the COS, Churchill wanted to go on the offensive against the Italian incursions. Churchill established another committee to examine this issue chaired by Anthony Eden, and Pug noted Churchill's various machinations to ensure the British built up their resources and, despite the invasion threat, to act against the Italians. To many of the military it was more important to keep soldiers and invaluable tanks at home for defence against the German Operation Sea Lion, rather than send them on a dangerous journey to North Africa. On the surface the number of Italian troops and resources made Churchill's policy appear dangerous. Pug, being the man he was, spent some inordinate time in his memoirs over Mussolini's easy occupation of British Somaliland and the neglect of his old Camel Corps, but the idea that this large area of neglected scrubland in the Horn of Africa was important held little interest in Britain, faced with a possible invasion.

It was an easy victory for the Italians who were delighted, congratulated by Hitler, ignored by most of the world, but encouraged Mussolini to instruct Marshal Graziani to turn towards Egypt, which Churchill rightly recognised as serious not just because of the canal, but the route to oil supplies, and for Churchill British prestige, not so much from the colonial aspect which was important to him, but to show the world, especially America that Britain could still fight. For a time, the news was good, the Royal Navy had attacked the Italian fleet at Taranto (11 November) using their air fleet. Such was the success of this attack that it has been suggested it acted as a guideline for the later Japanese assault on Pearl Harbor. Wavell also struck at the Italian Army and many Italian prisoners were taken and the threat against Egypt seemed less viable.

Pug recorded the temperature at the War Office rising again when Italy's attack on Greece started through Albania occupied earlier by

Mussolini. Chamberlain had offered a guarantee to Greece which put the British in a difficult position of whether to support them. As could be expected opinions were sharply divided and Dill (CIGS) and Eden were sent to the Middle East to examine the situation. As always, the situation changed by the day, the Italians were embarrassed when the Greeks resisted by forcing the Italian troops back into Albania and Hitler felt obliged to come to the rescue. The COS knowing that manpower and resources were extremely limited were concerned at Churchill's decision to assist the Greeks. Colville recorded that in this discussion Pug tended to side more with the COS, stating that 'there is nothing we can do on a sufficiently large scale to save the Greeks' and believing that air attacks would cripple the Greek defence as it had done in Poland and France.[28]

As such the year 1941 started with the British resources stretched to their absolute limit, with tensions between Churchill's views and his military, and he also had to explain to the Australian and New Zealand governments why their soldiers were being used in this seemingly remote part of South-Eastern Europe. General Wilson moved into Greece but a month later the Germans with their experienced military defeated the Yugoslavian army, and other British evacuations had to take place from Greece and Crete. When it was suggested that a plan should have been prepared for the possible attack on Greece by the Axis, Pug in his traditional defensive role pointed out that previous plans had depended on working in alliance with France which was now defunct.

Pug in his usual way looked at the situation from every conceivable direction. He knew, as he had expressed, that the venture would be a disaster, and he accepted that the responsibility fell to the War Cabinet, but he tried to find an excuse by claiming that it delayed the German attack on Russia by four to five weeks. This may have had an element of truth in so far that postwar it appeared that Hitler had delayed the attack on Russia, which had he not done so then he might have arrived at the gates of Moscow before the bitter Russian winter thwarted the final attack. A more cynical historian may note that the sooner the Germans attacked the Russians the better, because as alien as the Soviet system may have been to Britain, they were obliged to become a major collaborator in the war against Nazi Germany.

Pug was both military and political, but above all he was a constant admirer of Churchill, and he wrote that a 'military failure may be excused, but failure to keep a promise to help a friend in trouble is not easily forgiven or forgotten'.[29] Very few historians have supported Churchill's decision to squander men and material in this Greek episode, many would understandably disagree with Pug's apologia, but his views reflected an age of honour, of keeping promises even when made by politicians, and all this provided not only a valuable insight into Pug's character, but also Churchill with an attitude lost to the more cynical age of today. On reading a later explanation by Pug he draped the disaster in Greece into an acceptable form of explanation from his point of view: 'Originally the force was sent largely for moral reasons…and to secure air bases…the chances of a successful defence were recognised from the start as doubtful…and not helped by Greek delays'.[30] Many believe Churchill was fundamentally right about the Balkans as it was a constant threat to southern Europe and one of the keys to the Mediterranean and oil supplies. The Americans could never understand Churchill over his obsession with the Balkans, and the debate is still argued to this day by historians. Pug's first biographer wrote that 'it was a war waged entirely on his [Churchill] own direction and initiative, with Ismay's help', which is understandable as Pug's loyal support and admiration for his chief was considered as relevant.[31]

As 1941 gathered pace the threat of invasion remained in Britain in the early months, if only on the grounds that Hitler had already created a reputation for doing the unexpected. Rommel and his Afrika Korps had appeared in North Africa, and the bombing raids continued over British cities and ports. On 20 April Pug thought he had time to have a rest with his wife in Gloucestershire, only to be summoned by Churchill early next morning to Mr Ronald Tree's (MP) in Ditchley which he utilised in case the Germans bombed Chequers. On arrival Pug discovered that Churchill was demanding the COS should consider sending some of their best tanks to North Africa. They too, according to Pug, were somewhat disgruntled by the early morning summons and not convinced by Churchill's request. They discussed the rumour that Hitler was about to attack Russia, which everyone except Stalin seemed to know, (although Churchill, Russian agents and many others had warned him) and eventually decided it was safe to send the tanks, and the convoy left with only one ship sunk. Pug often refers to Churchill's propensity to call unexpected meetings at unsociable hours, General Brooke (CIGS) in his diary often complained of the late hours at Chequers as did many others, but as Pug often pointed out Churchill was relentless on himself, working all the time and it was a time of war and national survival. It would have been exhausting for some, irritating for others, but Churchill was the older man in years and set the pace, even the irascible Brooke admitted this as did most others, admirers and detractors.

The news of the war came with the same mixture of hope and despair, of news welcome and unwelcomed. The fall of Crete was a disaster, despite General Freyberg's troops fighting well and destroying many of the best German paratroopers, but there were serious naval losses in the evacuation.* There were problems in Iraq with whom Britain had signed an agreement in 1930, but under Wavell the problem was militarily resolved. Pug noted with insight that the Germans had missed a great opportunity as Iraq was critical in terms of oil supply, noting that 'we were in fact saved from a disaster of some magnitude by the ineptitude of the German High Command', a valid point often passed over in history books. Iraq also provided a route through which military resources could be transported into Russia. Wavell was then given the task of stabilising Syria from Axis interference, which led to the dreadful conflict of Free French troops fighting their own countrymen in the form of Vichy soldiers.

Pug noted the way that Churchill stayed in touch with his commanders such as Wavell, he knew that others saw this as bombarding the commanders with endless streams of messages and demands. Pug mentioned no names, but the inference was clear. As he had referred to those keeping diaries which should not have been published, he was again referring to General Brooke.[32] Time and time again Brooke was critical of the way that Churchill often bypassed the COS and sent instructions directly to commanders, seeing it as unnecessary interference with the commander on the spot. Pug accused such critics as failing 'to understand Churchill's motives' because apart from other reasons, 'he wanted them to feel that they were always in his thoughts, and that he was sharing their problems and their difficulties, their hopes and their fears, their failures as well as their successes'.[33]

---

* The navy lost three cruisers, six destroyers, with damage to three battleships, an aircraft carrier, and the army sustained some 12,000 casualties.

Pug was being overly generous towards Churchill, perhaps going 'over the top' in justifying his behaviour. He later added he thought that military leaders when they rose through the ranks became less prone to criticism and more likely to resent it when it occurred, whereas the higher the politician climbed he became an easier target for criticism and found it necessary to support his intentions and motives. Pug and Brooke were two very different men, Brooke, whose nickname was Shrapnel was a tough no-nonsense soldier chosen by Churchill as CIGS because of his strength of personality and dedication. Pug was Ismay's more affectionate nickname and was probably acceptable to Churchill because of his skilful administration and succinct way of writing reports, and because he was friendly and pleasant. Brooke admired and liked Churchill, but he was never afraid to tell the prime minister that he was about to make an error, Pug almost appeared to worship Churchill and would never criticise him. This attitude could be deemed a criticism which would be reasonable, but Pug in his role as a bridge between the political leadership and military authority regarded his post as one of remaining neutral in a delicate balancing act, though he often veered towards Churchill.

In terms of these two men presenting varying views of Churchill the historian must be careful as to which one presents the truer picture. This writer is inclined to believe that Brooke was correct, in so far that as a realist he knew of Churchill's proclivity to be at the front line in theory, and that he felt he knew better than the commander in the field. On the other hand, Pug was also probably correct in pointing out that Churchill wanted to encourage the commanders and he may have cared for them, because under the warlike belligerence was a man who felt a high degree of loyalty and compassion, as witnessed by the crowds who saw tears in his eyes at the sight of their bombed homes. As mentioned before, Pug tended to wear rose-coloured glasses, Brooke wore reading glasses, and to understand both men and their perceptions it is necessary for the reader to wear bi-focal spectacles for the optimum view.

In North Africa Wavell's Operation Battleaxe had failed against Rommel and Churchill believed the time had come to replace him by sending him to India. The relationship between Wavell and Churchill had never been easy, they were two very different men, with the suggestion that Wavell 'was too inarticulate…and his professionalism would not allow him to accept Churchill's romantic rhetoric, and sometime extravagant schemes'.[34] Wavell, according to Pug, accepted the move saying that the Middle East needed a new eye. Pug knew that many people were angry about what they regarded as Wavell's dismissal. He had conducted five battle areas, and some believed he was being used as a scapegoat for the Greek fiasco. He was deeply admired, and Rommel later said that he was one of the best opponents he had been obliged to face. The truth, as Pug perceived it was that Wavell was tired if not exhausted, which makes sense when reading of all his ventures, that Churchill knew this and Wavell accepted this as also the truth of the matter, prompting Pug to write that 'my narrative has shown that this accusation was groundless'. Pug had always been a close friend of Wavell and their relationship was widely known, and five years before Wavell died (1950) Major General Robert Collins was proposing to write Wavell's biography and requested Pug's help.[35]

Amongst the insights Pug provided was the peculiar Allied relationship with America which Churchill had been fostering for a long time. Britain's need for strong allies started to emerge in 1940. The first ally Pug described as the 'godless despotism' which followed Operation Barbarossa and the uniting with the dreaded Bolsheviks, the second was the support being given by America through the influence of Roosevelt. The American President had sent his adviser Harry Hopkins to Britain to find out what was happening and what the future might hold. He was not the distinguished looking envoy Pug had anticipated, describing him as 'deplorably untidy, his clothes looked as though he was in the habit of being slept in...he seemed so frail that a puff of wind would blow him away'.[36] However, as Pug soon discovered, the inner man was different, a sharp mind, clever, perceptive and above all he hated the Nazis. Churchill liked him and on this relationship was built the alliance as Hopkins was a man Roosevelt listened to with care. It makes a somewhat amusing interlude in his war memoirs to hear the upright properly dressed traditional British military officer Pug, meeting an American civilian intellectual and having to look behind his 'odd' apparel to see the real man. He travelled widely with both Pug and Churchill, even visiting Scapa Flow. On one occasion, Pug invited him for a walk on the beach, but Hopkins preferred to stay sitting. He later caught up with the surprised Pug and explained that he had found a comfortable seat on deck, until a polite naval officer told him that that it was unwise to sit on a depth-charge. This odd specimen, as many would have regarded him, was the herald of good fortune and was part of Churchill's 'secret circle' who ensured that Pug kept Hopkins in the military picture.[37]

Roosevelt was already supporting the British with agreements such as lend-lease, resources, and not widely known, he had advised the anti-British Vichy Admiral Darlan not to move the damaged battleship *Dunkerque* from Oran to Toulon for repairs, because it undoubtedly would have fallen into German hands. Pug often picked up these titbits of information because although a cog in the machinery he was there and observing with his trained eye the details of the day. While staying at Chequers with Averill Harriman, another important American envoy, he was woken in the night by Churchill's voice in the corridor. As he looked out, he saw Churchill disappearing down the corridor with Harriman's door still open. He popped in and asked what was happening only to hear that the German battleship *Bismarck* had sunk the *Hood*, which personally distressed Pug because he had been on board the *Hood* only a few weeks before and believed it was indestructible. He learnt that Churchill was confident the German ship would be sunk, which it was, causing Pug to ruminate that in the army when there was no further chance of fighting back to save life it usually meant capitulation. He noted that this did not seem the same with naval traditions, quoting the *Rawalpindi*, a small armed liner which had rammed a German battleship with the loss of all lives rather than surrender.

In early August Churchill and his party left on board HMS *Prince of Wales* for a major meeting in America with Roosevelt and his military men, but Pug was left behind because in Churchill's words he had 'to mind the shop' along with Brooke, so he waited in London and was able to reply to British urgent requests from America.[38] It is possible to detect from his words that he was sad not to be part of this expedition, but Churchill did take Pug's senior officers Colonels Hollis and Jacob.

Pug was excited that the Americans were backing the British, but he was unhappy with Stalin: 'how could we be friends with people like that? Apart from ethics, there were grave doubts about their military value'.[39] He reflected on a Russian General Putna whom he had liked, only to hear he had been executed in Stalin's purges, and he was worried this friendship had caused his demise, which was not the case. At first his belief that the Russian military was of little value was probably based on their conflict against Finland. It had certainly influenced Hitler and the initial success of Operation Barbarossa would have increased his doubts, but as was soon revealed the Russians had formidable manpower and they soon produced first-class soldiers at all levels.

Churchill had no love of the communist system, and had recalled that Stalin had joined with Hitler in the Polish occupation, but he was a man for winning and immediately treated Stalin as a comrade in arms offering support. Roosevelt was of the same inclination and with Churchill gave aid to the Russians. Harry Hopkins returned to discuss the situation and then flew to Moscow to meet Stalin himself, whom he found friendly and communicative, as Stalin would have been since he was desperate for supplies. Hopkins confided to Pug that 'I could hardly call Uncle Joe a pleasant man, though he was interesting enough, and I think I got what I wanted, but you can never be sure about that.'[40] Later Pug would have agreed with the sentiment that nobody could be sure about Stalin, many of his closest Soviet cohorts would have also concurred with this viewpoint. It was decided that an Anglo-American delegation be sent to Moscow with a variety of personnel including Pug. He explained his inclusion in this significant group with a letter from Churchill to be given to Stalin by Beaverbrook reading:

> General Ismay, who is my personal representative on the Chiefs of Staff Committee and is thoroughly acquainted with the whole field of our military policy, is authorised to study with your commanders any plans for practical co-operation which may suggest themselves.[41]

This would have delighted Pug, but it also underlined his importance even if he were 'a cog' and 'backroom bureaucrat', and he was pleased even if it meant travelling to the 'godless despot'. He offered some interesting insights in the way the party had to slip away quietly without being noticed. For his part he pretended he had influenza and his wife Darry left London to care for him in Gloucestershire so not to arouse suspicion by staying in London. The Royal Family met them and then they sailed from Scapa Flow on HMS *London*, following the same route as Lord Kitchener had done when his vessel was torpedoed in 1915.

Like many others he was not impressed by what he found in Moscow, the place felt dreary and the people appeared to Pug to be repressed. He made the comment that the one thing which pleased other long-term guests was that the hotel water was suddenly hot and not tepid as it had been before the arrival of the Western party.[42] They were immediately conscious that there was the constant danger that they were being bugged, and Pug disliked being tailed wherever they went. He was not an essential component with the visitors, his job was to liaise with the Russian military, but then and later it became abundantly clear that the Russian generals were no freer than the man in the street, and they were not allowed to discuss matters with their counterparts unless permitted by higher authority, namely Stalin. British and American generals were at liberty to talk with one another and share details and personal views, in Russia this was unheard of, especially after Stalin's purges of the 1930s when the military leaders had suffered for Stalin's paranoid fear of opposition. Pug found this annoying as his purpose for being there was evidently even more redundant than he anticipated.

Beaverbrook and Harriman at the political level did the real work, commendably as far as Pug was concerned, but in his memoirs he launched into an attack on Stalin's attitude towards the West by his bullying approach, which later emerged again with his constant demand for a Second Front, demanding more supplies, calling the West weak, all of which was to last throughout the war. There is little doubt that Pug remained deeply suspicious of Stalin because of his alliance with Nazi Germany in invading Poland. Later he noted that when Stalin became obnoxious over his demands, Churchill always turned the other cheek which Pug described as the 'Christian spirit'. This was typically Pug, always looking for the better side of humanity, especially when it involved Churchill, who was unquestionably being his usual pragmatic self in keeping Stalin on side because his forces were necessary for victory against Nazi Germany, not so much of the Christian spirit. Churchill was not a dedicated churchman, and he tried to follow the Christian ethos most of his life, but his distaste for Stalin and communism was well known, and it was the realistic approach which motivated Churchill in his strained relationship with the Russian leader.

Pug was bemused by the constant saluting of the Russian soldiers, all undoubtedly aware that they too were being watched by the authorities.

He also attended the banquets, noting the fear of the Russians when Stalin entered the room. He was smaller in stature than Pug had anticipated, realising his many portraits were produced to make him look larger than he was. Pug's memoirs reflected those of Brooke who also found the banquets involved too much food and vodka. Unlike Brooke, Pug was well-known for enjoying his food, once telling his colleague General Kennedy that 'eating was almost the only pastime busy people could have, and it was a good idea to concentrate on it', but even Pug found the Russian indulgence at this level too much.[43] In a lecture he gave in 1946 he wrote: 'I can assure you that, whatever you may have read about banquets at the Kremlin, and so forth, these conference meals were no picnic. Personally, I was out on my feet at the end of practically every one of them.'[44]

To confirm his feelings towards the Soviet Union Pug mentioned that the Russians presented them with a British soldier called James Allan, who had been captured in Calais, escaped the Germans, fled to Poland, made his way to Russia where he was treated as a spy, imprisoned, and beaten, and now the British were able to take him home.* For his bravery James Allan was awarded the Distinguished Conduct Medal, but the citation explaining what he had achieved was never published for political reasons. The Russians were seeking supplies which were agreed, and which the Allies always treated with the utmost energy and commitment, but Pug's role for being there for meeting the military was a worthless exercise. However, he had watched carefully what was happening at the political level and often heard of issues which he sometimes passed on. He gathered from a conversation with Beaverbrook that he considered the CIGS John Dill was not up to the task, and Brooke later commented on hearing this rumour that Beaverbrook had poisoned Churchill's mind against Dill.[45] Pug was not known as a gossip, but information about military colleagues he felt able to pass on to trusted sources, not expecting them to be published after the war.

---

* James Allan later wrote a book about this venture, see Allan, James, *No Citation* (London: Panther Books, 1956)

Chapter Three

June, 1941–1942, Three Problem Areas

American Allies

Within two days of Churchill hearing of Pearl Harbor, he and his selected party were heading towards Washington, basically to ensure that despite the Japanese attack the Americans would recognise Germany as the prime target, and to be encouraged to establish a combined COS (CCOS). Roosevelt had long been aware that there had been no American formal consultation apparatus between the two American forces, (their airpower was under army command), and discussions on this took place. It was also decided that the last CIGS, Field Marshal Sir John Dill was to stay as the permanent British link. Dill, according to Pug and many others, accomplished the task well, and because of his pleasant nature and military knowledge the Americans appreciated him.* The new CIGS was General Alan Brooke, and as noted, like Pug they were both disappointed to be left behind in Britain looking after the shop.

The CCOS system worked but frequently lacked harmony, and many decisions and disputes were resolved by Churchill and Roosevelt, with George Marshall often worried about Churchill's influence on his President. Pug pointed out that this Combined COS system was just America and Britain, other countries such as the Dominions kept their own authority but were often guided by the British COS, and there was no point in Russia being part of the ongoing consultations because no Russian general could dare come to a decision without first consulting Stalin.

In April 1942 George Marshall, accompanied by Harry Hopkins, arrived in London with an American strategy with which the British appeared appreciative but would not concur, and which remained a brittle

---

* He later died in post and there is a statue of him on his horse in Arlington cemetery.

tension for a considerable time. Marshall wanted to cross the channel and head for Berlin with an Operation called Roundup, and preparatory to that an operation called Sledgehammer which was to establish a large bridgehead in Brittany from where Roundup could be launched. Eisenhower wanted Mountbatten to lead the assault for Sledgehammer, Marshall supported him, and Eisenhower with Pug's support pushed this idea, who being Pug, thought more highly of Mountbatten than the COS who were not prepared to give their necessary backing.[1]

Pug, as always constantly saw the best side of all his many acquaintances. The British with some justification felt the Sledgehammer bridgehead operation was far too risky, and the timing was too soon because the Germans would be able to resist more easily unless weakened by their efforts elsewhere such as on the Eastern Front. Diplomatic politeness was undoubtedly expressed because the Americans returned thinking their plans had been well-received, which was far from the case. Churchill took a party with him to Washington including Pug and the CIGS General Brooke. Pug enjoyed the trip as it was on a comfortable Boeing flying boat and it was his first trip across the Atlantic, skipping through time changes so when Churchill asked for a meal at 8.00 pm., he was told that it was 4.40 pm., and he would be dining at the British Embassy. This was not good enough for Churchill who explained he did not go by 'sun time' but by 'tummy time'.

The next day Churchill went to the President's residence at Hyde Park while Pug and Brooke attended the CCOS meeting. Pug's observations of the Americans were interesting and differed very much from his colleague Brooke. He thought Marshall was a great leader, and although Brooke and Marshall became friends, in his diary Brooke made it clear that he thought little of Marshall's strategic ability. Admiral King was Anglophobic and proved difficult, and he was only enthusiastic about attacking the Japanese, but Pug managed to make a friend out of King which demonstrated Pug's friendly personality more than anything else. Another important element was the air force General Arnold, who said little because he was under Marshall's Army control, but he worked behind the scenes with Portal the air chief on the British COS, and was friendly, borne out by his nickname 'Hap'.

Both Brooke and Pug agreed that their own man John Dill was doing a first-class job as the British representative and liaison officer. They were not the easiest of days as the British needed American support, the Americans needed Britain as a launchpad if Hitler were to be defeated, and this commonality of purpose held the two Allies together despite differing strategic ideas. Nevertheless, despite all his efforts at trying to ensure the coalition worked, Marshall's biographer had the impression that Pug was critical of Marshall's 'global strategy', but Pug had admitted that the British should have come cleaner sooner than they did concerning their views on Operation Sledgehammer and the timing of Operation Roundup (Overlord).[2] As with Mark Clark and many other Anglophobic American commanders, Pug was to form a lasting friendly relationship with Marshall, who sent him a leg of ham for 1942 Christmas, a letter thanking him for assisting with his visit to Chequers in 1944, and even in 1950 sending Pug Christmas greetings.[3]

These days were not easy, as the inter-allied conferences were important for seeking an overall strategy for the war, and there were nearly always differences of opinion, sometimes cantankerous, if not bad-tempered, but generally resolved. The Americans had been shocked by the Japanese attack, believed only Russia was at war with Germany, and Britain was 'fiddling about in the Mediterranean' with suspicions about Churchill and the Balkans. The Americans found it 'trying' to come up against Brooke who was insistent that while a cross-channel invasion would happen, the timing had to be carefully selected to avoid failure, whereas the Americans hearing Stalin's plea for an immediate second front wanted to oblige. However, the Americans warmed to those generals who were pleasant gentleman, they were always fond of John Dill and Harold Alexander, and there is no doubt that a man like Pug fell into this same category to smooth the abrasions of debate. His friendly nature and understanding of the views of others was useful during these fraught meetings. George Marshall later wrote to Pug on his return stating that 'I want you to know that I considered it a great opportunity for us to have you here, and that you personally made an important contribution to our problems.'[4] It said much for Pug that he had made a friend out of George Marshall, known for his staunch views and deep suspicions about his British allies.

On Pug's 55th birthday (21 June) Churchill and Roosevelt returned to Washington, Churchill informing Pug they had reached an agreement over the atom bomb, and he had told the president about the plans for Operation Gymnast, which was the earlier name for Operation Torch, the proposed invasion of north-west Africa. Without knowing it at the time Pug would sometimes be criticised by later American historians and biographers for helping change Roosevelt's mind, one of Marshall's biographers writing that 'in search of compromise, General Ismay drafted a statement on offensive operations for the balance of the year. Ismay, a perfect oil can, gave with one hand while taking with another.'[5] Pug may well have drafted the notes, and may well have presented them, but he had not originated the concept and was simply doing his task of being the necessary conveyor belt. For many who did not understand his position in the British military machine he was often seen as being a major decision maker, which was simply misguided, though later the same biographer described Pug as 'the genial broker in arguments between Yanks and Brits'.[6]

Pug was curious about the relationship between the two political leaders who appeared as genuine friends in one another's company. Churchill took Pug with him to meet the President, and while in his office the British discovered from a message delivered to the President that Tobruk had fallen. Both Roosevelt and Marshall were genuinely sympathetic and generously offered to send 300 Sherman tanks to help.[7] Pug recalled that Churchill, unusually for him, winced and there was complete silence eventually broken by Roosevelt, who 'in six syllables epitomised his sympathy with Churchill, his determination to do their utmost to sustain him, and his recognition that we were all in the same boat. 'What can we do to help?' he asked'.[8]

However, Pug was also sympathetic to the fact that Churchill would now have to contend with a political attack on his conduct of the war in the House of Commons. Before he left for Britain, Pug recorded that Churchill sent a message to Auchinleck stating that 'you have my entire confidence and I share your responsibilities to the full.'[9] There was an eventual sense of agreement, and most importantly Operation Bolero was to be given full steam ahead, which was the massing of American troops in Northern Ireland and Britain. During this trip the British party watched some American army exercises, and Churchill asked Pug what he thought of them and received the reply 'to put these troops against German troops would be murder'.[10] Churchill disagreed and in a sense, Pug and Churchill were both right and wrong. Soon the battle of the Kasserine Pass in North Africa would demonstrate the American lack of battle experience, especially at officer level, drawing down criticism from many British officers, but the Americans rapidly learned and soon became first class fighters as they were blooded against the professional German military. Pug realised this feature of learning from experience more quickly than some of his colleagues, recognised that the Americans, to use his language 'had won their spurs', and he does not mention this incident of watching troops in exercise in his memoirs out of politeness to his American friends.

In London Churchill had to face an onslaught of criticism over the conduct of the war, with Pug noting that most of the problems had been because of lack of preparation, which could be laid at the door of the politicians now debating Churchill's future. The arguments varied with Pug recording one proposal that British generals should be replaced by French, Czechs and Poles, probably using parliamentary humour to stress the inadequacy of leadership. It transpired to be a storm in a teacup as Churchill won this debate with a vote of 475 to 25.

Pug was surprised that such a junior officer as Eisenhower should have been selected for the top command but soon grew to admire him. It would take until nearly the end of the war before General Brooke began to appreciate Eisenhower's qualities, but he tended to judge everyone by his strict military discipline and knowledge of strategy. Eisenhower was a man who was determined to make the coalition work, and Pug was impressed when Eisenhower's first endeavour was to ask him the best way to encourage good relationships between American troops and the British people, as he understood many American soldiers saw themselves as crusaders coming to rescue the situation.

Eisenhower like Pug recognised that for two years the British had been fighting a war and had been under constant attack. Pug was impressed that a military man should have such sensitivity towards the civilian population. Eisenhower was also insistent that there should be harmony between the Allies at every level. There was a degree of Anglophobia amongst some American generals such as Stilwell, Clark, Patton, Wedemeyer and many others to one degree or another, frequently brought about by the British sense of superiority, and this was often coupled with an awareness of British colonialism. Eisenhower was a man who overrode it, being determined that the two Allies had a greater cause in hand than historic debates. Pug recorded a time when Eisenhower was furious with an American officer who had called a British counterpart a 'son of a bitch' and decided to send him back to the States. The British officer tried to intervene saying 'he only called me a son of a bitch, sir', to which Eisenhower refused to listen pointing out that he had called him a 'British son of a bitch'. When in early 1943 Pug visited Eisenhower in Algiers asking about any news, he asked Eisenhower whether his intelligence officer was British or American, Eisenhower replied, 'I can't remember, but he is very good at his job.'[11]

The major difficulties arose over the strategy of dealing with the enemy. The Americans were constantly applying pressure to convince the British that the Channel should be crossed at once in 1942, or at least 1943. The British had a more realistic approach and knew that they would be meeting the German military which were by tradition highly professional. Already a battle-experienced Wehrmacht held most of Europe, and they could move huge numbers of troops more quickly than the Allies, who had to cross a turbulent sea channel. The British had already argued fiercely and refused to participate in Operation Sledgehammer, and they were demanding from the Americans that they first tackled the enemy in North Africa, projecting taking the war into Italy. The Americans were suspicious of the British propensity for fighting on the peripheries, wondered about the sense of the 'soft-belly' concept, and suspicious that the British were asking them to fight for colonial interests. The British had to argue that the Mediterranean was not colonialism but the protection of trade routes and oil supplies, all with the possibility of knocking out the Axis partner of Italy. Churchill for his part managed to convince Roosevelt that it was better for American soldiers to meet or be blooded against the German army in a desert area, rather than in a full-frontal attack on the French coast. It would be a cantankerous debate which created coalition tensions and would last for many months even during the various campaigns. It was only the common desire to eliminate the dangerous threat of the Nazi power which maintained a sense of common purpose.

From London the Americans told Roosevelt that the situation was one of deadlock, with Pug noting that perhaps Roosevelt 'always had a warm corner in his heart for North Africa'.[12] This was typical of Pug's generous almost homely observations, as Roosevelt was always suspicious of British motives and hated their colonialism. As observed above, Churchill was aware of the president's thinking, but he was convincing him that the new American army should meet their German adversaries on a more suitable battlefield before the main attack in Europe. Both Churchill and his forthright CIGS General Brooke held the same viewpoint. The American General Omar Bradley, after watching an American military disaster in North Africa (Kasserine Pass), had the grace in his memoirs to note that Brooke had been right:

> I came to the conclusion that it was fortunate that the British view prevailed, that the US Army first met the enemy on the periphery, in Africa rather than on the beaches of France. In Africa we learnt to crawl, to walk and then run. Had that learning process been launched in France it would surely have, as Alan Brooke argued, resulted in an unthinkable disaster.[13]

The Americans and British also debated not just the overall and campaign strategy but even tactics, which was not surprising given they were two very different nations despite a common but somewhat marred history stretching back to colonial days, which was probably the source of their distaste for colonialism. The Americans believed the Vichy French would not oppose them with the same degree of ferocity as they would the British, and they insisted on taking Casablanca as they wanted a port outside the Mediterranean, which made sense. The British warned the Americans that France would soon be aware of invasion movements, and although supporting the Free French under de Gaulle (whom Roosevelt intensely disliked) pointed out the Vichy element could not be trusted. The military, as Pug pointed out, would have argued to Domesday, but the political leaders of Churchill and Roosevelt resolved the situation, and the three areas of Casablanca, Oran and Algiers were decided.

Pug was pleased to note that when Eisenhower met General Alexander, he was pleased to have him as his commander of ground troops, being a man of such military experience and charm. Again this was Eisenhower at his best, not least because Alexander was a thorough gentleman like Pug and amenable. Alexander would have many criticisms levelled against him for his vague orders, for not getting a grip on such commanders as Montgomery and Patton, and not taking a firmer hand, but Eisenhower never changed his mind and much later in northern Europe when Montgomery was causing diplomatic mayhem, Eisenhower pondered having Alexander back as his commander.

Pug always managed to see the best side of other commanders. Within a few months Patton would be in trouble for slapping hospitalised American soldiers and calling them cowards, and overlooking the shooting of prisoners-of-war, but Pug simply described him as 'that colourful personality'.[14] Later he added that Patton 'was emotional and impulsive by nature and took a delight in playing to the gallery'.[15] Pug was rarely overly critical and found it somewhat ironic that Patton was a man with 'superlative courage' who survived the war, only to die in a car accident.

According to his first biographer Pug was not only useful on the military front, especially with the Americans, but was probably the source of other innovations, one being the appointment of Lord Swinton as British Resident in West Africa supported by Cabinet rank.[16] This post enabled easier communications across that part of the continent which was as divided as Europe. Pug's connections with the Colonial Office, the Foreign Office and others was important in his role as a 'bridge'. He may have played a part in planning the occupation of Madagascar, prompted by the fear of Japanese interest, and balancing the various issues with Vichy France. It could be argued that Pug was the 'bureaucratic bridge for agreements', which never grabbed the headlines like military triumphs, but which were essential for victory. His first biographer also indicated that Pug played a major role in the deception plans to hoodwink the enemy into thinking Allied plans were elsewhere, but how major his personal role in this sphere of activity is difficult to verify; the hush-hush nature of that activity did not help.

Desert War

To step back in time there had been considerable tensions regarding Churchill's interest in North Africa, with his demands for victory and interfering with the military, causing some friction between him and the COS. On 30 June 1941 General Sir Claude Auchinleck had arrived in Cairo to assume command of the Middle East. It was probably an unpopular posting given what appeared to be the growing failures in that area and the fear of Rommel's reputation earning him the name of the Desert Fox. Pug noted the military commanders were under continuous pressure from Churchill, who had been distressed by the failure of Operation Battleaxe and was desperate to announce a victory. Earlier in his memoirs Pug insisted that Churchill stayed in touch with his commanders to encourage and offer them support. Others interpreted that Churchill was pestering Auchinleck to move faster towards a victory, which reflected Brooke's frequent criticism of Churchill interfering with commanders. Auchinleck flew to London and the COS agreed with him that to move against Rommel too early could be a disaster, suggesting 1 November as the best time. There were evidently tensions between Churchill and Auchinleck, but Pug, as was part of his character tried to remedy the problems when the two of them were at Chequers, by explaining to his old friend that while Churchill was unusual, he was the best possible war leader and all his so-called rudeness, frankness of speech were part of his determination that victory should follow. On 28 August 1941 Pug wrote a letter to his friend Auchinleck trying to ease the tensions, in which he wrote:

> You needn't worry at all that his confidence in you has been impaired. I know it hasn't; but I do advise you most earnestly to write him a long private letter, telling him your hopes and fears more fully and more freely than is possible in a telegram or even an official letter.[17]

He later added that Churchill 'was a child of nature. He venerated tradition, but ridiculed convention. When the occasion demanded, he could be the personification of dignity; when the spirit moved him, he could be a gamin, later adding 'he had a considerable respect for the trained military mind but refused to subscribe to the idea that generals were infallible'.[18] Pug was already beginning to understand Churchill's nature better than most, and he was correct in so far that Churchill appreciated the personal friendly touch, and later Brooke would advise Montgomery to accept this when fighting in northern Europe. Pug was a man of intense loyalty to old friends and to his chief, and as such he was always caught in a personal emotional conflict which he tried to resolve with his usual kindness. He explained that although Churchill respected the military mind, he was always prepared to take a calculated risk. Pug was showing the positive side of Churchill's style of leadership, but it took someone like Brooke to stop some of Churchill's more reckless ideas born of his frustrated impetuosity. Pug admitted at this stage that Churchill had the habit of 'bombarding' his commanders with requests, advice, and demands, some of which Pug admitted might seem 'irrelevant or superfluous'.[19] Pug was aware of the sensitivity of his position, the bridge between his political chief and the military, and was always careful when Churchill asked about commanders, with Pug always refusing an opinion to Churchill's annoyance. Pug's reluctance to express opinions of others was mainly because of his sense of loyalty, and he also understood the Service Chiefs would not appreciate such interference. Pug had to work for Churchill but also alongside the military commanders. It must have been tortuous for him, because he had known Auchinleck for a long time, and years later (1959) he assisted John Connell in his biography of his old friend.[20]

Auchinleck returned to Cairo anticipating two operations, one Crusader to take Cyrenaica, and Acrobat to capture Tripoli, and he stayed in touch with Pug which seemed to help him under his immense pressures by others' expectations. In this world of commanders who had more men beneath than above, it must have been a genuine relief if not a pleasure to have a man like Pug with whom to communicate their feelings. Operation Crusader started well but then went badly wrong. Auchinleck went to the front line to investigate, and in London it was anticipated that Auchinleck would take personal control but instead he gave the role to his Deputy Chief of Staff General Ritchie, who according to Pug was a man of the highest calibre but with little experience of command. It was another disaster not helped as Pug noted, by Churchill in parliament paying tribute to Rommel's leadership skills. It may be tempting at this point to wonder whether Churchill was inwardly angry and wishing his generals were as good as the German commander. There was, as Pug noted, great concern over Malta because of its naval strategic position for communication lines in the Mediterranean.

The frustrations were increasing in Churchill's mind as he desperately needed some form of victory, not just for parliamentary success, but for the nation and as a signal to the Americans that the British could win. He decided to fly to the Middle East to see for himself, and then to meet Stalin but sadly for Pug he was not to go. Pug summarised the situation very quickly, that Churchill had gone to change Auchinleck for Alexander, and Montgomery was to take over the desert army (it was to have been General Gott who was shot down by a German fighter plane). In his memoirs Pug felt sad for Auchinleck but accepted that Ritchie may have been a mistake and was pleased that Montgomery was good, but adding that 'one could wish the victor of Alamein had acknowledged that his immediate predecessor in command of the Eighth Army had paved the way for his triumph'.[21] Later Montgomery would be criticised for this very point as his well-known ego irritated everyone.

Churchill was no fool, and he realised that Pug seemed to appreciate most of his military friends, and they liked him, and it crossed this writer's mind that Churchill took Brooke rather than Pug because 'Shrapnel' Brooke was the senior general and was tougher than the kindlier Pug. On 23 October Montgomery was successful at El Alamein and Churchill had the victory he had so desperately sought. Pug was over the moon in his adoration of Churchill writing that 'in the one case he steeled a nation to defy defeat; in the other, he laid the foundation of Allied victory'.[22] Churchill always deployed Pug to carry out the difficult task of explaining to the disconcerted Eisenhower the nature and reason for Churchill's propensity for sudden changes, as Pug was undoubtedly the best person for such a delicate task.[23]

Far East

During the latter part of 1942 the global crisis escalated with Japanese belligerence increasing. When Pug had previously worked for a few years as an Intelligence officer in the War Office, he had suggested that Hong Kong should be demilitarised in the event of a war against Japan, because maintaining an air force there was untenable, and a determined enemy would capture it with ease. His report was not well received and the garrison was kept at full strength. It eventually fell on Christmas Day 1941 with 12,000 casualties. Whether Pug had been correct or not is pointless to explore, but his notes on this underlined the danger that with the preoccupation with Nazi Germany, the Far Eastern situation had been put on a back shelf. Pug observed that Churchill had not let the possibility of problems in that area 'depress him too much'. The USA had been more aware of Japanese intentions and had imposed serious economic sanctions on that country.

It was decided that a Far Eastern Fleet consisting of the *Prince of Wales*, the *Repulse*, and aircraft carrier *Indomitable* should sail under the command of Admiral Sir Thomas Phillips. As with Churchill, Phillips was convinced that a well-prepared naval ship had nothing to fear from air attacks. Curiously, Pug while explaining he was not a psychic, claimed he often had presentiments, and as he farewelled Phillips was depressed because he felt that he would never see him again. In fact Phillips died in an aerial attack against his fleet. *The Prince of Wales* and the *Repulse* suffered a Japanese attack on 10 December 1941 by eighty-six bombers, and although the attendant destroyers saved many lives, Admiral Phillips and Captain John Leache went down with their ships. The Japanese had clearly demonstrated the tactical fact that air cover and attack were now part of naval warfare, and RAF fighters only arrived after the assault had finished.

John Colville recorded how Pug had told him that Phillips had held forth on naval invulnerability to air attack, infuriating Arthur Harris, who according to Pug thumped the table and said:

Phillips, you make me sick. I can tell you what is going to happen. One day we shall be at war with Japan, and you will be sailing across the South China seas in one of your beautiful battleships. Out of the cloud there will come a squadron of Japanese bombers and as your great ship capsizes, you will turn to your navigating officer and say, 'that was a whopping great mine we hit'.[24]

As Pug must have realised this was uncannily prescient, an ability Pug denied he ever had, but he had been apprehensive about Phillips' expedition as he said farewell.

Pug had been in the Carlton Hotel Grillroom when he first heard of the attack on Pearl Harbor, writing that had he 'not been in such a public place he would have shouted for joy'.[25] It is the nature of war that Churchill had befriended the hated Stalin, and now there was rejoicing that Britain's closest friend had suffered a dreadful attack on the cynical but realistic basis that it would draw America out from its hitherto sense of isolationism. By the end of December it was clear that the Japanese had control of vast areas of the seas and were threatening much of the Far East, with even the possibility of endangering Australia and New Zealand. Later, when Singapore was invaded (15 February) the Far Eastern situation looked totally dismal.

Chapter Four

1943,
The Year of Conferences

During 1943 a variety of conferences took place all round the world from the Middle East to America, Canada, Moscow, Cairo and Teheran, and to Pug's delight he attended them all, travelling some 40,000 miles and nearly half the year globe-trotting.* Roosevelt was keen on a military conference for all three allies, but Churchill pointed out again that the Russian generals could not express even an opinion without conferring with Stalin, and all their demands would focus on the necessity of an immediate second front. When Roosevelt pushed for a meeting of all three heads of state Stalin agreed, but he announced that the military situation was too busy and he could not leave Moscow, so they decided to go ahead without him.

Casablanca Conference

The initial trip to Casablanca (15 January) was the first of many conferences that year and codenamed 'Symbol', with Pug describing how 'junior' members of the delegation left earlier by ship, but others like him had to quietly disappear so not to raise suspicion. Pug sneaked out of White's Club 'like a thief in the night', driving through rain-filled pitch darkness to an agreed meeting point. They were put into larger cars and taken to Lyneham in Wiltshire. They had to listen to all the dangers, be strapped into parachutes, given Mae Wests (inflatable life jackets), supplied with currency for each country they flew over, and a gadget which gathered dew which could be drunk if they found themselves in a desert. Because of their seniority he and his companion Lord Leathers were given bomb racks in which to sleep, and it was a long uncomfortable

---
* Casablanca (January), Washington (May), Quebec (August) Moscow (November), Cairo (November), Cairo and Teheran (December).

journey, eventually landing to watch the Americans arrive in more comfortable and luxuriously appointed planes.

The Combined COS started the same day with Pug describing an atmosphere of 'veiled antipathy and mistrust'. It was the same dilemma as mentioned above. The British strategy was one of clearing the Germans out of North Africa, taking Sicily, invading Italy to knock her out of the war and to bomb Germany in preparation for crossing the channel. The Americans had yet to agree, with Marshall who saw the Mediterranean arena as a periphery and a waste of time. As usual Admiral King wanted more resources for the Far East and Arnold to bomb Germany into submission. The Americans were unified on crossing the Channel as soon as possible, and suspicious that the British were either delaying it or even did not want to risk the venture.

Brooke was informative and persuasive in his presentations, but his authoritative lecturing style irritated some Americans and Pug believed it was Dill, the British representative in Washington who helped save the day, and there is no question that Pug's pleasant demeanour also helped. Up to this time the Americans had not had the benefit of a COS which worked hand in hand with the political leader, and they had not experienced daily contact with Roosevelt having at that time no equivalent to Pug, who was the bridge between these two critical areas. It often led Marshall to wonder what Churchill was persuading the President to do when hidden away together in Roosevelt's home. However, there was always constant communication between Churchill and his COS through Pug.

The Americans were eventually persuaded that by invading Sicily it would take the pressure off Russia as would the continuous bombing of Germany. Pug believed the British started to gain a clearer understanding about the American concerns in the Far East, but there was heated discussion over Sicily or Sardinia preferred by the Americans, with Churchill throwing his weight in by saying 'I absolutely refuse to be fobbed with a sardine'. Later it was felt the British had won the arguments, but many of the Americans thought that the crafty British had led them down a garden path and that situation would not happen again. Later in the year Pug would explain to his friend Lascelles (King George VI's Secretary) the difficulty the British were having 'in trying to get the Americans to see eye-to-eye with us on various points of major strategy… most of them have never got over their distaste for campaigning in the

Mediterranean and are really only interested in the war in the Pacific'.[1] It was going to be a tension which would not go away and is still debated to this day. There was little time out for those attending the conference, but Pug enjoyed a few walks along the Casablanca beach watching the violent surf which Casablanca was renowned for, reflecting that when the troops had landed it was fortunate that for once it had been more subdued.

It was at the Casablanca conference that Churchill had drawn attention to the importance of Turkey and trying to induce that country into the Western Alliance, and although Pug thought it dangerous Churchill decided to go there and use his influence. Pug asked permission to visit Algiers to see Eisenhower before he returned to London, with Churchill agreeing but telling him not to 'loll about' there. Pug replied that since he met Churchill he had lost the habit of lolling about, but this possible joke by Churchill may have reflected a view of Pug who was not to all appearances a central or key figure in these proceedings. Pug was the bureaucrat, the mobile advisory information file, the collector of information, occasional adviser, the diplomatic balancer and for others he was the pleasant Chief of Staff for Churchill, a cog in Churchill's massive war machine, busy but on the edges of these major consultations.

It was at this conference that Roosevelt came up with the policy of 'Unconditional Surrender' which was to become a controversial issue in the years to come. In his memoirs Pug raised the issue with his usual careful diplomatic balance, but reading between the lines it was easy to gain the impression that Pug was not happy with this controversial statement, because the implications had not been carefully thought through, noting that Italy later managed to evade the issue, and an enemy faced by this clause would fight to the bitter end. Churchill made it known that Pug's reaction was similar to his own as he did not wish to apply the policy to Italy.[2] Churchill admitted in his history he had to give Roosevelt full support for the sake of coalition unity. Many observers, with good reason, thought it may have been an effort to keep Stalin onside by stating there could be no separate peace agreements with the enemy. Forever the diplomat, Pug eventually concluded on looking back, that he regarded himself as one of the few who did not think it made any material difference to the length of the war, simply because Hitler would fight to the bitter end because it was in his nature.

He went to Algiers for a brief meeting with Eisenhower, and not to be accused of 'lolling about' Pug made his way to Gibraltar, catching up with other conference members returning to Britain. It had been Pug's job to explain to Eisenhower the Casablanca decisions, and to convince him of British support for him as Commander-in-Chief. Eisenhower always appreciated Alexander because of his gentlemanly style and friendly approach, and he felt very much the same for Pug. Pug returned with Mountbatten and Admiral Pound in one plane, waiting for Brigadiers Dykes and Stewart following in the next, but later heard that their plane had crashed and both men were killed. Pug had regarded Dykes as a trusted good friend, and the only other person he could send to Washington in Dyke's place to advise of their account of the Casablanca conference was Lieutenant Colonel Grove who flew the next night, but he too was killed in a plane crash before he arrived. It must have been a sharp reminder that although Pug and his men were administrators, war and death were their constant companions.

Trident Conference

Historically it is now known that the Americans were unhappy about the Casablanca Conference, thinking the British had won the strategic tussle and they were being misled. Very much in the American mind was their concern over what would happen after the invasion of Sicily (Operation Husky), with the British convinced the next step should be crossing to mainland Italy, but the Americans had serious doubts. In addition to this Pug realised the Americans, with some justifications, were critical of the effort being made by the British in Burma, and were concerned about the possible collapse of China demanding more support for Chiang Kai-Shek. Pug was right and knew that although the British had a deep interest in the Far East, they were more concerned about the Nazi threat on their doorstep and limited by resources and manpower. Because of all these concerns a few months after the North African conference Churchill and Roosevelt decided on another meeting in Washington to be known as Trident. Churchill knew that the Americans were sensitive regarding Casablanca and in Washington would want to have more of their own way, so he collected a colossal staff for this next mission.

They left for America on the *Queen Mary*, which had been carefully deloused because of an onboard rat infection. It was a massive team and Pug mentioned a few in his memoirs, but curiously he avoided direct reference to the three Chiefs of Staff, especially Brooke who was so critical during these discussions. During the trip various meetings were constantly held to ensure they were all singing from the same hymn sheet. There was little time for strolling on the deck, except for a lifeboat drill during which Churchill demanded that a machine gun be mounted on his designated lifeboat because he would fight to the end. The liner was fast and able to zig-zag which made it an unlikely target for U-boats, and messages were flagged to accompanying destroyers to then transmit only when they had moved away from the *Queen Mary*.

On arrival they were well received, and all ate 'small steaks' offered on the menu which felt like a week's ration, drawing home the comfort of America when compared to the harsh realities in Britain. The conference started with Roosevelt taking Churchill away for their own personal consultations and a pattern was established, with the morning starting with the British and American COS meeting separately and then coming together an hour before noon. Pug noted that they shared meals and breaktimes together, which often helped ease the tensions from the frequent conflicts within the formal meetings. He also noted that the Combined Chiefs of Staff Secretariat helped it all run smoothly which was possibly something of an exaggeration. Some of the meetings were nothing short of turbulent and fractious as American and British viewpoints clashed, occasionally resolved by sending minor officials and administration out of the room so the critical chiefs of the combined forces could find a solution, and this tended to work. Pug was acutely aware of the tensions writing the reports on the main issues in his inimitably clear style.

The American point of view was their feeling that they had been led to believe their proposals for Operations Sledgehammer and Roundup had received British support, only to discover later that this had not been the case, almost intimating that they had been hoodwinked, and all matters had suddenly turned to the matter of the North African invasion, Operation Torch. They had agreed to Torch on the understanding they could launch an attack across the Channel in 1943, and yet there was no sign of this being prepared. They suggested the British idea of invading

Italy might be correct in taking that country out of the war, but it would not be a significant step to defeating Germany. The Americans boldly stated they were suspicious of the British interest in southern Europe, and they also mentioned the apparent British reluctance in crossing the Channel to France, implying that the British were trying to prevent this major operation.

The British counter argument, forcibly put forward by the CIGS General Brooke was equally clear. They were not averse to crossing the Channel, but with their experience of these seawaters, and fighting the Germans over two major wars, they felt the timing was critical and 1943 was far too soon to hope for success. The Germans had to be weakened by being pre-occupied elsewhere, exposed to serious bombing and military pressure, and to launch an amphibious attack against a well-fortified coastland defended by some of the best trained soldiers in the world would be a mistake if taken too early. It was not just the landing which would be difficult, but a structure for the constant supplies of men and resources had to be planned with care and foresight, which could not be accomplished in a matter of months. This venture also demanded total superiority in the air, German communications had to be seriously hindered, the landing troops had to be battle experienced with sufficient landing craft and naval support, as had been demonstrated in North Africa. Nor, the British argued, should the million plus troops be left idle before crossing to France but should be fighting the enemy and gathering battle experience. If, Brooke continued, Hitler had cause to be worried by the invasion of Italy he would consequently be more concerned about the Balkans, the oilfields, and would be forced to react taking the pressure off Stalin and giving time for the Allied Second Front in France.

These arguments racked back and forth and at times became angry, even when they widened to the Burma-China area of operations. There was agreement over the U-boat warfare and the conduct of convoys, and the need for an airbase in the Azores controlled by Portugal who would understandably try and remain neutral. A 'soft invasion' was proposed, but the British Foreign Office managed to persuade England's oldest ally to agree.

Nevertheless, Churchill was not entirely happy because the post-Husky strategy had yet to be finalised, and he decided to return to Britain via North Africa where he could speak with Eisenhower. He knew that it would appear to some he was trying to influence the American commander, which he probably was, and Roosevelt allowed Marshall to keep him company. Pug wrote that 'Marshall readily agreed' but not all believed Marshall was that happy with the proposed journey. They returned to Gibraltar with Pug sleeping for the entire 17 hours to Churchill's concern, thinking Pug should eat and wondering whether he had died. They flew the next day to Algiers, toured the battlefields, and Pug recorded that Marshall said he 'viewed Torch with a less jaundiced eye'.[3]

The British and American staffs met again, and it was decided to cross to the mainland. Eisenhower set two operations for planning, one to the mainland and the other to Sardinia.* Churchill claiming Sardinia would be a convenience, but Italy would yield an immense prize. It is now widely perceived that Trident was controlled by the Americans, who did not want to be cajoled again as they felt they had been at Casablanca. The British arguments were persuasive, but it was generally agreed that the Mediterranean theatre could continue with the strict agreement that France would be invaded in May 1944, and Eisenhower basically wanted to 'play it by ear' regarding Italy or Sardinia after Husky.

On their return Churchill asked Pug to take another plane because he was too heavy [!] but it may have been that Churchill wanted a private conversation with his fellow passenger Alexander. Pug had a risky flight to Gibraltar because one of the engines caught fire, and on his second flight to Britain his plane was approached by two fighters but with some relief it transpired they were Spitfires, thinking Churchill was on board.

First Quebec Conference

Within six weeks of the Washington Conference another was considered necessary following the success of Husky and the need to give a more defined shape to the plans for Roundup, now called by the more familiar name Overlord. The Burma/China theatre was not doing well, demanding better co-ordination between the Western Allies. Roosevelt, to Canadian delight suggested Quebec for the conference which would be known as Quadrant. It involved Pug and the others in another long trip in the *Queen Mary* with Churchill's wife and daughter on board,

---

* Sardinia was Operation Brimstone put in the hands of General Mark Clark.

with Pug noting how Mrs Churchill managed to keep her husband under control just by the way she looked at him. It was on these long journeys that Pug often made interesting observations of his fellow passengers. One was Orde Wingate with his history of the Long-Range Penetration Group, another was Wing Commander Guy Gibson, both of whom the Americans loved. They were taken to America by Churchill probably to show off experienced British warriors of different types. In his memoirs the presence of Guy Gibson launched Pug into a brief diatribe about the nature of bombing Germany. He was aware of the postwar debate over the morality and efficacy of such operations, but he arrived at the conclusion with which most would agree, that these actions demanded immense courage by the young bomber crews.

The journey also gave Churchill time to learn more about the plans for Overlord and discuss the fraught issue of South-East Asia. During this journey the decision was made to assign a different commander-in-chief for this area rather than leave it to the oversight of the Indian appointment. Pug was cross with himself when he later recalled he had once considered this in 1929 if a crisis of this order arose. The canvassing started and Admiral Lord Mountbatten was selected. Pug, however, was somewhat concerned that one man could take on such a huge task, and knowing Mountbatten personally believed he would need a good Chief of Staff to keep him in order. Mountbatten had a difficult task ahead of him and historically had many critics, his sense of self-importance was widely known and as soon as he arrived in the new post of SEAC (South-East Asia Command) many were aghast at the way he built up his staff to proportions which many thought grossly unreasonable. In December 1943 Admiral Sir James Somerville wrote to Pug about 'the proliferation of staff at South East Asia Command' and the 'nature of Mountbatten's command'.[4]

It has been suggested by his first biographer that it was Pug who put the idea of this new command area into Churchill's head, but not according to his memoirs, nevertheless, there may be some truth in this in so far that Churchill would often have quiet moments with Pug as they floated ideas.[5] When approached Mountbatten asked time to think the offer over and 'he went to Ismay for reassurance and advice. I feel as though I have been pole-axed', he began.[6] In all these spider-webs of discussion and interpersonal relationships Pug was always somewhere near the centre. Pug had described the appointment as a 'hot-potato', and in his written reply to Churchill, Mountbatten thanked him for the 'dazzling appointment', and he was grateful to record that all three of the COS and Pug Ismay 'are ready to back me with their own convictions'.[7] Brooke and his two service colleagues were probably happy to have Mountbatten away from the Western theatre of operations, and it seems that only Churchill's love of Mountbatten with his royal connections and the support of Pug had fulfilled Mountbatten's dream.

Later, when Wavell was announced as Viceroy, and Auchinleck was to be Commander-in-Chief of India, it was seen as a rationalisation of the war effort mainly implemented by Pug according to his first biographer.[8] Again there is scant evidence for this suggestion, but Pug and Churchill were the only two on board ship who had any experience of service in India, and again it may have resulted from their private conversations.

In Quebec Pug was delighted that both delegations were housed in the same building as he knew that when people met socially it made formal interchanges that much easier. The critical part of the conference was the planning of Operation Overlord with a target set for 1 May 1944, but they all agreed on three conditions. The first was the necessity of dominating the airspace, the second there should be no more than twelve German divisions in France, and synthetic harbours (later known as Mulberry harbours) should be prepared. There was some contention as to who should be in overall charge. Earlier the Americans had wanted one commander for all operational theatres, but the British had strongly objected along practical grounds, and with some sense in their arguments. Churchill had wanted Brooke but with the overwhelming forces supplied by the USA the choice had to be an American, with most thinking it would be Marshall. When Eisenhower was selected there was some surprise with considerable speculation as to why he was chosen. One suggestion was that Roosevelt always needed Marshall on hand, but it will always remain speculation.

Pug was delighted because he felt that Eisenhower was the right man, and he certainly was in the calm diplomatic way Eisenhower frequently held the fractious coalition together. Pug also thought his strategic ideas were excellent, though he noted in his memoirs that there were some who considered him an amateur. Pug thought the various criticisms of Eisenhower 'as unfair and unjustifiable', and in his memoirs launched into a lengthy argument in Eisenhower's favour.⁹ Once again Pug was attacking the publication of Brooke's diaries in which Brooke had made it clear, that along with his protégé Montgomery, he thought little of Eisenhower's military abilities. It was at this conference that Churchill decided he would send special emissaries to key areas, to represent the British government. One was Carton de Wiart to Chiang Kai-Shek where it worked so well the Chinese leader asked to keep him after the war. A second was General Herbert to General MacArthur, sadly Herbert was killed on the bridge of the battleship *New Mexico* when it was hit by a Japanese suicide bomber.

During many of these conferences when the temperature rose in the heated and cantankerous debates, not only between the Americans and British, but between Churchill's ideas which clashed with his own COS, it was Pug's task to act as a bridge. The word Pontiff (Latin root words pons/pont for bridge) applied to the Pope indicating the bridge between God and man, Pug was no Pontiff, but nevertheless, he was the intermediary between friends who so frequently clashed. It was his approach which often helped ameliorate strained relationships, but it was hard work, and like a bridge bearing the burdens, Pug would from time to time feel the pressure of that intense weight.

When the conference was finished and all returned to Britain and America, Pug stayed with Churchill who remained in Quebec for a week. While there he noticed that Admiral Pound was not well and told Churchill what he felt. Pound suddenly appeared better and Churchill dismissed Pug's views, but Pug was right, Pound resigned and died on 21 October, significantly for a naval man the anniversary of the Battle of Trafalgar. Unlike some others Pug launched into a kindly appraisal of Pound and criticised those who had accused Pound of sleeping during meetings, and for not being on the ball. Again, Pug mentioned no names, but it was his distaste at Brooke's diaries being in the public arena. It was not just Brooke who was critical of Pound, but Churchill as well, but Pound was determined to stay thinking Churchill wanted to replace him with his *bête noire* Mountbatten. As Mountbatten's biographer noted, 'Ismay, who knew Churchill's mind as well as anyone, had no suspicion that any such move was in question and doubted afterwards whether the Prime Minister could have been serious – he may well have teased Pound himself, but not more than that.'¹⁰

Pug was pleased to recall how good Pound's successor Admiral Andrew Cunningham was and Air Chief Marshal Portal as well. To balance the books, he also turned his attention to CIGS General Brooke, pointing out that he was the best all-rounder in the service, and had a well-deserved reputation for his military skills at Dunkirk. He pointed out that the Americans at first found Brooke's speed of speech, staccato language sounding like an authoritarian lecturer, difficult at first but they soon came to admire his military skills and later even liked him as a person. Over the eighteen years Pug had worked in Whitehall he thought Brooke was the best of all the CIGS, but this did not stop him being critical for publishing his diaries. What Pug probably did not know was that after the war Brooke was virtually impoverished, had to sell his house and move into the gardener's cottage, sell his favourite bird-books (he was obsessed with ornithology), and the diary publications may well have been a way to make some money.

On leaving Canada, Churchill and Pug spent some time in Washington, and when Roosevelt had to go to his home Hyde Park, he gave Churchill the use of the White House with the right to call upon the staff. Churchill held joint meetings there and Pug felt that with this trust it was beginning to feel more like a family. The trip home on HMS *Renown* was peaceful apart from the fact that Churchill's daughter while strolling the deck with an officer was nearly swept overboard, she held on and according to the relieved Pug looked like a 'drowned rat'. A curious note also appeared in the Ismay archives; a letter written by Alan Lascelles offering a suggestion which had been made that Ismay could be appointed Governor General in Canada; he had obviously made a good impression in that country.[11]

Moscow Meeting

Stalin refused to join Churchill and Roosevelt in conference and therefore a meeting of the foreign ministries was organised. Eden asked for Pug's company who was not that happy as he had only been back at home for less than three weeks, and it was essentially a political conference. Eden had received messages from Stalin, which Pug thought were highly offensive, complaining about the Arctic convoys which did not portend a happy meeting. Pug had the total support of Churchill who had written to Stalin telling him Pug 'is my personal representative on the Chiefs of Staff Committee and he is thoroughly acquainted with the whole field of our military policy and is authorised to study with your commanders and plans for practical co-operation'.[12] This underlined Churchill's trust in Pug but he was of little value as Stalin was more interested in other matters such as resources and a second front. Churchill was unhappy about Pug's redundancy in Russia, and in a memo to Eden he stated that Pug 'might have explained the facts and figures...how very foolish and physically impossible was the suggestion that we should send twenty-five or thirty divisions to the Russian front'.[13]

The journey involved a direct flight to Cairo, then to Teheran and on to Moscow where they were met by Vyacheslav Molotov, Maxim Litvinov and others in a friendly greeting which seemed to surprise Pug. The first session followed the next day and Molotov was voted into the chair with an agreed agenda. The main point for the Russians focused on the timing and whereabouts of the second front, which would have been no surprise to the visitors, because despite the fighting in the Mediterranean and Italy, the Russians were still bearing the main force of the German military machine. The next day it was Pug who gave an hour long talk of the timing of Operation Overlord, the expectancies, and the necessary requirements before the invasion was launched. Eden went to see Stalin about the Arctic convoy issues and found the Soviet leader, contrary to expectation, in good form and the issue of the Arctic convoys dealt with in a friendly fashion.

The rest of the meetings as far as Pug were concerned were purely political matters. The friendly atmosphere continued, with the Russians surprisingly agreeing to take China on board as a force against the Axis powers, something which hitherto they had ignored. There was also some discussion about how the situation in occupied postwar Germany would be settled, it had already been agreed that Russia, America and Britain would divide that country into three zones, and now they prepared the way forward for a meeting of the three top political leaders.

Then came a shock for Eden and his party when Churchill sent a message about the situation in Italy, Alexander was demanding more resources to win the Italian campaign which Churchill supported, and this meant telling Stalin that the second front might have to be delayed for a month. It is easy to speculate they must have had a feeling of trepidation as they took this news to Stalin and, according to Pug, Eden was at his best diplomatically, assuring him it was a brief delay and Stalin appeared to accept the news in good grace. The next day Pug was closely questioned on his talk about Overlord, and he appeared to answer the Russian questions in this secret meeting to their satisfaction. He must have made some impression because the Russians invited him to stay behind and visit their front lines, but Churchill demanded he returned to prepare for the next conference.

The conference had fared much better than they had expected, and most unusually for the Soviets they accepted an invitation to dine at the British Embassy, all of which impressed Pug so much he wrote that for 'the first time I was optimistic about our postwar relations with Russia', a feeling he kept at Yalta in February 1945 but which had 'evaporated' by Potsdam in July of the same year.[14] This was all so typical of Pug who always wanted to see the best side of people and a situation. They had trouble leaving on time because the local airport said the weather was too appalling to take off, the British pilots disagreed, so they appealed to Molotov who cleared the way only to find they had not been given time to warn the anti-aircraft guns that a friendly plane would be passing overhead. Pug wrote in his memoirs how difficult officialdom could be at lower levels unless one had friends in higher places, but he added that 'perhaps these habits are not unique to Russia, or even war-time!' and he was undoubtedly right.[15] When they returned to London, Pug and Eden, according to Lascelles, were convinced 'that they [Russians] can never rehabilitate their appallingly devastated country without our help'.[16] This help was mainly American and some British resources mainly conveyed with the Royal Navy through the Arctic waters which Stalin badly needed, which is why he probably broke old habits and ate in the British Embassy.

It is clear from archival material that Pug was not entirely redundant as he claimed. A copy of a telegram from Eden to Churchill read: 'I must put on record how deeply in debt I am to Ismay. He helped us at every stage in Moscow and here [Cairo] and played a chief part in inducing faith in our intentions. Thank you so much for his help.' In the New Year Eden wrote a personal note to Pug stating 'I hope that you know how really valuable your help was to me in Moscow. I believe we did a good job together, and I <u>know</u> that we could not have done it without you.'[17]

Back in Cairo they met a Turkish delegation in the hope of negotiating a way to bring that country onto the Allied side, but the Turks, despite Eden's assurances of help, argued that if they did so the Germans would sweep in. There would be many attempts at various times to try and influence the Turks, but they persisted in their neutrality and many would have some sympathy with their stance. It was not until 7 November that Pug was back in his office reporting to 10 Downing Street.

Cairo and Teheran Conferences

Pug arrived in England only to find that four days later he was off again to Cairo for the Sextant Conference, then onto Teheran for the Eureka talks. They set sail in HMS *Renown* arriving in war-torn and bombed out Malta on 17 November. Lord Gort was in command of the island, using a bicycle and receiving the same rations as the other residents, indicating that he was a man of principle. Churchill stayed with him but did not enjoy the spartan existence and soon developed a cold. Pug suggested he should return to the ship, but Churchill refused, having found an opportunity to meet all the service chiefs in the Mediterranean, and he insisted that they met with the COS all crowded into his bedroom. The discussions varied over the Italian campaign, the possible capture of Rhodes and partisan operations in Yugoslavia, none of which would have pleased or interested their American counterparts. A cable arrived from Roosevelt suggesting Khartoum would be a safer meeting place than Cairo. The British memory of Khartoum was somewhat coloured since the death of General Gordon there in 1885, which Roosevelt would probably have known.

Churchill asked Pug to investigate the matter, who had the Khartoum facilities checked and found them wanting, and he felt that the Cairo security measures were strong with British squadrons available to stop Luftwaffe attacks and Roosevelt accepted the British views.[18] They continued their journey on HMS *Renown* to Alexandria and then flew to Cairo on 21 November where at least the amenities were good. According to Pug they were surprised and disappointed to find Chiang Kai-Shek and his wife already present. The Americans were putting great store in the forlorn hope the Chinese would help demolish the Japanese enemy. They had wanted to discuss these issues with the Chinese after Teheran and not before, with some on the American side thinking it was a good idea since it would stop the Soviets thinking the British and Americans were 'ganging' up against them, which irritated Pug who believed that the Allies should have been more blunt with Stalin. He argued this in his postwar memoirs, but whether he thought this at the time must remain speculation.

The British constantly opposed the American wish of a global United Chiefs of Staff on the grounds that the Chinese were understandably not overly interested in the European conflict, and once again Russian generals would always need Stalin's agreement even to express a mere viewpoint. In the first plenary meeting they all met Madame Chiang Kai-Shek who often helped with interpretation, with Pug suspecting that she sometimes expanded the translation by inserting some of her own opinions. Nevertheless, he described her as a charming interpreter, whereas Brooke in his diaries was bemused by the fact that the younger officers were more bewitched by her feminine shape enhanced by her national costume. Mountbatten gave a talk on his planned operations for Burma even though they had yet to be discussed at the COS level, and Chiang Kai-Shek wanted more including the immediate capture of Rangoon which demanded a large amphibious operation. Pug also discovered that the President had promised Chiang Kai-Shek a large Operation called Buccaneer to capture the Andaman Islands, despite the warning this would consume too many resources at a critical time, with Pug explaining it by later writing that 'great men have a tendency to brush aside any practical objections which they find inconvenient, and make concessions to expediency'.[19] Pug also noted that it often led to difficulties which it did in this case.

The second plenary session next day took part without the Chinese in which the British pleaded that landing craft in the Mediterranean, due to be sent to Britain for Operation Overlord (sixty-eight in number), could be kept in Italy until 15 January. This request was evidently for Operation Shingle for the landing at Anzio to which Pug made no reference. Because Overlord was dominant in American eyes, they objected but were eventually won round. However, when Churchill asked for some help in taking Rhodes the Americans were much firmer, probably recalling Gallipoli and raising their long-held suspicions about Churchill and his obsession with the Balkans, always wondering whether he was trying to delay Overlord. Thereafter there were more discussions on South-East Asia, leaving no time for the two Western Allies to reach a mutual understanding on Overlord before they met the Russians.

On 27 November they flew to Teheran and were housed in the British Legation which Pug described as somewhat rundown, and whose gardens joined those of the Russian Embassy. Roosevelt and the American party were to go to their legation a mile away. The Russians then surprised them by claiming they had unearthed a plot of enemy agents in the area determined to kill at least one of the three political leaders. They then offered the Americans a building within their own heavily guarded embassy to keep them safe. Most believed this to be a Soviet ploy to move the Americans into a building which was undoubtedly bugged, but just in case the Soviets were telling the truth it was decided to accept the offer. Nobody could verify if the Soviets were being honest, but years later a Russian secret agent called Sudoplatov mentioned that Otto Skorzeny was ready to launch an attack on Tehran which the Russians thwarted, although there is no supporting evidence.[20]

Lavrenty Beria, head of the Russian secret service was obsessed with security and had arranged for as many rooms as possible to be bugged. Later when Stalin was invited to a meal at the British Embassy Beria led the NKVD on a methodical search of the area where the event would take place. Beria also ensured that the rooms were bugged with listening devices in order that private conversations could be overheard. It was at Teheran that Sergo Beria (Beria's son) 'manned the recording equipment bugging their rooms and was surprised to overhear FDR level a counter-accusation at Churchill for trying to engineer an anti-communist government' in Poland.[21] Beria's son was clever and spoke both German and English which gave Beria the necessary excuse not to sacrifice him on the frontline. Stalin needed a daily appraisal from Beria's son as to what was being said, and as to whether it was being spoken in a way which was genuine, or whether Roosevelt was aware that he was being bugged. They later used directional microphones to hear Roosevelt as he was wheeled around in the open areas. Roosevelt always suspected that his conversations were recorded. It appeared Churchill was not fooled by Beria; various other reports on meeting Beria have surfaced from time to time, and while some found him convivial most felt his coldness and desire for power to be the dominant feature of his personality. For many he represented the dark and unknown side of Stalin and Kremlin life. The whole ploy of moving the Americans had probably been Stalin's manipulative way through Beria's expertise of controlling the meeting.

Away from the devious machinations of the Soviet spy machine Pug was thrilled to see 'the Big Three sitting round the table at long last'. He reported that Roosevelt looked the picture of health and was in excellent form, whereas Churchill was suffering from a cold which did not help his voice, but he managed well. On the other hand, Pug described Stalin looking like a professional poker player with an 'expression as inscrutable as the Sphinx'. Stalin could see no point in the military experts meeting next day as decisions were made at the table of three. As Pug noted, Stalin was accustomed to being the master of 'his house' and all decisions emanated from him. He pointed out that his military experts were elsewhere, but he offered Voroshilov who wore the uniform of a Marshal of the Red Army, who left Brooke, as reported in his diaries, totally unimpressed, and stunned everyone by claiming that crossing the English Channel was no worse than what the Red Army had done in crossing wide rivers.

The main bulk of the conference as viewed by the Allies concerned Operation Overlord, because it would offload the German resistance on the Eastern Front and expedite the fall of Nazi Germany. It was clear that there was no point in Allied soldiers being idle in Italy, taking Rome was evaluated as good, but then to hold a line in northern Italy, leaving some troops available for a landing in southern France. Others proposed the policy of moving northeast towards the Danube and encouraging Turkey into the war. On the other hand Stalin showed no interest in the Turkish situation, he thought Rome was desirable but not important, but what he deemed critical was Overlord along with the operation to land in the south of France at the same time, if not before or immediately after Normandy, which remained his on-going argument. Pug later thought that Stalin was as imperialistic as the Tsars and wanted the Anglo-American forces away from the Balkans. It was agreed that Operation Anvil would take place though later it would create more Anglo-American tensions.

On 30 November the last day was Churchill's 69th birthday and all were invited to his party in the British Legation, but only after American and Soviet security had checked the whole place. Pug was grateful he was not important enough to give a speech but enjoyed relating how a waiter while listening to Stalin's speech, let slip a huge cream cake onto the head of the Russia translator Pavlov, who was covered from head to toe but who continued to translate as if nothing had happened. These were, according to Pug, exhausting days, so as a form of break they invited the Americans to visit Jerusalem and stayed at the King David Hotel. The talks continued in Cairo where the British tried to dissuade the Americans from using valuable landing craft in Operation Buccaneer but came up against a stone wall. Churchill later tackled Roosevelt and failed, but succeeded later. By the end of this exhausting period Churchill was ill at Carthage and unable to return to London until January. Pug was himself unwell from bronchitis and was looked after on HMS *London* as they took him back to Britain. This illness from which Pug suffered was the start of future health problems for him.

Chapter Five

1944, Overlord and More Conferences

For Pug the year 1944 was all about Operation Overlord describing it as 'the year of destiny'. He kept close to his boss Churchill, but in his recollections he dwells almost entirely on Normandy D-Day, occasionally revealing details of curious interest. Pug was sometimes claimed as the overseer of the various plans of deception, he may have contributed ideas, but his main task was to coordinate the ideas, administer the experts and report their findings when and where necessary. The intense bombing of Germany, the Monte Cassino battles and the Anzio beachhead, as with many other features of the war, all faded in Pug's view into the background with the potential ramifications of success or failure with Overlord. This viewpoint by Pug would have been shared by many others, and although it was all top secret few would have failed to guess what was being prepared. Interestingly Pug wrote to Wavell in India explaining how:

> Feelings at home are very mixed. There are a number of people who go about talking as though all is over but the shouting; on the other hand, a lot of people who ought to know better are taking it for granted that Overlord is going to be a bloodbath on the scale of the Somme and Passchendaele. Never has there been an operation so widely advertised.[1]

Pug himself was convinced that Hitler would withdraw his troops from other theatres of war to block Overlord on the beaches and unleash his much-vaunted wonder weapons. He was also convinced Hitler would use his considerable resource of slave labour to build up the Atlantic Wall. The Germans knew this second front was being prepared, but were uncertain as to timing and place, and both sides of the divide had considerable problems to face.

The general plans for the invasion had been established by a body known as COSSAC (Chief of Staff to Supreme Allied Command) and approved at Quebec, though some concerns had been expressed at its limitations. Montgomery was responsible for the initial invasion until Eisenhower had time to establish his own headquarters overseas. Montgomery, as he had done in the plans for Operation Husky, was immediately critical, this time more correctly and demanded a wider assault area, a deeper bridgehead and total control of the skies which all demanded immense resources, all of which Eisenhower supported. Pug reflected how correct Stalin had been at Teheran when he said Overlord should be planned and executed by the same person. Montgomery had once made the same point to Alexander over Operation Husky.

Montgomery's plans demanded more landing craft, more vessels such as minesweepers, more aircraft and bombers to hit the communication hubs, otherwise there would have to be a delay, something the COS and the politicians needed to avoid. Churchill decided he would preside over a weekly meeting of the Overlord planning, this annoyed some, but Pug, a great admirer of his boss, regarded this as the key to the way forward because Churchill had the authority to reconcile differences and move along at speed. There were many clever people involved in building the mobile harbours, not least Commodore Hughes-Hallett who originated the idea, but Pug insisted that Churchill's part should not be ignored. It was, Pug argued, Churchill's drive and initiative which brought all these projects to fruition. There was some truth in Pug's claims, as Churchill had supported General Hobart's 'funny tanks' against military conservative opposition.

One of the more curious aspects of Operation Overlord which Pug dwells upon in his memoirs was the reasoning for the precise timing of date and hour. The paratroopers needed darkness to conceal their approach but moonlight to spot their drop-areas, demanding a late-night rising moon. The tide had to be low to expose the underwater obstacles, but not too long to make it a long and dangerous haul across exposed beaches. H-Hour had to be three hours before high water, and only the 5–7 June fitted these demands. Pug recorded an amusing anecdote at one of the meetings concerning details of timing, when Churchill asked if anyone knew when William the Conqueror landed, Pug had fallen asleep and said 1066 not realising Churchill had asked for the time of day. He was surprised when everyone roared with laughter and Churchill somewhat pityingly said 'Pug, you should have been in your basket ages ago.'[2]

One of the major planning efforts was top secret, as it was intended to mislead the Germans on timings and place. The German and Japanese embassies in Dublin were carefully isolated, and no civilians were allowed to cross the Irish borders. As is widely now well known a false army with air-filled rubber planes and tanks was established in East Anglia, all associated with General Patton, described by Pug as 'that apostle of the offensive *à l'outrance*', and who after the war many Germans agreed that they thought Patton had been the best of the Allied generals. Whereas East Anglia was wide open for inspection, the West country and many of the coastal areas were under virtual lockdown. They even found Montgomery's *doppelgänger*, dressed him up as Montgomery and packed him off to Gibraltar where they ensured a Spanish spy for the Germans could not mistake that it was Montgomery, and let the Germans know that he was there and not in Britain planning a cross-channel attack.

There were other issues with the two bomber commands under Air Chief Harris and the US Strategic Air Force under General Spaatz. Harris complained that his forces were more used to bombing large target areas, not the specific points Normandy D-Day demanded, and Spaatz that it would be better pursuing his policy of hitting oil plants than mere railway junctions. The combined COS listened but decided Overlord was the priority and they would respond to Eisenhower's requests. Churchill was concerned at the possible number of French deaths which might occur by the planned bombing and he asked Roosevelt for support, only to be told by the American president that success in Normandy came first. Pug noted that French casualties were fewer in number than expected and it was not resented. This was Pug's rose-coloured glasses again, as it is now known that quite naturally, there was a degree of resentment from those areas which suffered most, even if some did feel that anything was worth ridding themselves from Nazi oppression.

The American troops were in the southwest and the British in the southeast and once exposed to the plans, they were according to Pug 'hermetically' sealed in with no comings and goings to avoid any spies discovering what was afoot. It was at this juncture in his memoirs, that he recalled an amusing anecdote in which, to befriend the British public, the Americans raised money to rebuild a bombed church. When the rededication service took place after the war, the general who helped in this effort was furious to hear over the radio the bishop who preached stating they were lucky 'in having this *succour* [sucker] from America'.³ This joke can be found in various writings and whether Pug was relating it as a point of amusement, or it was genuine this writer would love to know.

The whole of southern England became armed camps with huge depots of ammunition, with Pug recalling the understandable sense of tension for those preparing and those ready to go and fight. For some, time passed too slowly because of the sense of impatience, for others too fast because of the fear of failure and concerned whether all the preparations had been appropriate. Pug attended the major conference at St Paul's School attended by King George VI and everyone else, where he believed Montgomery was at his best. By this he probably meant that Montgomery was always self-assured which can be a blessing before a risky venture is undertaken. Even the administration details were outlined with Churchill later expressing his concern that only appropriate material was taken, as he had 'heard' that in Operation Torch dental chairs had been landed on the beach and at Anzio hymn books. This was a widespread rumour but how far it was true was difficult to identify. Pug was instructed to write a memo to Montgomery saying the Prime Minister was concerned about the number of non-combatants and non-fighting vehicles landing on the beaches. General Brooke was also aware of Churchill's argument that the army needed too long a tail, to which the ornithological Brooke replied when this arose at Chequers, that the peacock was a beautiful bird with a long tail, but it was necessary for a sense of balance.

Pug recorded the moment when he found Churchill closeted with Admiral Ramsay concocting a plan for Churchill to travel across on D-Day. At first Pug was horrified that the top man should not so much be close to danger, but he should be at the centre if any critical decisions were suddenly needed. Unlike Brooke, Pug was not a powerful personality and agreed with Churchill to keep quiet because he promised Pug he could come as company. The intention was to sail on HMS *Belfast*, to this day moored on the Thames in London. Eisenhower protested to no avail, and Pug was becoming worried and beginning to think of informing the COS, but King George VI who had also wanted to go, now tried to persuade Churchill otherwise with Pug feeling guilty about letting the cat out of the bag. When the monarch failed first time Pug phoned the king's personal secretary, Sir Alan Lascelles and suggested another attempt which worked. It was, according to one of Churchill's biographers, Pug 'who made the rather clever point [to Lascelles] that the problem was not so much safety as being cut off from communications during a short period when crucial decisions might be necessary'.[4]

They travelled down to Southampton where Pug was impressed by the attitude of the troops, had his head 'bitten off' by Churchill when he suggested they should return to London to be more central, and was offered a place on a headquarters ship by an old fox-hunting friend. He declined for fear of Churchill's wrath and when he told him later Churchill asked him why he had not taken the opportunity. Pug had travelled with the left-wing politician Ernest Bevin who, despite their possible differing politics, admired him and noted the soldiers called him Ernie and asked him to look after their wives and kids while they were away.

When the news filtered through that the invasion had been postponed because of the weather it is not difficult to imagine the sense of agitation and nervousness. It was Pug who went to Churchill with the bleak news and at half past one in the morning Churchill decided to go to bed, instructing Pug who would sit and wait not to wake him up. At five in the morning Bedell Smith phoned Pug that the invasion was on, and being obedient went to bed without waking Churchill, who woke himself half an hour later and sent for Pug who told him the news, Churchill later writing that Pug recalled 'I made no comment'.[5] Many would have found Churchill a difficult man to work for with his change of mind and instructions, but Pug seemed to accept it all 'as one of those things'.

It must have been a great relief when Eisenhower decided to launch on the somewhat tenuous advice that the weather would probably improve the next day. De Gaulle had arrived having been kept in the dark in Algiers because of communications being locked down, and although Pug never mentioned it, because the French camp was suspected of having 'leaks', and de Gaulle was furious. Pug admitted de Gaulle was a difficult man, but rightly pointed out that as a Frenchman whose country had been occupied by the Nazis, he had some of Pug's sympathy.

As the news filtered through that the landings were going as planned, except for the fighting on Omaha Beach, the main concern was whether the German military commander von Rundstedt would move his divisions from the Calais area, but as Stalin gave directing orders from Moscow so the Germans were waiting for directives from Hitler. By 10 June Pug was pleased to note the bridgehead was some 60 miles in length and some 12 miles in depth. By 12 June Churchill had his wishes fulfilled and with the COS and others visited the beaches, and three days later Pug visited with the king. It was on their return they discovered the dangers of the V1 pilotless planes known as Doodlebugs, which as Pug noted created more fear than bomber raids because the people below felt more helpless with their fear increasing once the engine stopped making any noise. There were constant bombing raids to hit the launch pads of these weapons, but the sites needed to be overrun to eliminate the problem entirely. The same problem arose over the more dangerous V2s which again underlined the importance of 'boots on the ground' to eliminate this dangerous crisis.

These were momentous days, full of risk and danger, the battle was raging in France, Britain was being attacked by the wonder weapons and there was a great deal of expectancy matched by uncertainty in the corridors of power and across the world, but Pug still found time to write a letter to his friend Mountbatten in South-East Asia. Mountbatten had been much earlier involved in some of the discussions on Operation Overlord, but very much on the periphery. Nevertheless, Pug wrote his congratulations to Mountbatten: 'If anyone had told us two years ago that we could throw ashore a million men, two hundred thousand vehicles, then three-quarters of a million tons of stores, across open beaches, in none too favourable weather, in thirty days, we would have dubbed him mad. So that's a great feather in your cap, Dickie.'[6] In many ways it was undeserved praise, but it demonstrated Pug's fundamental belief in friendship. Mountbatten's biographer Philip Ziegler believed this note was sincere, and Mountbatten found it the nicest communication he had ever received.

In the meantime, Operation Anvil, the invasion of the south of France was creating tensions. In Italy the American General Mark Clark against Alexander's orders had captured Rome (which Pug naturally described as 'Alexander's overwhelming victory'), and the Italian campaign was losing troops to Anvil which was not well received.[7] According to his own memoirs Alexander was unhappy about Eisenhower's decision to remove troops for southern France, but Eisenhower remained firm. This conflict regarding the overall strategy of the Italian campaign has been long debated, as it inevitably became known as the backwater war while D-Day Normandy was opening the doors of mainland Europe. Some argue that all that was necessary was to establish a drawn line in northern Italy and hold it, others that it could lead to a breakthrough into Austria, which was unlikely, or head north-east towards the Balkans. There were clashes at every level, between the COS both sides of the Atlantic and between Churchill and Roosevelt, the latter not budging an inch. Churchill was more concerned about the potential Russian surge, but Roosevelt was determined that the Nazi collapse came first. Operation Anvil now renamed Dragoon took place on 15 August and there were few casualties with Marseille being captured intact.

Churchill and Communism and the Octagon Conference

According to Pug, and probably correctly, Churchill was more far-seeing than many others and was growing suspicious of the renewed threat of an expanding Russian communism. He had befriended Stalin out of sheer necessity to overcome the Nazi threat, but he had not forgotten the menace which Stalin's form of communism raised, and he foresaw the dangers as the Soviet Army surged through Eastern Europe, thus his concerns over the Balkans. To all appearances America at this stage seemed little concerned about the postwar era and the dangers of communism; if anything they were more concerned with British imperial plans, but Churchill was somewhat despondent about emerging Soviet hazards, especially over the tensions of a future Poland.

Pug recalled that at the end of July the Russians had appeared outside Warsaw and on 1 August General Bór-Komorowski started the Warsaw uprising, which after some sixty days of bitter fighting was crushed by the Germans. As is well known the Soviets sat and watched, Warsaw was too far away for sensible air support by the Western Allies (though they tried) and Stalin refused them landing support. It was crystal clear to Churchill and others that Stalin's behaviour was based on not wanting to encourage a free government in Poland which he intended to occupy as a communist country. At that time Pug had not realised how deep Churchill's concerns were about the dangers of a communist occupied Europe and his fears of Stalin's expansionist plans. When he looked back it dawned on him that this provided the reason for Churchill's preoccupation with Greece, at a time when many believed everything should be concentrated on the war in northern Europe.

Communism was stronger than before, even in France where the communist-led partisans had been the most prolific and brutal, with the same implications in Italy and in Greece where, as far as Churchill was concerned, it had now reached a crisis level. Churchill had explained to Roosevelt that he had made an agreement with Stalin that he might hold Romania, but Greece should remain within the Western sphere of influence with American endorsement. The Americans eventually agreed, and Pug found them somewhat sanctimonious about 'spheres of influence' because postwar this would become for them a politically dominant issue.

It was not until 12 October that the Germans left Athens and a British force of some 5,000 was sent in under General Scobie only to find itself involved in a bitter civil war, house to house fighting with partisans of various hues made difficult by not wearing identifiable uniforms. The British were instantly criticised for becoming involved in Greece's business, especially as the major war was raging elsewhere. Alexander told Churchill that he could not afford to send more troops, so Churchill took himself to Greece with Eden, met Alexander, the British Ambassador Leeper, while sleeping aboard HMS *Ajax* for safety. He called a meeting with the American Ambassador present, the Russian representative, members of the communist factions and Archbishop Damaskinos (1891–1949) who was finally accepted as Regent, and it appeared that Greece was again a free country. Pug recorded how the free world owed much to Churchill's interference, who had foreseen the problems, bothered to rush out there to resolve the possible dangers, and although condemned and criticised for his actions, at least in 1952 Greece and Turkey were able to join NATO.

On 5 September the British COS were back on the *Queen Mary* sailing towards Canada for the second conference there, code-named Octagon. The trip across the Atlantic was fraught with difficulty and not helped by Churchill being under the weather, but it did not stop him and Mrs Churchill having lunch and dining with Coleville and Pug, with the former noting that 'both meals were gargantuan in scale and epicurean in quality; rather shamingly so'.[8] Nevertheless, Churchill seemed to be in a bad temper most of the way and was continually at odds with the

COS over various issues, especially the Far East strategy and Churchill's conviction over taking Sumatra, to which Brooke and his fellow service chiefs strongly objected, and it seemed Churchill would not be moved by their advice.

It was so fraught that there were suggestions they would all resign and as Pug later wrote to Eden, 'the resignation of these great figures at that particular junction would have spelt disunity at home...I therefore stepped into the breach by saying that I would resign and that even if Winston accepted my resignation no one had heard of Ismay...it was in that context that I duly sent a formal letter of resignation.'[9] It was evident that Churchill had exploded and seemed to have once again used Pug as his anvil, but Pug made few comments on this in his memoirs. It is only by looking at General Kennedy's account to whom Pug had obviously spoken that Churchill had accused Pug 'of being a bromide in trying to get settlements and agreements. He had told Ismay that his job was to prod him and help him to make rows and oppose his advisers, or words to that effect.'[10] To resolve the problem between Churchill and the COS Pug had suggested to the angry and unwell prime minister that he should point out that it was more a political rather than a military matter, but Churchill ignored him and the COS meeting became overheated.[11] Brooke noted in his diary that when he was asked by Pug whether to send the resignation letter, Brooke had told him it was his decision, 'but that it would probably bring Winston to his senses'.[12] This was typical of Pug's sense of duty that cohesion was essential even if it meant his end days, and his statement that 'no one had heard of Ismay' was part of his natural humility.

After the conference he wrote to his wife explaining how Churchill had handed the letter back to him saying: 'don't write me this sort of rubbish, dear Pug: we are going to the end, together, you and me. I'm sorry if I get angry, but you must admit I have a cause', with Pug asking why he vented it on him, and giving him the impression he could do nothing right, but adding that Churchill 'was really rather sweet'.[13] This 'quarrel' would never have happened if Pug were just a messenger boy, but there were frequently times when he had to defend Churchill to the COS and *vice versa*, which inevitably led to tensions and a sometimes uncomfortable job and lifestyle. He later wrote to his wife that whatever happened in the postwar years nothing would induce him to be a go-between again and be asked to mirror other people's opinions. It was unlike Pug to boil over, and some have suggested he came close to a breakdown, but his sense of frustration was clear because of the nature of his thankless task. Brooke later added a note to his diary which described Pug as 'dear old patient Pug had at last reached the end of his tether and could stand Winston's moods no longer…of course Pug always got the worse of it', and in many ways it was amazing that Pug lasted the war's duration; like Brooke, both men were loyal and dedicated servants to their nation.[14]

His letter to Eden explained it clearly, whatever the personal cost the war-machine had to work, and work in unison. Later Harry Hopkins wrote to Pug with the words, 'as I look back upon it, I think your mellow advice and charming approach to the bitterly controverted opinions contributed incalculably to the amicable settlement of differences and to the gradual growth of mutual confidence'.[15] Harry Hopkins like everyone had his critics, but few have doubted his shrewd perceptions of events and people. They arrived to be greeted by the Roosevelts and the American contingent, and Pug felt it was like a large family gathering. He was, however, shocked to see that Roosevelt looked very ill as did their military representative John Dill. Pug noted that seven weeks later Dill died, as did Roosevelt seven months after this conference.

The British were now concerned about the Japanese conflict and having relied on the Americans for defeating Germany, did not want to be seen as selfishly interested in Burma, Malaya and Hong Kong, their old colonial interests, but asked to join with the Americans in the attack on Japan itself. Until Germany was defeated British land forces would not be available, but the Royal Navy was ready. It was known that for several reasons Admiral King was not enchanted by the proposal, so Pug was taken aback when Roosevelt accepted the offer. The involvement of the RAF created some technical problems which had to be sorted through. Pug was of the opinion Japan was nearly finished, but realised the Japanese people regarded their monarch as almost a deity and the demands of Unconditional Surrender meant they would fight to the last man standing. It was a short conference and ended on 16 September, and for once Pug recorded that he enjoyed the journey home and for the first time was able to stroll around the promenade deck.

Moscow and Paris

As soon as he returned to Britain Pug discovered that Churchill wanted to take him to Moscow to meet Stalin, with the intention of raising the Polish issue and the question as to whether the Russians would fight the Japanese. Roosevelt was busy fighting an election, so he sent Harriman to represent American interests. They left on 5 October and for the first time could fly across France without being harried by the Luftwaffe, landing in Naples where a brief conference was held with Alexander, Brooke, General Wilson, Macmillan and others, from which they gleaned the Italian campaign had suffered from the loss of troops to Operation Dragoon (originally Anvil). The next stop was Cairo and then straight to Moscow where it all felt like 'goodwill', and Stalin even dined outside the Kremlin in the British Embassy. As Churchill and Eden were involved in political discussion the rest were given a box at the ballet, where both Pug in his memoirs, and Brooke in his diaries expressed bemusement that two sergeants in the party were not allowed to enter the box because of their rank. Both men were curious that communism was supposed to be based on a 'classless society', but they overcame this by two brigadiers taking the stall seats.

On 14 October Stalin came as well, sitting with Churchill and Harriman in the 'royal box', and in the interval asked Churchill to stand up and receive the applause of the audience, and when Stalin then stood up beside him the cheering became explosive. Brooke gave, according to Pug, a brilliant survey of the Western Allied campaign, the Russians offered their side, and Stalin promised to fight the Japanese as soon as the Germans had been defeated. The political talks over Poland were not so successful, Stalin was determined that Poland should be part of the projected Soviet empire. The Soviet dictator had gathered obliging Poles with him for the occasion, who according to Pug, were just his 'stooges' to do his bidding. The Americans were not that concerned as mentioned above, but only keen that Russia should fight Japan. Pug later wrote to a friend (Lew Douglas) explaining he could not understand Russian mentality, that they obviously wanted to be friends but warning that unless that friendship is retained 'there is little hope for the peace of the world', which was indeed prescient.[16]

As also recorded in Brooke's diary, they were astonished that their plane was loaded with caviar and vodka which they understood to be presents which they all duly divided with immense pleasure, only to discover later that they had been intended for the Russian Embassy. Fortunately, the British Foreign Office came to the rescue replacing the vodka with whisky.

Pug was pleased that following an invitation from de Gaulle to Churchill to attend Armistice Day (11 November) in Paris he was invited to attend by Churchill. There were some concerns over safety as there was a possibility of German agents who might welcome an opportunity to assassinate Churchill but Churchill, being Churchill, would not hear of this concern. The prime minister and his wife were made special guests of the French Government and Pug with Brooke stayed at the Continental Hotel where Pug noticed there was little hot water. The next day he was happy to record that when Churchill appeared there was a sustained roar of appreciation from the crowd. Later Pug and Brooke met with the French generals Juin and Koenig who asked for their help to persuade the Americans to aid them to equip eight new divisions, which Pug thought important so that France could play its part in the defeat of Germany.

It is worth noting at this point the close working relationship with Brooke, and their friendly relationship with one another. Churchill and Brooke with de Gaulle then left to visit the front line and Pug flew home. He described the 'rude shock' of hearing about Rundstedt's unexpected push through the Ardennes, later dubbed the Battle of the Bulge. This unexpected attack took everyone by surprise and was something of an embarrassment. After the battle was finished Montgomery gave a press interview in which his ego inflated too far as he gave the appearance that he had saved the Americans. It was a tense moment in the coalition balance and others, including Churchill, had to calm matters down because although Montgomery had been given charge it was the American soldiers who fought, not least with General Patton suddenly thrusting his armoured divisions forward. This was almost scandalous, but Pug with his diplomatic niceties and charm made no reference to this coalition embarrassment, but he pointedly remarked that Rundstedt failed 'thanks to the magnificent fighting of the American troops'.[17]

Chapter Six

1945,
Yalta and the End of the Road

Following the Battle of the Bulge it was amply clear that Germany had lost, but the fanaticism of Hitler ensured the Germans fought to their last doorstop. Their factories, resources, cities, towns and homes were devastated, and the time had come to examine what the post German war situation would be. The three major victors needed to discuss the immediate and long-term future with its ramifications when possible. Pug was aware that Churchill remained deeply concerned about Poland, not least because Britain and France had gone to war to support that country which had been carved up by Germany and Russia, and now it appeared the Soviets would stay in Poland, the one of the two neighbours whom the Poles historically despised the most.

Once again Stalin would not leave Russia and the unwell Roosevelt and an exhausted Churchill were expected to travel to Yalta, not only a substantial distance, but not the easiest of places to reach. Churchill wanted a meeting with Roosevelt first at Malta, he refused on matters of timing, but a combined COS meeting took place. The main issue was the final assault on Germany where there were some coalition differences. The Eisenhower plan was for a wide front closing off the length of the Rhine, then crossing it at several points to serve as bridgeheads and then advance into Germany on a broad front. The British, led by Montgomery's thinking and endorsed by others (Brooke) was a single rapid thrust to Berlin, if only to beat the Russians there. The Americans disagreed with what they described as a 'pencil thrust' and the debate was acrimonious. Marshall stood firmly behind Eisenhower and the British had no choice but to accept. Pug had warned his friend Lascelles that the Americans would have their way, although Churchill himself was inclined for the immediate capture of Berlin.[1]

Pug admitted later that Eisenhower's plan worked, but as to whether it shortened the war or not or would have forestalled the Russians taking

Berlin, can only be speculation; he acknowledged that such debates could never be resolved. When the Russians did occupy Berlin, it cost thousands upon thousands of lives, Russian and German, and whether the Germans would have fought so hard against the less dreaded Allies will always remain a question of speculation. The COS meetings in Malta were strained, and it had started with Walter Bedell Smith sick in bed with ulcers, and seemingly depressed that the British would win all their arguments. This was duly reported to Pug who took a bottle of champagne to Bedell Smith's sick room, which with Pug's easy-going friendship and gentleness persuaded the American patient that the British had every faith in Eisenhower. Brooke and others did not, but once again Pug smoothed the way, and it was clear that Eisenhower and Bedell Smith regarded his influence probably more critical than it was, but Pug's lotion worked.

In the archives remains a letter from Pug to Bedell Smith in which the American had been furious with Pug, and to which Pug replied explaining what had happened, and then adding in his difficult handwriting the postscript 'I must add Bedell, that I required 4 aspirins, 3 gins, and a bottle of port to recover from your onslaught! Seriously though, I do hope and pray that your stay in hospital will be short…I shall come and pay you a visit.'[2] It seemed on reading this letter that Pug would not let personal attachments slip away. He would maintain a long friendship with Bedell Smith, and they would remain close long after the war ended. In the archives there are endless letters written by Pug to old friends such as Bedell Smith, George Marshall, Eisenhower and countless others, many of his notes are difficult to read because of Pug's cramped handwriting, and in one interesting letter (in October 1949 when Bedell Smith was the Commanding General 1st US Army) he forwarded to Pug his attempt at deciphering a hand-written letter from Pug which had caused problems to read.[3]

Pug's friendly and easy-going personality helped smooth the way in the often-strained relationships in the Anglo-American coalition, and many of the Americans found his company almost medicinal.

Pug noted that when Roosevelt arrived, he looked very ill and later told Lascelles he was convinced that Roosevelt would not live much longer and 'that he was more than half gaga'; according to Lascelles Pug had felt this a few months before.[4] Pug was correct that Roosevelt's health was failing, and he died a few months later. They then flew at a great height for a long distance, and even after that it was an eight-hour car journey to Yalta. The area had been badly hit by the war, and although senior members of the delegations were well housed others had to survive under barrack room conditions. Pug was more accepting of conditions and in a letter (17 February 1945) to Mountbatten wrote that prior to their arrival, 'all our information suggested that it would have been impossible to have selected a more unsuitable rendezvous from every point of view – climate, accommodation, accessibility, and so forth – but we had a wonderful break in the weather, and so forth – but the Russians had done miracles before we arrived'.[5]

Pug always tried to see the positive side, but later summarised the meeting in an interesting sentence: 'The Conference lasted about a week. From the gastronomical point of view, it was enjoyable: from the social point of view, successful: from the military point of view, unnecessary: and from the political point of view, depressing.'[6] Roosevelt, according to Pug, likened the meeting to a large happy family, which Pug may have agreed with once, but now had his doubts. At previous conferences the military personnel had been, according to Pug, the *prima donna*, but this was more a political meeting and Pug admitted that he found it difficult to find sufficient work to fill his time. The civilians had the hard work and it was agreed that France should have a zone and be a member of the Control Commission. This was undoubtedly down to Churchill who was desperate to have as much Western influence in occupied Germany as possible. Stalin agreed to fight against Japan, and it was established that all the Russian rights which had been lost in the 1904 Russo-Japanese War would be restored. The main problem was the demand for free elections in Poland, with Stalin insisting that country was necessary for Russian security. Pug added in his memoirs that on looking back they should have seen the red-light warning of Soviet intention; it is highly likely that Churchill had. In some ways Yalta was a tragedy as Stalin, who had once united with Nazi Germany in attacking Poland, was now able to control most of central and eastern Europe. The euphoria of victory in Europe and a weakening Japan had obscured the long-term designs of Stalin's policy to build his own empire.

Pug was astonished that instead of taking a peaceful cruise home Churchill decided to fly directly to Athens to see how matters were progressing. Pug praised him for this sense of duty, but after the Polish debate Churchill was probably intent on ensuring Greece stayed within the Western sphere of interest. Pug and the group paid an historical visit to Balaclava to view the site of the charge of the Light Brigade, immortalised by Tennyson, then while Churchill was driven to Saki to fly to Athens, Pug was boarding the *Franconia* and enjoying life in the cabins which had been prepared for Churchill.

On his return to London Pug was concerned that Churchill was going to have to explain Yalta to the Commons, especially regarding Poland, suggesting that Churchill may have been going too far when he explained the Russian government had to be trusted. This was probably Churchill's parliamentary defence mechanism, because unlike many, especially the Americans, he was highly suspicious of the Soviet communist system under Stalin, despite the diplomatic bonhomie approach when they met socially. As Pug noted the British had risen to the defence of Poland as it was occupied by an enemy, and it still was, but by a different version. Pug noted that the Americans at this stage were all too trusting of the Soviets, but Stalin was determined that Poland would remain a Soviet satellite. It would have been politically and militarily difficult to oppose Russia at this time. Since Barbarossa Stalin, often called Uncle Joe to his annoyance, had been painted as a good friend, and the Russian soldiers as fighting to the last man. The British and American public would have been appalled had Russia suddenly been declared an enemy of peace. It was a serious conundrum for the West and nobody wanted the war to continue once Japan had been defeated. It would not take long for many historians to look at the statistics, and it became abundantly clear that Russia's losses in the fighting, both military and civilian were much more than all the Western forces combined. The more cynical, and probably the more realistic, realised that Britain had survived the war, bolstered by American support, aid and resources, using the British islands as an unsinkable aircraft carrier to launch into Europe, and thereby stopping the Soviet army sweeping west into France to rid the country of Nazi forces; there was a possibility that most of Western Europe, let alone Eastern Europe could have been Soviet dominated.

The Russians called the Second World War the Great Patriot War because in their opinion, and with some justification, they had been the victors. Stalin was until his death a tyrant and oppressor not that much different from Hitler, making Mussolini and Franco appear mild. Nevertheless, in 1945 being critical of Russia was an unacceptable view, certainly not prevalent in the public mind, Uncle Joe and the Red Army were popular, and falling out with them at this stage for most was inconceivable. As Pug pertinently noted, the failure to bring freedom to Poland 'brought shame on the Western democracies' but 'must in fairness bear in mind the circumstances of those days'.[7]

As Churchill was defending Yalta, a coup d'état was happening in Bucharest as Soviet troops entered Romania's capital and this was followed by a communist government. The war was drawing to its close and in early March Churchill, Brooke, Pug, and others visited Montgomery's forward position, setting foot on German soil, stayed at Venlo watching the battle and crossed the Rhine. It was not all triumph because on 13 April they were told of Roosevelt's death. The pace was gathering, Himmler had offered unconditional surrender to the Western Allies, but it was refused, Mussolini was killed by partisans (28 April), and Hitler committed suicide (30 April). Two days later the German Army surrendered in Italy, Montgomery accepted the surrender of German forces in the northern regions and on 7 May the unconditional surrender of Germany was signed at Rheims and the definitive text signed in Karlshorst, Berlin on the night of 8 May.

Pug, hearing the news at three in the morning at home with his wife, wondered whether Churchill knew, but his phone had yet to be disconnected from Rheims, so he had to go in his dressing gown to a public call box to phone No 10, only to discover Churchill was aware. Pug had a reputation as a great sleeper, but that night it eluded him as he pondered the problems with Japan and the future of Europe. At Stalin's request the announcement of Germany's surrender was not broadcast for a day, with Pug irritated that Stalin always had his own way, but Churchill gave lunch to the COS and afterwards they had their photograph taken in No 10 Downing Street's garden, with Pug standing behind as had been his custom, the necessary administrative tool in the back row.

His work was not finished that day as Churchill's victory speech needed checking which according to Pug still needed supplementary material. Churchill, famous for his style of English and presentation always depended on Pug to ensure the correctness of fact and ensuring any major points had not been omitted. Pug noted that in his speech Churchill referred to the dangers of having rid Europe of 'the Hitlerites' that justice and law should rule, and no more totalitarian and police states should emerge, with him wondering how many of his listeners would have picked up the warning of Churchill's fear of Stalin and communism. Afterwards they were all driven to Buckingham Palace where King George VI made a point of congratulating Pug and Sir Edward Bridges, the King saying they were the only three who kept their jobs for the duration of the war. Pug compared the rejoicing which followed the war as more restrained than that in 1918; there was a sense of relief and gratitude with the hope that the Japanese conflict would soon end.

Churchill contacted President Truman seeking another meeting with Stalin, expressing his anxiety about the future and his concern about the Yalta conference and Russian intentions. The famous Potsdam Conference was thereby organised for 15 July, later than Churchill had anticipated, and he used the time to try and encourage Truman to keep American forces in their forward positions, but Truman point blank refused telling Churchill the zones had been established at Yalta. On 1 July the Americans and therefore the British troops started to withdraw leaving the Soviets in central Europe.

In Britain the Coalition Government came to the end of its life in May, with polling day fixed for 5 July but extended because of the many overseas postal votes. This necessary delay meant Churchill and Atlee had to return home, giving Pug time to explore Germany. He was surprised at the quality of some of the better off country homes which had not suffered war damage, concluding well-off Germans had not suffered as much as most; he could have added that there were similarities in Britain, but did not. At a splendid luncheon the Russian military led by Marshal Zhukov presented Eisenhower and Montgomery with awards followed by some excellent speeches. This caused Pug to ruminate that if the Kremlin, namely Stalin, reflected the sentiments expressed that day the world would have been a better place.[8] Eisenhower had also been presented with the Freedom of the City of London and according to Pug gave an excellent speech, and even his military critic Brooke admitted that on hearing this he saw Eisenhower in a different light.

Pug spent time ruminating on the long growing tension between Churchill and his COS over their Far Eastern policies. The military wanted their forces based in Australia operating across the Pacific under

American command. Churchill preferred to operate across the Bay of Bengal, occupying Sumatra to strike at Malaya and disrupt Japanese communications with Burma. In his diaries Brooke often fumigated against this strategy, describing it as 'a mad idea'. Pug admitted it was probably Churchill's hope of restoring British prestige. The arguments had been heated with the threat of resignations, which Pug pointed out that such a breach at that time would have been catastrophic. However, the British under General Slim had accrued some success (Imphal and Kohima), Admiral Halsey had all but destroyed the Japanese navy, MacArthur had cleaned out the Philippines, by May 1945 Rangoon had fallen to General Slim, and by the Potsdam Conference the urgency of the debate had calmed down. The first days started with the COS meeting in the early morning and coming together with each other in the afternoons. Pug took a bet with General Arnold that the Japanese would fold by the end of the year, which happened after the atom bombs had been dropped. He later received 'a novel form of paperweight, two silver dollars mounted in a block of polished walnut wood. It was inscribed: "*To Pug Ismay from Hap Arnold. Thank God I can pay this now*", adding 'It is one of my most cherished mementoes of the war.'[9]

Another memory Pug recalled was watching an ADC handing Marshall a telegram which he read then placed face down. He then called for a secret session and announced that the atom bomb experiment in New Mexico (the Manhattan project) had been successful, with Pug feeling thankful this experiment had eluded their enemies, but according to some it was obvious that Pug felt revulsion at the new weapon.[10] However, he later told Lascelles 'that an invasion of Japan would cost us and the Americans half a million men, and he didn't think it was worth it', which reflected the main argument for using nuclear weapons against the Japanese.[11]

With a small party he visited Berlin and was shocked by its destruction, stating there was a sense of depression with only elderly Germans slowly moving around the ruins, surrounded by the smells of death and decay. He entered the old Nazi Chancellery and had 'the feeling of being in the presence of evil'. He saw in a room hundreds of Iron Crosses and ribbons strewn across the floor, 'a symbol of utter defeat and degradation'. In a personal and friendly letter to Anthony Eden, Pug wrote a postscript about his Berlin experience noting 'This place is full of ghosts. I find it hard not to cry sometimes.'[12] He had found the trip into Berlin highly distressing and returned to a hot bath, a strong drink, and later would turn down the opportunity of attending the Nuremberg Trials. Beneath his uniform it was clear that Pug was a deeply sensitive and emotional person. That same evening Churchill gave a dinner-party with Truman and Stalin as the chief guests, and Pug was impressed by Truman's speech and the man himself.

Two days later he returned to London with Churchill and Atlee for the election results, full of praise for the graceful way Churchill acknowledged the surprise defeat, at least in public. Pug returned with Atlee who now held the reins but at least he had been alongside Churchill during all the war years, but now with a new Foreign Secretary in Ernest Bevin who also impressed Pug. The conference ended five days later and they all returned to London.

The pace speeded-up with the atomic bombs dropped on Japan, Russia declared war on that country, a face-saving formula regarding the Japanese Emperor was devised, and on 14 August the war against Japan concluded. Pug was exhausted stating that 'a great weariness descended on me like a pall', and he wanted to retire at once. Atlee suggested he took a long holiday and then do twelve more months. He and his wife decided to visit America once again sailing on the *Queen Mary* which was returning the 35th US Division, all too happy to sleep in crammed conditions on deck floors as they were returning home. They travelled around America, visited among others his wife's aunt and many old war acquaintances where Pug said they were nearly killed by kindness. They discovered how shocked the Americans had been by the British expulsion of Churchill, not understanding that Churchill was adored for his war leadership, but he was not necessarily deemed the best man for restoring war-ridden Britain for the benefit of the working classes, who recalled their dashed hopes after the Great War and the ensuing poverty. Conversely, Pug was surprised to hear the occasional criticisms levelled against Roosevelt. When he returned, he told his friend Lascelles that in America there was universal 'apprehension of Russia's intentions', a view long held by Churchill, and this concern was to prove correct.[13]

When Pug returned home the main issue was the future organisation of defence, and although Churchill as Prime Minister and Minister of Defence had worked well with what Pug described as his small 'handling machine', now there arose the vexatious question of the Prime Minister retaining supreme responsibility as well as the post of Minister of Defence. Pug, being deeply conservative was sad to see the title 'imperial' disappear, but the COS remained as an integral part of the system. When he retired from his post in November 1946 he concluded by writing 'I had had an eventful and very lucky innings.'[14]

When Churchill's resignation honours list was published, the three COS members received peerages but Pug a CH (Companionship of Honour) which naturally pleased him, but it raised many eyebrows elsewhere. Pug was a military man and Churchill's Chief of Staff and yet was awarded what was primarily regarded as a civilian honour. Churchill was more annoyed at Montgomery being awarded the title El Alamein which he thought was more deserved by Alexander, but with which Pug disagreed.[15]

Atlee later rectified Pug's small award and he appeared in Attlee's last victory list on June 1946 as a Knight of the Grand Cross of the Bath (Military Division) and in 1947 was gazetted as a Baron for 'his many years of distinguished and devoted service'. Attlee even wrote a personal letter to Pug grateful for his long-term service and commitment.[16] For many it might have appeared that Attlee was more generous in his appreciation than Churchill, but the latter was notorious for not being overly bothered about awards, and was often critical of the system. In the meantime, Pug remained busy with different types of commitments, and he would be frequently called to address matters of a delicate nature, as in late 1945, Halifax, Ambassador to the USA asked Prime Minister Attlee that Pug cross the Atlantic to address the Foreign Policy Association in New York.[17]

Picture of Ismay. (*IWM TR 2839/Public domain*)

A Combined Chiefs of Staff discussion at the Potsdam Conference; Charles Portal, Hastings Ismay and Leslie Hollis. (*NARA*)

Ismay with Brendan Bracken and Mary Churchill in a saloon carriage of a train used for Winston Churchill's tour of North America. (*IWM H 32957*)

Ismay talking to Sir John Simon at a farewell dinner for Admiral Stark at the Royal Naval College, Greenwich. (*IWM A 30046*)

Casablanca Conference, French Morocco, 14–24 January 1943. Churchill with his chiefs of staff, Ismay behind him. (*Public domain*)

Somaliland. (*Flickr*)

Whitehall: corner of the old War Office. (*Paul the Archivist via Wikimedia*)

Battle of Britain Monument detail. (*Derek Mayes/Creative Commons ShareAlike 2.0 (CC BY-SA 2.0) license*)

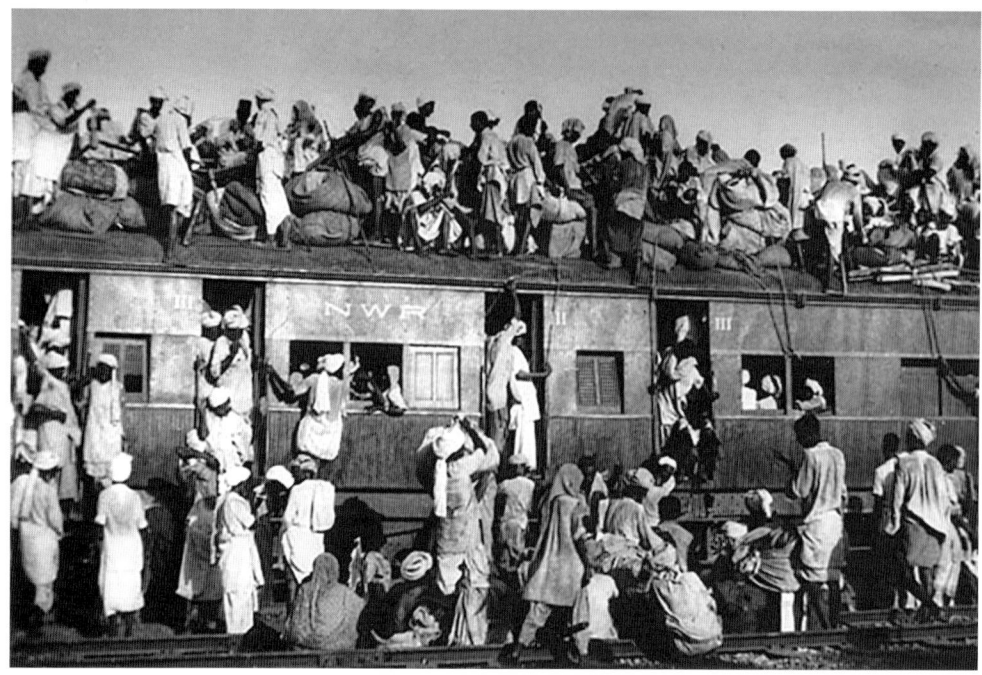

Overcrowded train during the partition of India, 1947. Considered to be the largest migration in human history. (*Public domain*)

Villa Saïd. (*Polymagou – CC-BY-SA*)

Winston Churchill sharing a joke with Joseph Stalin and his interpreter, Pavlov, at Livadia Palace during the Yalta Conference in February 1945. (*IWM NAM 229/Public domain*)

Lord Ismay in the Netherlands, 25 October 1952. (*Public domain*)

Lord Ismay, Secretary General NATO, in the Hague. (*Dutch National Archives*)

Chiefs of Staff, 1945. (*IWM*)

American and Allied leaders and Chiefs of Staff at the Quebec Conference, with Pug being light-hearted. (*Public domain*)

Pug Ismay.

Code-named *Terminal*, this was the final Big Three meeting of the war. (*Public domain*)

Charterhouse School. (*fotosforfun2*)

Somaliland Camel Corps. (*Netherlands Archives*)

Polo in India. Pug was well known for this sport. (*Public domain*)

Allies' Grand-strategy Conference in North Africa, 14 January 1943, near Casablanca. (*IWM A 14131*)

Maurice Hankey. (*Public domain*)

Lord Moran and Ernest Bevin c.1940. (*Public domain/Wellcome Images*)

British War Cabinet 1939–40 with Chamberlain and Churchill. (*Walter Bellamy*)

British Prime Minister Clement Attlee inspects the guard of honour, consisting of Scots Guards, on the lawn of his residence during the Potsdam Conference. (*NARA*)

Franklin D. Roosevelt and Churchill at the Quebec Conference. (*Roosevelt Library/Public domain*)

Churchill in Dover. (*IWM H 3509*)

Churchill with the Polish Government in Exile, 1941. (*Public domain*)

Stalin, Roosevelt and Churchill in Teheran, Iran. (*Roosevelt Library/Public domain*)

Chiang Kai-Shek, Roosevelt and Churchill in Cairo. (*US National Archives*)

Octagon Conference. (*National Film Board of Canada. Phototheque/Library and Archives Canada/C-026921*)

Tehran Conference. (R to L): General Voroshilov, Stalin, interpreter, Harry Hopkins, General Sir Archibald Clark Kerr and George C. Marshall. (*US Army Signal Corp Photograph*)

Yalta Conference. (*Public domain*)

Churchill, Averill Harriman, Stalin and Vyacheslav Molotov, Moscow 1942. (*Public domain*)

Roosevelt, Churchill, Ismay and Mountbatten at Casablanca. (*German Federal Archives*)

Stalin, Truman and Churchill together for the first time, just before the Conference at Potsdam. (*Public domain*)

Lord Mountbatten meets Nehru, Jinnah and other leaders to plan Partition of India. Pug behind him. (*Public domain*)

General Brooke, who worked with Pug Ismay throughout the war. (*Dutch National Archive*)

Casablanca Conference. (*National Museum of the US Navy*)

Part Three

India, Nato, and Other Posts

After the war Pug Ismay was busy with voluntary work, but desperate to retire and care for his beloved Jersey cows. This was not to be the case as he went as Mountbatten's aide to India in 1947 to oversee the controversial independence and partitioning of India and Pakistan, which resulted in a phenomenal loss of life in the ongoing communal massacres. Mountbatten at the time and since has been the subject of much scrutiny and criticism for the way he handled the fiasco. Pug felt the pain of this disaster for most of his life thereafter; he tried to account for why it happened, and never criticised Mountbatten but some of his personal letters to his wife are revealing on this subject. On his return to Britain, he took on once again many voluntary roles, spoke from the cross benches in the House of Lords, and was asked by Attlee to be the Honorary Chairman for the Festival of Britain, as well as spending much time with Churchill as he wrote his history of the war.

When Churchill was returned to power, he promptly brought Pug back into the political arena as Secretary of State for Commonwealth Relations, but this was more a pretext because it was apparent Churchill needed his expertise in defence. Very much against Pug's wishes Churchill insisted he became Secretary General of NATO, a post he worked hard at with travelling, speeches, writing a booklet, organising an efficient administration, dealing with problems relating to the European Defence Community and supporting West Germany's admission to NATO. He had to deal with the habitual American complaints about European financial budgets, the Cyprus issue, and the fiasco of the Suez Canal, eventually retiring in his 70th year.

Following his return to his Jersey cows Pug remained busy with correspondence, writing his memoirs, involved in other peoples' publications, always defending Churchill, Mountbatten, and at one time Eisenhower, and even took up the cause of Polish officers unable to return to their homeland. In 1963 the Prime Minister Harold Macmillan called upon him for help with defence policies. He died in 1965 the same year as Churchill.

The final part of the book explores Pug through his ongoing relationship with Churchill during the war years, and afterwards he was constantly assisting Churchill not least in some of the more delicate matters arising in his history of the war, with Pug always protecting Churchill's reputation and dealing with correspondence which raised issues over Churchill's account. Pug is further explored by a brief study of how his contemporaries viewed him, fellow generals, the Americans, senior civil servants, a politician, and with one exception (Lord Moran) all describing him in a pleasant if not kindly light. The book concludes with an overview of Pug's strength and drawbacks both as a man and his place in history.

Chapter One

1947,
Post War and India

It was a new beginning for Pug, more relaxed and hoping for some genuine time at home, this was at least his hope and anticipation when the war ended. He attended his old school Charterhouse on Founder's Day and gave the annual speech with the opening lines:

> On this the first Founders' Day Dinner since the end of the war, our first thought must be remembrance – remembrance for those Carthusians who have given their lives. They have a home in our minds for ever, and we will see to it that their children and their children's children are never without friends.[1]

On reading the speech it was clear that under the circumstances of the day he always hit the right note, even referring to the French asking for RAF fighter support and the necessity to keep them at home for the defence of Britain. He finished this section with a note on Churchill concluding that:

> Had Churchill not hardened his heart and refused to send more fighter squadrons to France, the whole of Europe would have been plunged into slavery and there would have been no possibility, within any measurable period of time, of rescue coming from the New World.[2]

He repeated this task the following year, this time speaking on his war experiences and the profession of his faith.[3] He always proved to be an excellent orator and he was constantly asked to give speeches and contribute to BBC broadcasts. He became involved as chairman of the National Institute for the Blind and was President of the Gloucestershire

British Legion, but he really wanted to look to his 'neglected farm' and his Jersey cows.[4]

When Montgomery went to the War Office in June 1946, he wrote that 'I soon discovered that the Chiefs of Staff Committee as a body was not the efficient machine that it had been in the past. The departure of General Ismay, Sir Ian Jacob, and some prominent members of their staff, had severely weakened the Secretariat.'[5] It was clear that as Pug wandered around his old school premises being entertained and enjoying new social contacts, he was being missed 'back in the office'. Even Brooke appeared to miss his company as he wrote a letter to Pug thanking him for the advice and the assistance he had given, and with the use of the word 'advice' it was a clear reminder that Pug and been more than a bureaucrat.[6] Pug replied to Brooke the next day (25 June 1946), admitting to the occasional difficulties of working with Churchill, which Brooke would have more than appreciated.[7]

Nevertheless, despite his attempts for an easier life, Churchill would constantly call upon Pug for help and assistance, not only over the next few years writing his extensive memoirs and history of the last war, but in many other matters. In December 1946 Churchill called for his help on a speech he was preparing which concerned the relationship of Prime Ministers and Chiefs of Staff, the vexed problem which Brooke had referred to and which Pug knew all too well.[8] However, Pug remained determined in 1946 to take a significant break and if possible, to retire and farm his beloved Jersey cows.

At the end of 1946 he was writing letters and making plans for him and Darry to visit Australia and New Zealand, a hope he had held for many years having been invited by the prime ministers of both countries.[9] It was never going to be straightforward for him as life was about to become hectic once again. As the new year of 1947 started he received a letter from Montgomery, now Chief of the Imperial General Staff, with a request that he accept the vacancy on the Royal United Service Institution's Council left by General Ronald Forbes Adam.[10] This was not to engage him with work, but 1947 would be consumed by him returning to India at the time of independence and the partitioning.

Background to India

India had been regarded as a major component of the British Empire, and the British Monarch had long accepted the title of Emperor based on India being regarded as the 'jewel in the crown', but it was a highly complex and volatile continent. During the colonial period the British had eventually cleared the Indian sub-continent of Portuguese, Dutch and French interests. However, they found themselves with a massive area deeply riddled by many religions and their various sects, and academic search for India's indigenous history had fed the natural rise of nationalism among Indians who wanted the control of their own land. As early as 1900 the Congress emerged as an all-India political organisation but unsupported by the Muslim elements. India was a enormous land space with a huge population divided on serious religious grounds and difficult to control for the British. It had a massive Hindu population, this religion itself having many different sects and cults, ranging from monotheism to a vast polytheism with different styles of worship, conduct and fundamental beliefs. A large minority of the Indian population was Muslim with a different theology and philosophy. In addition to this were the Sikhs and the Pathan and Baluch tribesmen, all with various forms of government. The means of government was just as divided, ranging from the almost democratic provinces to princely states hemmed in by a deep social class system including the Untouchables.

As early as July 1905 Lord Curzon the Viceroy had ordered the partition of Bengal on the grounds of facilitating administration, but it was really to quench insurgent nationalism which in turn outraged the Bengalis. It was during this decade that Pug was serving in India and would have been aware of this situation. In 1909 there was a Christmas Day plot to destroy the British administration by an attack on the Viceroy's Ball for the Governor of Bengal, when the Viceroy would be present. A few years later the Delhi-Lahore Conspiracy was hatched in 1912 to assassinate the Viceroy Lord Hardinge. The Viceroy was injured but this attack was followed by British efforts to destroy such activities amongst the Bengali and Punjabi revolutionary groups.

Just prior to this in 1906 the All-India Muslim League had been formed and from that time on would propose the creation of a Muslim state to be called Pakistan. During the Great War the Germans tried to unsettle the delicate situation, sometimes referred to as the Hindu-German conspiracy, for nationalistic groups to attempt a Pan-Indian rebellion against the British Raj. It caused minor and major disturbances such as the Ghadar Mutiny in the British Indian Army. After the war Gandhi appeared from the Indian nationalist movement in South Africa, and from 1920 to 1922 started the Non-Cooperation Movement, and despite British efforts his pacifist approach had wide effects across the sub-continent and were reported by the world press.

In 1917 the Montagu Declaration had implied Dominion status in due course, and an Act of 1919 allowed a degree of self-government in the provinces. In 1927 the Simon Commission proposed further devolution followed by a series of roundtable conferences in London. Many Indian politicians were more than aware that these promises were to keep India in the box, but men like Gandhi were soon making a demand for action.

In his memoirs Pug makes the defensive point against the common American opinion that the Indians were correct, and Britain was hanging on as a colonial power. Pug believed the British were not deliberately making difficulties, but with the benefit of historical hindsight it could be argued the British were in no hurry, especially with growing issues in Europe, and the sub-continent was considered amongst the great national possessions. Roosevelt hated the idea of colonialism, often suggesting that the British exaggerated the so-called communal problems (that is, hostility and fighting between the different religious sectors), but he died before independence in 1947 which proved such problems were all too real. It was a vast country and according to the 1941 census, India was divided between 255 million Hindus, 92 million Muslims, six million Christians and five and a half million Sikhs. These massive figures of the divided society are almost suggestive of potential communal problems if not civil war as the feelings ran deep.

Pug was equally convinced that the British could not have ruled 'for one week without the consent of the vast majority of the population'.[11] There was possibly a degree of truth in this, but an organised revolt in such a large country would have been difficult to organise and the British had trained a loyal Indian Army. Though Pug knew that the political classes wanted the British out, he admitted they carried 'little weight' with the masses who were probably more interested in surviving.

When in 1939 the Viceroy Linlithgow declared India's entry into the war without consulting the provincial governments, the Congress asked for all its elected representatives to resign and Muhammad Ali Jinnah, president of the All-India Muslim League demanded the adoption of the Lahore Resolution for the division of India into two states, Muslim and Hindu sometimes referred to as the Two-Nation Theory. Partitioning had been in the mind of many Muslims for years. By August 1942 Gandhi was demanding self-rule and the civil disobedience movement started under the *Quit India Movement* (*Bharat Chhodo Andolan*), and for some Indians the Japanese enemy seemed to offer a quicker way to freedom.

The Second World War was the critical factor in accelerating Indian independence and it also led over the next twenty years to the major decolonisation of over thirty other countries, much of it propelled by the American demand in return for their financial support. For years the British had known that independence would have to be accepted one day, and 'the problem of the future government of India had been pursued in Whitehall in its usual leisurely fashion'.[12] The Viceroys Halifax and Willingdon (whom Pug had served) had constantly focused on this issue, but all were acutely aware of the latent religious antagonism. India, for the British public was often viewed with a degree of pride, a source of wealth, romantic notions, but it was not within most people's horizons. Many politicians realised that India had to have its independence, apart from the more traditional colonial types such as Churchill. Men like Churchill, apart from his imperial background to which Roosevelt to Churchill's annoyance kept referring, were also conscious of the military aspects. The Indian army was both Hindu and Muslim, and as Pug had once noted it was not divisive as both components saw it as a high calling of warrior status. Churchill was concerned that the loss of the Indian army would affect morale. However, everyone recognised that when it happened, it would be a difficult process because of the bitter religious divisions. To keep India onside Stafford Cripps had been sent there in 1942 to look at a constitutional settlement explored in Whitehall, and naturally it failed.

When Attlee took over from Churchill in 1945, he was more ideologically driven and the Labour government started to look with more determination at India and other potential liberated territories seeking independence. Had Churchill stayed in power he might have felt obliged to travel the same route, but it would not have been so rapid. Attlee sent out a small team to encourage the Congress Party and Muslim League to form an agreed pattern for independence. There could be no agreement and there were horrific riots in 1946 Calcutta, portending the future problems, and the army had to restore the shaky equilibrium. This focused the British politicians on the knowledge that not only was the task extremely delicate and difficult, but could result in more bloodbaths, with Wavell deeply concerned about the near future. He knew that with the British Army gone there would be no resource for policing the communal riots and mayhem. There was no central government organ in which the political parties could be involved because the Muslim league simply refused to participate. As such Wavell had proposed that the British withdraw in stages leaving the difficult areas of the Punjab to the last moment, but Attlee and others, including Pug and Mountbatten, rejected the idea and may have been mistaken if the 'what-ifs' of history could be explored. The Whitehall perspective was one of wanting to maintain what they called a unitary India.

Independence and Partitioning

Pug had been anticipating going to Australia and New Zealand following their invitations, and had been in his office planning this break when Mountbatten had arrived, telling him that Attlee had appointing Mountbatten to travel as Viceroy to India to resolve the issues of independence. As a matter of historical curiosity Stafford Cripps had hoped to be appointed and Pug had also been considered for this role.[13] Pug realised that Mountbatten had arrived with ulterior motives which he mentioned the next day, and prompted Mountbatten by saying, 'You must have had some special reason yesterday for coming to see me, I believe you are going to ask me to go to India.' Pug was not keen, but being a man of national duty said 'If you are going out to play the last chukker twelve goals down, count me in on your team.'[14] In his memoirs there is a sense he was sorry he had been asked, stating that his 'first reaction was that it was one of the most delicate and perhaps distasteful assignments imaginable', but 'it was difficult to refuse' although it was unattractive.[15] He was a man of service, but he wrote that Darry's sense of duty was much stronger and she had been the one who suggested he should offer his help.

Pug was tired from his ceaseless round of work over the previous six years and needed his long holiday, and he knew little of India in recent years being so Europe orientated, but he had more knowledge than many having served there in his earlier years. He had started his military life in India, had worked for the Viceroy Willingdon, and he knew the great sub-continent as well as anyone. Even in March 1944 he had been kept in touch to a certain extent by Wavell, informing him that there were disturbing food shortages in India and Wavell's inability to help the situation.[16] It was followed by another letter underlining the importance of sending food to India.[17] A year later in March 1945, Pug received a letter from Richard Gardiner Casey, the Governor of Bengal, referring to the problems in that province, the increasing friction between Muslims and Hindus, his working relationship with Wavell the Viceroy and the widespread dislike of Churchill with all the various reasons.[18] In another letter Casey also mentioned the Muslim idea of a state to be known as Pakistan.[19] Churchill was of course irritated by both Mountbatten and Pug taking on what he saw as a shameful posting, it was Mountbatten's task to accomplish the task, but Churchill knew that Pug had the background knowledge to help. Pug knowing Churchill so well realised he would find this work objectionable.

He explained to Darry that he felt it was a matter of duty, which she had emphasised herself, and Attlee wrote a reply on hearing that Pug had cancelled his visit to the Antipodes. Pug wrote to Auchinleck (Commander in Chief, India) about his appointment as Chief of Staff to the Viceroy with his intention of having little involvement with military matters; the course was being set. In this letter he also expressed his own feelings:

My dear Claude, I expect that you are as surprised as I am to find myself returning to the land of my youth. God knows it's about the last thing that I wanted to do but if I can be of any help to you and Dickie in the terrific task which confronts you, I shall be well content to make the personal sacrifices that it is going to involve.[20]

Pug worked closely with Sir Eric Miéville, who was well known to him as Miéville had worked with him as a private secretary to Lord Willingdon in India, and because of Attlee's trust in Pug they were able to review all the papers. The gathering team were given rooms in India House so they could study the situation as closely as possible. It was an immense task with Pug already understanding many of the background features, as India had an estimated 390 million people, speaking 370 different languages, with so many religions and cultures which meant over the centuries it had never achieved unity. In a curious way independence became an issue when this complex jigsaw of a country found itself controlled by one nation which existed some four and a half thousand miles away.

There immediately appeared an issue between the Government of India and the Treasury over the terms and financing relating to pensions and compensation for returning British officials, and Wavell suggested it should be resolved before they left for India. There was some heated political debate and when the Cabinet Secretary informed Pug that it would be unlikely to be resolved, Pug retorted that if that were the case he would not commit to going, and it was likely Mountbatten would feel the same. He had no idea if Mountbatten would have taken this line but the threat worked and the politicians agreed.

Pug and Miéville left Britain on 19 March and Mountbatten and his team followed the next day. Darry did not accompany Pug but two of his daughters would later follow to help their father. Pug was pleased when he arrived as Auchinleck was there to greet him, and they went to the same house which Miéville and Pug had occupied when working for Lord Willingdon. There Pug met an old servant Abdur Rahman Khan who had been his orderly for nearly twenty-five years, and to whom he had been paying a small pension, which again illuminates his character. Abdur had travelled from Delhi to meet him.

At this stage Pug only hoped they could settle the differences between Hindu and Muslim and retain the Whitehall dream of a unitary country, or peacefully manage to organise two states all of which seemed possible as they set out with high hopes. The government had informed Wavell to transfer his responsibilities at the airport. It lacked a sense of dignity, so he refused and it all happened at the Viceroy's House. Over the next few months Pug would travel around India, meeting all the leaders, trying to bring some form of political reconciliation and calm ruffled feelings. He never mentioned in his memoirs or papers the smoothing of emotions he had to do in the Viceroy House, once writing to Darry 'both Dickie and Edwina are dead tired, nervy as they can be right across each other. So that in addition to my other troubles, I have been doing peacemaker and general sedative work…it's very wearing for them, and for me.' In the past, the two had been able to manage separate lives, but now they lived and worked together.[21] Naturally competitive, 'Edwina was jealous of her husband's new priorities, suffered from the heat and felt unsettled. These domestic tensions only added to the pressures Mountbatten faced.'[22]

As they had been travelling to India trouble had broken out in the two areas which had always been, and would remain the most dangerous zones, the Punjab and the N.W.F.P., (North-West Frontier Province). In the former following the collapse of the Union Government there had been widespread rioting, and in the latter a Muslim Redshirt Congress opposing the Muslim League found itself against total opposition, especially involving many of the tribesmen prevalent in this area. It was beginning to cross their minds that a two-state system was the only viable option. None of this confusion was helped by the poor communication links between London and Delhi and the other Indian hubs of importance. Mountbatten had been cautious to explain to Attlee that he was preparing for a unitary state, but other alternatives might have to be considered and it was projected that November 1948 should be the time for the transition of power. Mountbatten had not been warned about the problems relating to the Indian princes and their fiefdoms with their close relationship to the British Crown, making the whole scenario both delicate and potentially dangerous.

In his memoirs Pug had noted that in the initial stages he had thought they had all been given too short a time for this transition of power, but he soon changed his mind on arrival. He discovered that the communal bitterness had reached a serious level, describing a dinner party where he had a Congress member on one side and a Muslim on the other. He regarded both men as intelligent with 'impeccable manners' and well-educated, but both men would not stop speaking to him in loud voices about the 'inequities of the opposing community'.[23] This account by Pug creates its own political cartoon, that without the presence of a British general between them they might have used their knives and forks as weapons. However wrong the so-called British ownership of India may have been, at least there was some possibility of control between factions awaiting to massacre one another. It was, as Pug thought many times, like sitting on a powder keg.

The 1946 massacres in Calcutta had raised the level of provocation and another outbreak was feared. Pug also thought the 'administration of the country was going to the dogs', and the old control system had been replaced by an Interim Coalition Government over which the Viceroy presided. Their only interest was that Britain should quit India, this came before any other business, and 'all were racked with anxiety about the future'. Nehru had complained the system was unfit for governance, and over the years the British had, according to Pug, 'divested themselves of power'.[24]

Pug and Auchinleck, with whom he had been at Sandhurst, were both concerned about the future of the Indian Army, as its reconstruction would take time, and it all depended on the final settlement. There was a shortage of British troops who in normal numbers may have been able to police the trouble spots. Pug, like many others recognised the situation was fraught with danger, and in a letter to Darry just after his arrival he wrote:

> The situation is everywhere electric, and I get the feeling that the mine may go up any moment…to make matters worse the economic situation is bad. All the servants say that they cannot get food or clothing and that there is no security of life and limb…we've been in messes before now and got out all right. And we will this time, perhaps after going into deep waters and dark places.[25]

Three days later he wrote to Darry the warning that 'if we do not make up our minds on what we are going to do within the next two months or so, there will be pandemonium. If we do, there may be pandemonium.' These letters written before the crisis came to a head further indicated that Pug was a realist and knew it was a no-win situation, and his views seemed to reveal that time was of the essence for not just political purposes, but for safety reasons. Later, as will be shown, there was immense criticism directed at Mountbatten and his team because everything was too hurried, but in his letters to Darry, and not with the benefit of hindsight,

Pug seemed to forecast the whole situation would be a disaster sooner rather than later.

Mountbatten had met the Hindu leader Nehru in 1946 and liked him, probably from the time Nehru had refused to lay a wreath at the monument for fallen Indian soldiers who had fought for the Japanese. Some had regarded these Indian dead as heroes and even martyrs because they had fought against the British and not for them. Nehru had been educated at Harrow and Trinity College, Cambridge. Like Nehru, Jinnah was fluent in English and British ways, and both understood their colonial masters and what they stood for which made communications that much easier. However, Jinnah was aware that Nehru had more of Mountbatten's sympathy, and he had undoubtedly picked up on the well-known rumour that Mountbatten's wife Edwina was having an affair with Nehru, or at least they were on very close friendly terms. Nehru and Jinnah were both strong political leaders but like many politicians to this day they knew little about daily life in their communities and the necessary administration, and Jinnah remained deeply suspicious of the Nehru-Mountbatten friendship, constantly remaining obdurate in his arguments, persistently arguing for a state of Pakistan as he had done for many years. Mountbatten met and talked with them, but it soon became clear that even his social charm could not resolve the gigantic problems between the two sides, nor the other myriad issues of the day.

According to Pug, Mountbatten had tried every conceivable route to maintain the unity of India, but it soon became clear that the Muslim League would not agree to anything which did not involve the creation of Pakistan as an independent state, and Congress refused to discuss any form of partition. Mountbatten had many discussions with leaders and the Governors were invited to Delhi. Two factors emerged, that speed was of the essence, and a united India was out of the question. New plans were drafted then redrafted and a picture slowly emerged of a two-state system, but which meant that the provinces of the Punjab and Bengal had to be partitioned, under the oversight of a Boundary Commission which had a British chairman (Sir Cyril Radcliffe) with one Hindu and one Muslim member.

Pug, as was his custom in this post, travelled to see for himself the nature of the situation, selecting the two most vulnerable areas of the Punjab and NWFP, seeking information and trying to assess the critical issues to find a way forward. He was already arriving at the conclusion that a two-state independence was the only way forward. The two places he visited were both dangerous areas especially for unwelcome visitors, notably Nehru, who against advice went and experienced for himself the bitter antagonism. If India were to become independent Pug studied the advice that the NWFP could not remain a no-man's land for warring tribes, encouraged by Afghanistan sharing the same border. Pug wrote to his wife Darry explaining his visit to these two dangerous provinces, describing them as hectic, and 'on the verge of civil war with intense emotionalism'.[26]

Pug returned to Delhi where he and Mountbatten realised that they were not only trying to deal with a new situation, but one which daily changed its shades of colour. They both realised that beyond the political situation the British military manpower would not be able to handle a massive internecine war, and both concluded that this would involve a massive retreat. When later Mountbatten was criticised for the over-hasty transfer of power, Pug would often defend it by referring to this nightmare of insufficient troops, the communal hatreds, a tired Civil Service, and no one certain which was the best way forward. Those in India at the time could see for themselves the bitterness within the divided communities, expressed not only by debate and argument but in the bitter riots and appalling murders down the streets and alleyways. From Pug's point of view, it seemed an insoluble situation and despite the later criticisms often containing some elements of truth, it is possible to have some sympathy with his viewpoint; it was as he had predicted a potential disaster one way or the other.

Pug with George Abell, an Indian Civil Servant and private secretary to Wavell in his time, knew India well, and they tried to devise an acceptable plan and started a series of consultations with the government, the Muslim league and Congress. In doing this they were trying to assess the key areas and the difficult issues. They recognised that the critical problem was how a two-nation independence could be achieved without bloodshed. The administration and Indian military were a mixture of all sides of the religious divides, and a question of their allegiance arose while the new borders were being prepared, which could lead to the disintegration of the whole sub-continent. The evolving plan was a matter of timing, and unlike Wavell's ideas was expected to be much quicker. The provinces would unilaterally and simultaneously be granted independence, the east and west to the Muslims, the centre and south to India (or Kindustan) to India which would mean dividing Bengal and Punjab. It was anticipated there would be a strong central government in Delhi.

Pug worked hard at the details and with Abell was sent to London (2 May) with plans which had not been shown to Nehru or Jinnah. Pug had to persuade the Attlee government to accept the concept of two states, describing it as a 'Hobson's choice'.[27] The plans stated that:

> For each of the 11 provinces to decide their own future, Bengal and the Punjab to choose being split between India and Pakistan, to join one country entirely, or go it alone…the aim was to release the text 24 hours before Indian leaders next met on 17 May, thereby reducing the amount of time they could suggest amendments.[28]

Mountbatten was convinced that it had to be accepted as he believed with too much time the two parties would fall out again. Pug wrote to his wife about the need for haste, adding the significant line that 'We have made almost innumerable alternative drafts under all these heads, but it is impossible to get Dickie [Mountbatten] to go through them methodically. He's a grand chap in a thousand ways, but clarity of thought and writing is not his strong suit.'[29] This opinion shared with Darry underlined many of the criticisms aimed at Mountbatten in future years, but it would be the haste that would one day emerge as the focal censure. Pug had expressed much of this in an early letter to Darry, writing that he had held conversations with Gandhi, Nehru, and later with Jinnah indicating the dangers of delaying a decision.[30] The impression gained is that Mountbatten and Pug sincerely believed that the moment they had an acknowledgement of agreement it had to be nailed down at once.

Pug, using his persuasive ways, managed to encourage a shocked Cabinet to accept the possibility of a two-state India. Later Churchill asked if there were an alternative to which Pug said it would require at least two divisions of British troops, which after six years of war even Churchill realised was unrealistic. Churchill was worried about the time limitations and was probably right to ponder this problem, especially cutting all the united services and he was concerned that partition would fragment India. He said:

> How can we walk out of India and leave behind a war between 90 million Muslims and 200 million caste Hindus? Will it not be a terrible disgrace to our name if we allow one fifth of the population of the globe to fall into chaos and carnage? Would it not be a world crime that would stain our name forever? We must do our best in all circumstances but, at least, let us not add by shameful flight, by a premature hurried scuttle to the pangs of sorrow so many of us feel, the tint and smear of shame.[31]

Annoyingly, not that Pug stated it in public, he had just accomplished persuading the British government when Mountbatten suddenly telegrammed him, warning that the whole issue was back in 'the melting pot'. Vappala Pangunni Menon, an Indian civil servant, who had served under Wavell and who had been a Constitutional Adviser and Reform Commissioner to three viceroys, including Mountbatten, had pointed out that the plan now in London was potentially dangerous. He suggested that Wavell's plan had speculated on two central governments of Pakistan and Hindustan based on dominion status for both, and he believed this plan had a better chance of success. Nehru when consulted had also disagreed with the plans in London, which Pug believed emerged from Nehru's deep distrust of Whitehall, whereas Menon's ideas were more acceptable. Menon drafted the new plan and Nehru agreed. In his memoirs Pug admitted that 'by this time I was bewildered, out of touch with the situation in India, and useless as an envoy'.[32]

This confusion meant that Mountbatten and Menon had to leave for London at once, prompted by Pug who was amazed at the sudden change of course. The second plan based on Dominion status was probably the better of the two, whereas under the original proposal the provinces would declare their own independence from the Commonwealth, and Attlee and his government agreed at once. Pug wrote to Darry expressing surprise and some concern about the proposed date of independence which was drawing closer, the original dating being June 1948, and they were now looking to December 1947 if not earlier, even though Pug expressed concern that the civilian and military components would have to be reorganised.

As noted above this speedy departure has long been a matter of debate, and the letter to Darry clearly indicated Pug's concern about Mountbatten's hurry. However, it appeared that Mountbatten and Pug both believed the sooner the transition had to happen the better, otherwise Britain would be faced with rebellion in India. It was now a matter of returning to India to present their plans to the Indian parties, but neither Mountbatten nor Pug in trying to avoid an outright rebellion had envisaged the chaotic mayhem and slaughter which would ensue. Pug was exhausted with these fraught issues and the travelling, writing in his memoirs that 'I woke up on 2 June feeling like I had done on the various D-Days during the war; but on this occasion I had less confidence in the result.'[33]

Mountbatten's task was to convince Nehru and Jinnah to accept the plans, Pug was busy with how to divide the military and the administration, the military aspect causing him and his friend Auchinleck not only many problems but great sadness. The Indian army was old and deeply traditional and part of Pug's lifeblood and the situation was a logistical nightmare, causing some clashes between Mountbatten and Auchinleck, the latter being rightly concerned about future dangers in the wider community. It seemed that the British Army had to stay to monitor the situation, but it had already been moved out of the Punjab. Once again Pug was in the typical Chief of Staff role acting as a communicator between Mountbatten and Auchinleck. Jinnah accepted the British Army should stay but Nehru objected. It was an understandable reaction by both leaders, but both Auchinleck and Pug felt the Indian Army would not be able to retain its cohesion. Auchinleck feared for British lives, Pug disagreed on this point, and was generally correct. The date for the transition of power was set for 15 August. Pug had no role in trying to persuade the various princes to accede their powers either to Pakistan or India, as past arrangements were ignored and set aside. Many of the princes hoped that Britain would support them, but later military force was applied by the newly established governments.

Another issue was the British assumption that Mountbatten would remain as Governor-General to both states, and he would provide the necessary authority for liaison and combine them in foreign and defence policy, which with the benefit of hindsight was somewhat naïve. Nehru agreed but Jinnah decided he should be Governor-General, and possibly correctly did not regard Mountbatten as impartial, who, in turn, felt he should step down from both with which Pug disagreed. Pug had to return to London as Attlee's government was somewhat shaken that Mountbatten should only hold the position in India. Jinnah's determination not to agree over the Governor-General situation had, according to Pug, hit London like a bombshell.

He met with Attlee on 7 July and managed to persuade him and even Churchill whom he met the next day. A day later Sir Cyril Radcliffe arrived in India, with the allocated and impossible task of dividing the Punjab and Bengal provinces between the two new proposed states in barely a month. Gandhi in the meantime had denounced the whole concept of partition. The Punjab would be the most difficult because in addition to the Muslim and Hindu populations there were the Sikhs, who were also powerful landholders. Pug was deeply concerned about the Sikhs describing them as a 'warrior sect, which provided many thousands of splendid recruits for the Indian Army and had every cause to feel aggrieved'.[34] It was for this reason that many British officials in the region had been against the partition, especially the Governor of the Punjab Sir Evan Jenkins. This province was potentially one of the most viable areas for future growth, with its agriculture, the British canal system and its electric power systems, which partition could possibly destroy. It was clear that Radcliffe was aware of this issue, but like so many others he was under instructions.

Mountbatten was under the impression that a good military force could prevent such an outcome, and they prepared this policy under Auchinleck, to be known as the Punjab Boundary Force, but there would be a time with no civil power which any military force needed, nor did they have any idea at this time where the boundary would be placed on the maps. The existence of the Boundary Force was a forlorn hope, and the power of words would not resolve the intense bitter issues. On 20 July 1947, Pug wrote to his wife expressing his forebodings at the perceived 'lack of problems'.[35] The future must have felt totally insecure, like entering the 'great black hole' and 'rarely had optimism been so unrealistic'.[36] Jenkins had asked that the Radcliffe Awards, as they were known, should be published before 15 August, the designated date for the transfer of powers, but Mountbatten decided it was not to be released until after that date. There was always a suspicion by Pakistan that Mountbatten had changed some of the Awards in favour of India. When some details were confirmed Pug noted there were merely ten weeks to create a new administrative machine and to divide all the assets, and as Pug noted 'there was a tendency on the part of politicians in India to regard all the British members of the Civil Service as bigoted, scheming bureaucrats, and the Indian members as mere stooges of their British colleagues'.[37]

Pug was probably right, but it was a reflection of the legacy from much of the behaviour of the past. His concern for dividing the Indian Army along communal lines was always his deepest concern, not so much because of his love of the traditional military past, but because a unified military would be necessary to control much of the population's outbursts. He talked to Jinnah about the situation writing in his memoirs that 'I asked him to remember that an army was not merely a collection of men with rifles and bayonets and guns and tanks: it was a living entity, with one brain, one heart, and the Indian soldier was, generally speaking, a dedicated man whose loyalty centred on his regiment.'[38] Pug suggested dividing the army on numerical lines, but he failed, perhaps understandably, to convince Jinnah.

The night before 15 August, Independence Day, Pug was taken ill with a bout of dysentery, which he later described as a 'providential dispensation' as he thereby avoided the dissolution of the empire.[39] It was in his words a painful experience 'but not altogether unwelcome. I was convinced that the right thing had been done, but I was in no mood for unrestrained rejoicing.'[40] He flew with his daughter Susan to Kashmir for some rest and recuperation, but he was soon recalled to Delhi as the news was flooding in of numberless massacres. The Punjab Boundary Force was in a helpless situation and the now divided army remained loyal to its allotted governments, but the Indian army probably stopped a total rebellion, and the reduction of India to a mass of fiefdoms and warlords.

Underlining the violence of those days, Pug's daughter Sarah had travelled with her fiancé by train which had been attacked, and all the Muslim occupants slaughtered but Sarah hid her fiancé's Muslim bearer below her seat.[41] According to Pug this servant was the only Muslim to arrive safely at the station.[42] He wrote to his wife explaining that he had asked Sarah not to travel by train and suggested that Darry should not make arrangements to come out to India as she planned, writing that 'before you sail, and I am beginning to wonder whether you should sail at all. I am literally being rushed to death, and the situation is very critical.'[43] Pug may well have misused the word 'literally', but he may well have been worried about his immediate future as he watched the descent into chaos and blood-letting.

He wrote again a few days later describing his difficulties in talking with Jinnah, but Pug was already becoming known for refusing to take sides in the conflict. He explained to Darry that:

> Our mission was so very nearly a success; it is sad that it has ended up such a grim and total failure…I have written to Dickie asking him to release me immediately the battle is over; since with communalism having reached its present extremes, there is no reason in high places for anyone who is determined to be absolutely impartial…but naturally I can't quit while the storm is raging.[44]

Everyone in the British administration was in a sense of deep shock, but in such a huge, populated country where different religious neighbours had lived side by side under British authority, suddenly to be told that some must move not just house but out of the area, leaving possessions and livelihoods behind them, it was almost understandable and should have been foreseen that it would promptly provoke hatred and fear. It was for many an unwelcome forced migration to places unknown and not necessarily welcoming. In northern India with its long-settled village system, Hindus and Sikhs had to travel one way and Muslims another, leading to immense confusion. Delhi, the central government and all the British were caught by surprise and set off balance by not foreseeing or understanding the consequences, and it was a matter of retreat. Many British made rapid plans to leave, and Pug felt the campaign, as he called it, had been lost. Mountbatten set up an emergency committee, Nehru and Jinnah, according to Pug, did their best to calm the situation, but 'neither had the knowledge or experience to deal with a cataclysm of this kind'.[45] Pug spoke to Jinnah who was in a state of shock, and he watched Nehru charge into a crowd slapping faces and trying to calm it down. It was beyond their control and no person or entity could stop the massacres and the rioting.

The precise figures of those uprooted will never be known and the various efforts to speculate have varied widely from ten to twenty million. Those who died from violence and starvation also remains unknown, but probably ranges between one and two million. These figures were known at the time to be astronomical, and Mountbatten when later back in Britain gave an address at India House, and he 'appalled some of the guests by his speech when he proclaimed that *only* 100,000 people had died in the riots'.[46] Many were horrified that Mountbatten should refer to 100,000 deaths as 'only'. Pug himself was upset on hearing of the speech and in a letter to Darry he described it as unrealistic, pointing out that 'the crucial facts are that there is human misery on a colossal scale all around me – and millions are bereaved, destitute and homeless, and worst of all desperately anxious and almost hopeless about their future.'[47]

Pug's neutrality never stopped him from trying to help and his compound was full of Muslims seeking shelter. Later Congress and Nehru would acknowledge his impartiality.[48] He flew to see Jinnah to seek help as Nehru appeared to be able to do nothing to stop the mass slaughters. He found Jinnah charming and was probably the first guest to stay in his house, but what was happening was now beyond control. He flew back to England in October and managed to calm some of the fears but he did not hide the dreadful facts and the general situation. The press in Britain was publishing the accounts of the massacres and mayhem and being critical of Mountbatten. Pug tried to convince the government that the two states were doing their very best to bring matters under control. While he was away trouble broke out in Kashmir, and Mountbatten acquiesced to Nehru's demand which left that area of the north-eastern part of Punjab with an ongoing war which would flare up time and time again for years ahead.

Pug returned to Delhi at the end of October hoping to find matters had improved, but he was greeted with the news of yet further trouble. The Maharaja, in a state of desperation, signed an accession agreement for the state of Kashmir to India, and Mountbatten had accepted this even though it was such a highly populated Muslim area, and it had been anticipated to go to Pakistan.* Pug had visited the Maharaja Hari Singh

---

* Maharaja Sir Hari Singh was the last ruling Maharaja of the princely state of Jammu and Kashmir.

to encourage him to hold a referendum for his people to choose their state, but he had always been evasive and seemed to refuse to accept what was happening on his doorstep. Pug, understandably, could never understand why Pakistan was not consulted, which had increased Jinnah's suspicion of Mountbatten's Hindu prejudice. From all the accounts Pug was noted for his neutrality, but Mountbatten it appears, was much more inclined to his friend Nehru. Pug made every effort to try and manage to bring India and Pakistan together over the issue of Kashmir, but as could be expected, he failed.

As it had been decided that Mountbatten would be Governor-General in India but not Pakistan, with the anticipation that when Mountbatten was in one country Pug would be his representative in the other there was no point in him staying. Because Mountbatten was only to be in India he would naturally be biased towards that country, as Jinnah had long suspected. Jinnah was struggling in his new area with a smaller army, and Pug persuaded Mountbatten to allow Jinnah a Dakota plane for rapid transport. Pug was becoming understandably restless at living in a country where he felt they had failed, and curiously he wrote to his wife following an interview with Gandhi whom he found interesting but pessimistic about the future.

According to one source, Pug was indignant when he discovered that, without consultation, Mountbatten had listed him for a Knight Grand Commander of the Order of the Star of India. He already held a higher order, but apart from the lack of courtesy in not having been consulted, he told Mountbatten:

> You should have asked if I was willing to be recommended to a lower order. But that is not the point. Nothing on earth would induce me to accept an honour for the most painful and distasteful episode of my career. I must ask you to delete my name at once.[49]

Auchinleck declined a peerage, saying that he would accept a Knight of the Order of the Garter but not if it came on Mountbatten's recommendation. Pug returned to England just before Christmas of 1947. It is clear from this account that he was not at ease with all Mountbatten's work but being Pug, he remained in firm friendship with Mountbatten until his death, and it was Mountbatten who would read the lesson at Pug's funeral service.

It had only taken Mountbatten seven weeks to obtain Cabinet permission, three weeks to announce it and only eleven more to transfer power to the two new states. On reading the various accounts it appears that Mountbatten rode the storms of disaster with his usual confidence and aplomb, but it had badly upset Pug. Since the disaster the whole episode has been deeply criticised, not least Mountbatten's role with his need for haste. It has even been claimed that he left India 'at the height of the trouble to attend the wedding of Elizabeth and Philip. Rubbing salt into wounds being his speciality and swept away with the overwhelming sense of triumph as London celebrated the union of the Mountbattens and Windsors.'[50] There was some truth in this which was reflected in Pug's letter to Darry:

> Edwina has been dreadfully tiresome lately…there have been daily scenes about Dickie's decision to go home for the wedding. Personally, I think it's advisable on every count. It's good for the government of India because it will show them that they can do without him: it's good for Pakistan because it will show them that he is not as they charge, the Supreme Commander of the Kashmir offensive: and it's good for Dickie himself as he badly needs a change.[51]

The debate over Mountbatten's efficacy and character was already being raised in the press, national and international, and has been the subject of hostile criticism to this day. One historian noted:

> Mountbatten was headstrong, convinced that he was always right and unless they could be useful to him, he was not interested in other people or their views; he was above all else interested in promoting himself. In many reckless actions throughout the war, he had demonstrated a complete indifference to the consequences of a succession of rash decisions…in an ironic twist, Mountbatten, who had seemed untouchable in his irresponsible wartime escapades, was to adjudicate a culture where to be 'Untouchable' (to use the contemporary term) was quite the opposite of the privileged and protected standing in his own society.[52]

Many historians and observers have criticised Mountbatten and his judgement and character, but Pug's more sympathetic approach in his memoirs throws some light on the situation which at the very least emphasises the nature of the problem. Pug immediately recognised the various dangers they faced, the bitter divisive split between Hindu, Muslim, Sikh, and many other sects with their ways of life. The split was not just religious or philosophical but social and ran deeply amongst all levels of society, and he was aware that unless a resolution could be mapped out India might well descend into an open rebellion and internal war. The religious hatred and suspicion reflected the religious wars of early Europe, but the simmering of pure hatred was reaching boiling point. Whether there had been partitioning or not the consequences would probably have been the same, but the arguments still rage on. Many refer to Gandhi who was against the partition, some that an Indian government equipped with a united army, police and administration would have resolved the issue. This is not a study to explore this complex issue, and the truth or the causes may possibly be found in the way Britain controlled India over the previous century. Pug at least had seen that in 1947 it was beyond human redemption and although he felt 'bad' at being involved no one, including Mountbatten, could carry out a peaceful transition under the circumstances of 1947; the influences and forces of India's history were overwhelming.

For many years Mountbatten felt the pressure of criticism for the 1947 disaster, and journalists and critics were in hot pursuit; although Pug was unhappy about the results he always gave Mountbatten as a friend his support and advice. At times Mountbatten was seething with anger and asking Pug how to deal with yet more in-coming criticisms, who calmly wrote back (1 October 1948) stating it would be a mistake to use higher powers to speak to the 'Press Lord', that the men behind were only 'blatherers and cut no ice', so 'in all the circumstances, therefore, I feel that it would be better that neither you yourself nor anyone acting on your behalf should make any move in this matter'.[53] This problem would haunt Mountbatten and even Pug for the rest of their lives.

Chapter Two

1948–1952, Some Minor Roles

For the few years after India Pug was busy in the House of Lords, working privately for Churchill, Attlee at an official level and with many other commitments ranging from Lloyds Bank to the army. When in July 1948 he was made Honorary Colonel to the 532nd Light Arms Artillery Regiment he gave a five-page speech, all of which must have occupied a considerable amount of his time. His first biographer wrote 'that this did not take up too much of his time' but when any researcher looks through his speeches and addresses in the archives during these years it is simply unfathomable as to how he found time to write and prepare so much, let alone his correspondence.[1] It was during this time that he was busy assisting Churchill with his memoirs, which will be touched upon later, but sufficient for the moment to note that every chapter was sent to Pug for checking and revision, especially because Pug's memory was often better than Churchill's. As noted, he admired and loved Churchill as a person and nearly always responded to his requests, but it also meant that Pug was almost too busy and would never have a lengthy or normal retirement.

India continued to unsettle him, especially when news came through that Nehru had authorised the occupation of Hyderabad by armed force which, following the bitterness over the Kashmir case, caused Pug to write a protest to Mountbatten and Attlee, threatening to speak on the subject in the House of Lords where he sat on the 'cross benches', a term signifying the member was not allied to any one party. It was typical and correct of Pug as a military man to remain neutral in politics as he had remained neutral in the hotbed of the Hindu-Muslim conflict, but Nehru's action had more than irritated him. Attlee tried to dissuade Pug, but it was unnecessary as he had to stay at home with influenza. He rarely spoke in the Lords, but he rose to his feet about India and was always listened to on matters of national defence. He was regarded as having a specialist ability in this subject and was respected for his views. On 14 December 1950 in the Lords, he gave a lengthy speech covering various subjects related to the Second World War including defence, the Washington talks, the plans by Gamelin for the French response, all indicating that history had its lessons for the future.[2] Six months later he had an article published in *The Daily Telegraph* on the defence of the free world, and relating to what he saw as a grave hiatus at a recent summit, and an urgent plea for co-ordinated action, along with the need for freedom loving nations to unite and avert a third world war against totalitarian states. He wrote as an introduction:

> All the freedom-loving nations are resolved to preserve their freedom at all costs. Menaced as they are by the Totalitarian States. Their immediate aim is to avert a third World War. And they are agreed that the best, if not the only, hope of achieving this aim is for them to develop so great a united strength that no aggressor will dare challenge them. But the mere piling up of armaments, on however a colossal scale will not itself provide a deterrent.[3]

He may not have been part of the government, he was no longer in the higher echelons of the military, but he always had a constant interest in world affairs, Britain's defence system, and expressing such views in public would soon once again envelop much of his life. Both sides of the House listened to his views, and even Churchill came along once to hear him, as he argued for a close relationship with America, of maintaining the Chiefs of Staff system, and on what would be the most vexatious problem of the free world, facing the threat of Russian communism.

In Britain people were still suffering from the economic backlash of the last war, and although Britain and France had signed the 1946 Treaty of Paris against a possible resurgence of German power, the world was changing. It was soon realised that the main threat was communism and instead of holding Germany down it was now considering the possibility of letting West Germany rebuild its industry, keeping her onside and acting as a buffer state to the east, encouraging the free world to unite. Pug was aware of these wide-ranging issues, and on 4 April 1949 the North Atlantic Treaty was signed, giving birth to NATO. Britain knew many countries were critical of America when the Korean war started, but Britain and the Commonwealth joined alongside the Americans. On 22 February 1951 Pug rose again in the Lords and gave a speech on a state of war existing between the free world and communism, on the British Commonwealth defence, on the structure of command in the North Atlantic Treaty Organisation (NATO), and he encouraged all political parties to understand the dangers ahead.[4]

Festival of Britain

As a result of his unpleasant experience in India, when Attlee asked to see him at Downing Street, Pug 'went in fear and trembling'...expecting to be asked 'to undertake some sort of overseas appointment', but when asked by Attlee to chair the Festival of Britain he relaxed.[5] This festival was intended to mark the anniversary of the 1851 Great Exhibition, and Herbert Morrison was to be the Minister in Charge, but Pug's future role was an honorary post involving mixing with people in the intellectual world of music, writing and the arts in general, as well as business and politics. He was happy with this feeling 'relieved at not being asked to go abroad again, and I accepted at once'.[6] Many people after serving the duration of the last war and then working non-stop in India would have announced their retirement, but Attlee knew that Pug was a man of service. The Festival of Britain Council held its first meeting on 31 May 1948 and was addressed by Princess Elizabeth who reminded them that the 1851 Exhibition had been organised by her great-great-grandfather, the Prince Consort Albert. All towns, cities, and villages were to be prompted to organise their own little festival and Pug noted that 'we promised that the Festival Office would help them at all times and in every possible way, except in the matter of finance'[!].[7]

They were to have a combined Exhibition on the south bank of the Thames which stands to this day. It opened on 3 May 1951 with a service at St Paul's attended by the royal family, and Pug found the occasion very British and inspiring. That evening there was an inaugural concert at the Royal Festival Hall, and Pug and Darry went with the Lord Mayor and other dignitaries, only to find that they were trapped in a faulty lift, and they could not attract attention until the Lord Mayor hammered the lift door with his shoe. They had to be rescued in a somewhat undignified way as the lift was about six foot short to the landing. Pug later noted that what added 'insult to injury' was 'nobody had noticed that the boxes of the Lord Mayor of London, the Chairman of the Festival of Britain and the Director-General had been empty throughout the whole of the first part of the programme'.[8] Mountbatten, who had entertained Malcolm Sargent to dinner, had written to Pug using his influence for tickets to the concert to which Pug responded positively as usual, and so Edwina and Mountbatten at least heard the whole performance.[9] The next day the royal family and others including Churchill visited the site and saw all its features. Pug was also amused that Churchill found the new escalator fascinating and having never seen one went up and down several times. It said much about Churchill's lack of use of public transport because escalators had been used in the London underground since 1911.

The Festival of Britain involved Pug in many social occasions in which he was always made welcome because of his pleasant easiness in company and he gave many speeches. He delivered a lengthy speech on the Festival to the Council, as the Chairman, among other speeches by Princess Elizabeth, Herbert Stanley Morrison, and Gerald Barry the Director General of the Festival.[10] The following month he gave another speech to a meeting of the heads of local government of England and Wales at the Guildhall, which included references to planning Operation Overlord, accompanied by speeches from Gerald Barry, and Sir George Aylwen, the Lord Mayor of London.[11] It may have been an honorary position but the archives with his many speeches made it clear he was a busy person whose oratory was always welcomed. He travelled to many of the major cities to give these addresses and talks, and watched their festivities, the list was endless, but it seemed that Pug enjoyed the experience. The festival came to an end on 30 September with concern about the king's health.

Secretary Commonwealth Relations 1951–2

Pug had given his last speech at the ceremony of the Festival of Britain on 30 September 1951, aged 65 years. He had every intention of retiring, but the 1951 election had taken place. It had been won by Labour with a slim majority and Attlee had called the 1951 election to increase their small majority. During these elections the Socialists had branded Churchill a warmonger, with Labour suggesting 'a third labour government or a

Third World War?' The Labour Party lost, and Churchill was elated by having gained an electoral victory in his own right. All that he now required was to make his happiness complete by the return of the old familiar faces with those who remained, with Pug asked 'to supervise Commonwealth Affairs, Alexander Minister of defence and Colville as his private secretary'.[12] Or as Churchill's bitterest historical critic Nigel Knight expressed it, 'Churchill immediately inducted his cronies into his cabinet, regardless of their aptitude and experience'...'It is undeniably true that circumstances in 1951 were totally different from those existing in 1945, but Churchill began by trying to re-create the situation as he had left it six years before.'[13]

When the results had been announced Pug decided on an early night when the telephone rang with Churchill asking if he had been asleep. When Pug affirmed Churchill's suspicions that this had been the case, Churchill responded 'well, I only want to see you for five minutes', and so Pug used cold water to wake himself up and was with Churchill within quarter of an hour.[14] Churchill promptly offered Pug the post of Secretary of State for Commonwealth Relations, Pug claimed he was overjoyed to be working for Churchill again, and the next afternoon received the seals of office from the king. He then went to his official office, which was the old Colonial Office where he had once gone looking for leave as a young man, but this time he noted the red carpet was laid out. As Colville wrote in his diaries, Churchill's 'faithful associates, General Ismay and Lord Cherwell, were brought into the Cabinet against their own better judgement'.[15]

The whole world was very different from 1945, Roosevelt was dead, and in Colville's words 'Stalin was an ogre' and 'Churchill stood on a pedestal wearing a halo'.[16] Pug's appointment was right, and despite the cynicism of some critics, this was a level-headed and an appropriate appointment given Pug's personality and reputation. However, there are many hints that Churchill was being somewhat cunning as it has been suggested he wanted Pug in the Cabinet more for defence reasons, and the available evidence leans in this direction.[17] Pug himself wrote that 'I found myself more closely involved in defence matters than is usual for a Secretary of State for Commonwealth Relations.'[18] He and Churchill talked almost at once about defence matters, with Churchill asking Pug to update himself. Pug had always kept a watching brief on international matters, but the main concern they pinpointed was that Russia was going very much in the direction Churchill had once predicted with his Iron Curtain speech in Fulton, America. It was an expression first used by Goebbels, but with Churchill it became significant.

When in October Pug received a telegram from Christopher and Mary Soames congratulating him on joining the Cabinet, how far he was pleased to be there was another matter, but he was content to be alongside Churchill again, probably especially when he was involved in defence matters rather than those of the Commonwealth.[19] When Field Marshal Lord Alexander eventually returned from Canada as Governor-General at Churchill's wish for him to join the Cabinet, he found politics dirtier than war. There were moments which would have delighted Pug, as when the *Gloucester Echo*, *Sunday Times*, *Western Daily Press*, and *Birmingham Post* contained articles reviewing the granting of the freedom of Cheltenham to Pug. The ups and downs of the high social life Pug found enjoyable. On Boxing Day 1951 he enjoyed a meal with Churchill on board the *Queen Mary* when Mountbatten arrived from his home in Broadlands to join them. According to Colville, Mountbatten spoke 'arrant political nonsense' which Churchill found amusing but Pug was evidently annoyed. Churchill always gave much value to Mountbatten's royal connections but like Pug, he was less enamoured by his views.[20] Lord Moran was involved and again appears as one of Pug's few critics writing that on the *Queen Mary*, it was like being in the war again, 'The P.M. is still talking and there, opposite him, is Pug, still listening to him with his mouth open, as if he would not miss a syllable, uttering the same throat gurgling sounds of mirth. Pug, anyway, has not changed. Everything else seems different.'[21]

He was right in so far that Pug had not changed, and it was his consistency of character which people loved and respected. Not just because of his pleasant nature, but his loyalty, his neutrality in home politics and his ongoing years of service. Many understood his closeness to Churchill, and when in early 1952 (22 February) there was chatter about Churchill's ability to remain prime minister various ways were discussed as to how he could be shifted into the House of Lords, various names were suggested, even the Queen, with Moran noting that 'various names came into his [Lascelles] head; he dismissed them one by one, though for a moment he hesitated when he said Pug'.[22]

Pug's new post was short in duration, and it was clear from his memoirs and archival notes that his main concern was discussing the world situation and the Soviet threat with Churchill. The critical concern was their estimation that Russia had 'the best part of one and a half million men on a war footing, and the threat of overwhelming military strength, combined with political cunning, had enabled them to get control of one country after another without recourse to arms'.[23] Pug concluded that only the threat of the American atom bomb was the real deterrent. He knew the Americans understood the situation, but their constitution seemed to block them from alliances except in wartime. However, the Vandenberg Resolution (proposed in June 1948 by Senator Arthur Vandenberg) which recommended 'association' and collective arrangements for the sake of national safety, amounted to the abandonment of their traditional isolationism. It had enabled the signing of the NATO treaty with the critical premise that an attack on one of NATO's members was an attack on all. This meant, as Pug noted in his memoirs, unlike Hitler the Soviets could not 'pick off one country at a time'.

In April 1951 Pug spent time with Eisenhower as he took over command of the NATO military, and he was impressed 'by the team spirit which already animated the members of his international staff'.[24] This had always been Pug's dominating drive to surround himself with a cohesive team dedicated to its work. Just prior to King George VI's death Churchill asked Pug to travel to Lisbon for a meeting of the political wing of NATO. It was not the best of times to travel as Pug was attending his youngest daughter Mary's wedding, and he had to dash to the airport changing from his wedding attire while in the car. The one official moment in Lisbon was Greece and Turkey formally acceding to NATO, with Pug proudly noting in his memoirs that 'it was ironical that their accession was particularly warmly welcomed by those who had castigated Churchill for having saved Greece from the clutches of the Communists in 1944'; once again, he was entitled to say: *I told you so*. But that was not his custom.[25] He was a constant supporter and admirer of Churchill even in his private moments.

Chapter Three

1952–7,
Secretary General to NATO

Writer's Note: In his memoirs Pug mentions his appointment to NATO but hardly refers to any aspects of this work, apart from a few social details, and how he landed up in the role. He wrote that 'to tell the story of those years in full would overload these memoirs: to tell them in part would be misleading.'[1] Only two speculative reasons may be deduced from this statement; either Pug was becoming tired, (his health was faltering at this stage) or more likely he felt the issues at this time were too close to events and therefore somewhat sensitive.

When he had travelled to Lisbon with Eden for the NATO Conference, Pug thought the political, financial and myriads of other committees were too complex, describing these bodies in Lisbon as 'a mixture of the Tower of Babel and Bedlam'.[2] The political structure of NATO obviously needed clarification in its organisation and one of the resolutions was that a Secretary General should be appointed with a strong Staff Secretariat. The British Ambassador in Washington had politely declined, and the post seemed unfillable until Eden suggested Pug to Churchill. Pug was stubbornly opposed to the idea, so Eden called in the prime minister and Pug was categorically overruled by Churchill who insisted it was his duty, with Pug later writing that he felt like a naughty schoolboy being told to stop being defiant by his headmaster. Churchill used the word 'duty' because he knew Pug would respond, especially to him, thus he was announced as Secretary-General (12 March 1952) to the political structure of NATO.

On 24 March Pug surrendered to the Queen his Seals of Office which he had received from her father only six months earlier. He tried various manipulations about changing the nature of the post and failed, but it was agreed that he could initiate and prepare agendas. He later recalled that General Alfred Gruenther amusingly reminded him years later that as he was leaving the Lisbon meeting, he had said 'This is the first that I have seen of NATO and thank heavens it's the last.'³ Pug had landed up in a post of which he was uncertain but was now committed. There followed a flurry of telegrams informing the world of the new appointment, Eden telegrammed Canada, and Pug asked Churchill to make sure all the Commonwealth countries were informed thereby explaining why he was leaving that post.⁴ Many in the Commonwealth were sorry to see him go, and it was best expressed in a letter from the New Zealand High Commissioner in London, stating that 'I need hardly tell you how much I have valued your enthusiasm for a grasp of everything connected with the Commonwealth, as well as your personal friendliness.'⁵ Yet again it was Pug's friendly demeanour which often made him successful even in a post he had held for a brief time.

Churchill's secretary John Colville watched all this unfolding of events, noting that 'after the war he [Pug] looked forward to a peaceful life, caring for his herd of Jersey cows, it was not to be. In 1951 Churchill inveigled him, against his wishes into becoming Secretary of State for Commonwealth Relations and in 1952 NATO.'⁶ Colville returned to this theme writing that 'I lunched today at the French Embassy, a party in honour of Pug Ismay who is going, strongly against his original wishes, as Secretary General of NATO'.⁷ It was widely known that Pug had been reluctant to take on the new role. Lascelles, the King's secretary gave an amusing insight in his memoirs, recalling that:

> In April 1952 Winston gave a luncheon party at No. 10 for Ismay and Bridges, Ismay was about to go to Paris as Secretary-General of NATO, and, in an admirable speech, said how much he regretted leaving his home in Gloucestershire, and his beloved herd of Jersey cows. Winston ejaculated loudly from the chair, 'Quite easy. Milk the cows in the morning, fly to Paris and milk the Americans in the afternoon.' I don't think there were any Americans in the room.⁸

For their part the Americans were discussing Pug's appointment, and a memo of a telephone conversation by the Special Assistant to the Secretary of State read:

The Secretary telephoned Mr Lovett to say that he had just received a telegram on a top-secret basis from London which informed us that the British were suggesting Lord Ismay as Secretary General of NATO. Mr Lovett said he thought that this would be all right; that Lord Ismay was very favorably disposed toward this country and had a very excellent sense of history. Lord Ismay might not be the best possible choice but had many advantages that some of the others who had been suggested did not have.[9]

After this note the Secretary then phoned a Mr Pearson who had heard the news and informed him that Pug 'was a great figure and very close to the present Government of Britain which would make him an acceptable choice, although he was afraid that Lord Ismay's military background' might be awkward.[10] Pug's personality would overcome this issue, but it was clear that the Americans were happy for once with a British general. Those Americans who knew Pug from previous years welcomed him with open arms. General Alfred Gruenther the US Army Chief of Staff wrote on 13 March 1951:

Dear Pug, I will not congratulate you on your appointment as Secretary General, but I certainly want to congratulate the North Atlantic Treaty Organization for its far seeing wisdom in selecting you. I know that the new appointment will interfere with your personal plans and that it will involve many sacrifices on your part. I do, however, want you to know that the entire SHAPE organization is overjoyed with the appointment. We all stand ready to help you in your important assignment in any task that you see fit to give us. [Gruenther always signed off as 'Al'.] [11]

On 14 April 1952 he and Darry moved to Paris and at first stayed in a hotel while the staff and secretariat were installed in temporary buildings in the Palais de Chaillot. Pug recalled that the British had wanted the NATO headquarters in London, but with the bomb damage and limited housing he had little sympathy for this viewpoint. The hotel was pleasant enough but not as private or secure as Pug would have liked, and eventually he and Darry found their own place at No.10 (a number which probably made him smile) Villa Saïd which was just about suitable and would be used for entertainment and could dine nearly forty people. As their new home became more important, they brought over their old butler and his wife from Wormington to assist. This proved to be useful because in time they would entertain many important figures including such royalty as the Duke of Edinburgh and the King and Queen of Greece. It took longer to find better accommodation for the offices and during most of his time he worked from the temporary accommodation in the Palais de Chaillot.

He set to work at once and was active. An archival letter from Eisenhower on 12 April 1952 referred to Ismay's assistance in attempting to ensure Italian presence in NATO, an issue which concerned Eisenhower who was already grateful for Pug's help.[12] More to the point Pug found to his immense pleasure two men in place with whom he had worked with before, Richard Coleridge in charge of the office, and an Admiral Dick, both of whom spoke excellent French. France was the country hosting them, but was again in political turmoil, and with their traditional attitude insisted on advising on all appointments which led to considerable intrigue. The French had more interest in their involvement with the European Defence Community (EDC) which later transpired to be something of an abortive attempt by Europe's Western powers to counterbalance Soviet strength and potential threats. Its influence started to lessen by the mid-1950s. The French were wary of Germany and wanted their forces, if they were re-established, under French command and not as a separate power. Many suspected de Gaulle of interfering; he was not in power at the time, but he may have been wielding some influence.

Pug always felt that NATO was the only sensible key for defence and therefore peace in the west and believed the way forward had to be a sound understanding between the Military control in Washington and the Political Council in Paris. Both sides he argued should keep one another fully informed, which sounded like simple common sense but Pug had to work hard to achieve this result. He had thought he was a stopgap measure, but this appointment was not his anticipated duration of two years but five, taking him through to April 1957 when he would be 70 years of age. The more he became involved with the work and the ensuing problems the more he realised what had to be done and he became strongly dedicated to the task. He worked assiduously at building up the efficiency of the administration and during his time a huge number of airfields were built, along with fuel pipelines which the public and press knew little about. Pug made a friend of Geoffrey Parsons who was the Chief Press Officer and decided work was needed on public relations. Parsons was able to assist and offer advice to Pug about press-conferences and how to present the nature and intentions of NATO.

From the moment he arrived it was clear from archive research alone that Pug was frenetically busy, not only travelling but preparing speeches and addresses nearly every day. He spoke in Copenhagen (19 July 1952) on the necessity of making NATO a success and with variations repeated this effort in all the member states.[13] In September he decided that good propaganda was essential and prepared an address entitled 'Towards a better understanding of the North Atlantic Treaty', which was only one of a series depending on the audience.[14] He worked at a major speech for the officers of SHAPE (Supreme Headquarters Allied Powers Europe) expounding on the North Atlantic Council and its function as an international cabinet for NATO affairs, and the responsibilities of the council towards the military authorities.[15]

It would take pages just to list the titles and places for delivering his speeches, and because he loved the social life and horse-racing it is almost incomprehensible as to how he found the time to write so much. His love of polo had transformed into horse-racing and many people thought he had an excellent eye for the winner. He also became something of an expert at news conferences, interviews, newspaper articles and broadcasting. As early as December 1952 the *US News and World Report* produced an interview with Pug entitled 'Can the North Atlantic Treaty Organization (NATO) army fight now?'[16] This related to the strategic difficulties in Europe's defence, indicating that Pug was aware of the all-round logistics of this Cold War tension. He travelled around the European member states, giving radio broadcasts in nearly every country selling the importance of NATO. As early as 18 July 1952 his notes revealed his interview in Denmark, with the interviewer asking him if this were his first visit to this country. He answered:

> Yes, it is and I cannot tell you how delighted I am to be here. I admit that it was a great wrench to give up my last post in the British Cabinet in order to take up my new appointment with the North

Atlantic Council. But my Prime Minister, Mr Churchill, whom I served as Chief of Staff throughout the last war, told me that it was my duty. How glad I am that I took his advice! The responsibilities are immense: but so are the compensations: and not least to visit Denmark that I have wanted to do for a long time.[17]

Only Pug with his open expressions of warmth could try and endear himself to a country with which he had next to nothing to do with before, though his friendly approach often attracted the most cynical comment.

He was already making his mark, and as early as September 1952 Churchill gave a speech which is worth quoting:

I forbear to call him by his pet-name, because I might be thought to be showing disrespect to his international status. But it seems to me that Lord Ismay is doing the same sort of thing for NATO as he did for us – as he did for me, and I am sure Mr. Attlee will agree with me, as he did for us – in the war to make all things go as well as possible between the military and the politicians and to weave together many diverse elements into the harmonious structure of a machine capable of giving decisions for millions of men.[18]

Churchill was also aware that in that first year Pug had visited six countries giving endless broadcasts and press conferences. He toured in the north in such places as Norway, south to Portugal and Italy, and many in-between. When he visited, he was inevitably welcomed by the head of state, but when it came to England the Foreign Office was uncertain about the Queen receiving one of her own subjects, but after the usual Foreign Office debate they gave way and Pug officially met the Queen in his NATO role. In Germany he met the Federal Chancellor and opened the discussion on West German forces in NATO. The next year he visited America and Canada, then Greece, Turkey, and others; it was a formidable timetable and workload.

Pug more than most was aware that it was essential that NATO was not just military and he established work-committees to explore the ways and means of co-operation. Their reports led to adoption by the fourteen member nations giving a cohesive structure and thereby making communication lines essential in the event of war. Members of the political structure moved around Europe and were present at NATO manoeuvres and exercises. His knowledge and understanding of NATO's function and future importance was growing and his expertise was acknowledged. In April 1952 he had given a lengthy press conference in Paris, relating to the views of NATO held in the USA and Canada and touched upon the NATO Annual Review.[19] A few months later he produced a text for a broadcast he was going to make through the BBC called 'Insurance for peace', and later another broadcast stating the necessary reasons for establishing NATO in the first place.[20] In 1954 he was still preparing for many BBC broadcasts, writing and checking the scripts, as this was a major effort on the fifth anniversary of the signing of the North Atlantic Treaty relating to the reasons for the formation of NATO; these efforts often stemmed from other notes, but he invariably had to check and update them.[21]

Pug produced another text ready for a television interview with himself and US journalists over questions on NATO's ability to function without a German contribution to the West Europe defence, whether the vital aspect of NATO's development was in the past or the future, and whether the lessening of tension in Europe would weaken NATO. It concluded by asking whether NATO had succeeded in giving Europe political and military stability.[22] He repeated the same theme in a speech in the Houses of Parliament relating to the aims, structure, and operation of NATO.[23] He gave an important press conference which related to the consequences of Stalin's death and Russia's change of tactics which might involve NATO's involvement in economic and political fields, and the need for further military expansion.[24] After this he wrote a paper for publication in *The Scotsman* entitled 'The causes, purposes and hopes of the North Atlantic Treaty Organization'.[25] He was the spokesman, the propaganda wizard, but above all the human face for much of NATO through his speeches, broadcasts, press conferences, newspaper articles, and researching through his prodigious amount of papers was almost exhausting, especially understanding the notes in his handwriting.

His new home at No.10 Villa Saïd had become important. Pug naturally led an active social life and joined the French Jockey Club and the Travellers Club in Paris, and he pursued his love of horse racing for which he was known as something of an expert in his judgement of horses. However, the most relevant times at Villa Saïd were the informal lunches he held for many of the national delegates. Around the lunch-table trust and friendship could be extended and informal discussions could take place without immediate ramifications. Pug was starting what is now known as business lunches, where people could express their views with notes being taken by various secretaries for later use; it was a matter of clearing the air and feeling free, which all proved valuable at later more formal discussions. Pug himself had to tread with care because he was the neutral international chairman and not representing British views which at times, being Pug, he must have found difficult. The British appointments sometimes led him to clash with the British Foreign Office who made such appointments, especially when they went ahead without first notifying him. On one occasion he objected to their selection of the British Ambassador to NATO, and the appointment was held up until Pug was certain it was the best possible choice.

He frequently had to travel to America, not least because they were financially and militarily the major partner. On 12 March 1953 he was closeted with the President, Secretary Dulles, and Douglas MacArthur. The President (Eisenhower) started by asking for Pug's views as to whether the allied countries were 'making a maximum effort both in terms of their resources and capabilities and in terms of their will to face up to some of the hard decisions which must be made if NATO is to continue to make progress'.[26] This would vex many American administrations over the decades to come, most recently with President Trump. Pug answered by stating that most of the NATO countries were 'straining themselves to the very maximum of their capabilities and resources', and he pointed out the French were weak in government because of the composition of their present parliament.[27] The President thought Denmark could make a greater effort with which Pug agreed and thought the same true of Belgium. The President believed the Belgians had done the right thing by introducing a 24 months military service conscription and had been disillusioned when others had not followed their lead. There was a discussion about the relationship between the NATO military and the civilian authorities. Pug pointed out that matters had evolved since the President was the last Supreme Commander. Nevertheless, Eisenhower felt the Supreme Commander and Pug had to stimulate all the governments to make maximum efforts. This and many other meetings underlined the difficult tasks that faced Pug, but it also indicated the trust others felt in him and his opinions.

One of the main issues confronting him during his time in office was the question of West Germany. NATO was primarily in place as a defence mechanism against Soviet domination and possible war, and for many divided Germany was beginning to be seen as an essential component despite the hostility less than ten years before. The fraught question was whether West Germany could now be integrated into Europe and be re-armed, which was a strategic necessity if a Russian threat were to be effectively countered. During 1953 both America and Britain were looking to a time when Germany would not be occupied and their rearmament could start, and NATO, and not the EDC would be regarded as the main area of coordinated defence on a large scale. The EDC was outlining the possibility of a supranational army, but one which would subsume West German forces into a European military organisation. This was regarded as resolving the tendentious problem of German rearmament. However, to achieve success in this momentous change meant treating West Germany as an ally which, in Pug's opinion and from what he had experienced in the last war, could only be resolved by a meeting of agreement by the heads of the major states. He set about organising this for a summit of the three western occupying powers of France, Britain, and the USA in Bermuda with Pug in attendance. It was not easy to arrange but was finally settled for early December 1953. Churchill informed Pug it had been arranged and late in the day he had to pull all the stops out to rush to the airport to ensure he arrived on time. It was a major conference covering many topics, but NATO and the Russian danger were central to the agendas.

At the conference Pug pointed to the necessity for NATO considering a 'new look' or 'long haul' concept regarding defence build-up, stating 'we should know what we want and how to obtain it', noting that by mentioning this issue was 'not caused by pessimism over defence build-up' because it was satisfactory, but certain facts had to be considered.[28] The most important feature Pug underlined was that the military requirement levels could not be attained on current peace-time economics.

Pug had played an important role in Bermuda painting the picture of NATO being the main bulwark with the EDC part of that framework, and his arguments were accepted. He was still acting as a bridge no longer in a passive style, but a bridge with directions on which way to go, which included plans to bring West Germany into the framework with the other fourteen nations. It was also decided that NATO needed a 'new look' with the build-up of NATO power for what Pug had described as 'the long haul'. This meant extending Western European influence in West Germany and an acceptance that atomic weapons may well have to be used. This event was often regarded as Pug's most important contribution, and at the end of the session he had lunch with his old friend President Eisenhower. They both hoped that France would ratify the EDC treaty and bring that body into the NATO structure, but in August 1954 the French refused. This meant that the objective of bringing West Germany into the fold appeared to have failed.

It did not stop the impetus and on 28 September 1954 an agreement was made for ending the occupation of West Germany, who with Italy were invited to become members of NATO. It was Pug and his team who rapidly drew all the drafts for the agreements and clarified the situation and the necessary machinery for the way forward. As such on 9 May 1955, there was a formal meeting of the NATO Council which the German Chancellor Konrad Adenauer attended, and Germany became the fifteenth member of NATO, and a tribute was made to Pug's contribution. It prompted the reactive creation of the Warsaw Pact, a feature of the Cold War which was further emphasised when Pug had long retired, with the building of the Berlin Wall in 1961.

At a Churchill dinner there was much talk about the Bermuda Conference and Lord Moran reported that 'Pug felt the strength of the Russians had been exaggerated. In the event of war, they would have long lines of communications, and would always be looking back over their shoulders at Poland and the other satellite countries.'[29] Churchill agreed in principle, but he replied that if they had only one third of their forces, there were no real defences in Europe which was a growing concern and had been part of the impetus behind the conference. The fear of an imminent attack was never far from their minds, and in a letter from Pug to Churchill he related a conversation between himself and Gruenther, who was then Supreme Allied Commander in Europe, in which Gruenther reiterated his opinion on the likelihood of a Soviet attack on Western Europe, confirming that he shared the views of Montgomery and Lord Alexander.[30] There was a great deal of anxiety prevalent at this time and only a few months before Pug had prepared a speech to be delivered to the 'think tank' of Chatham House, relating to the reasons for the formation of the North Atlantic Treaty Organization and its structure.[31]

Life continued at a hectic pace as Pug not only maintained old friendships, but was constantly being asked by Churchill to test various waters, even in his domestic parliamentary life. Moran recorded that when he had once called by No. 10 Downing Street in case Churchill needed him, being told 'that Pug Ismay, Norman Brook and Jock [Colville] were closeted with the P.M.', preparing Churchill's reply to Shinwell for the next debate.[32] Mountbatten, always ambitious had long harboured the desire to become First Sea Lord, his father having been dropped from the role because of his German name in the Great War, and it was clear he had sought Pug's help, who received a letter from Edwina Mountbatten thanking him for his assistance regarding the appointment of her husband as First Sea Lord.[33] Pug was involved in many matters and in the lives of his numerous friends.

Both Pug and Montgomery realised that NATO was no longer a temporary arrangement to avert the Soviet danger but was going to be a long-term structure. This would mean wider budgetary controls and expansion which led to some friction with the French still certain about the value of the EDC which Montgomery considered 'dead'.[34] Montgomery was always in the background with his strong, sometimes opinionated views. He was highly critical of the various NATO problems, the nature of the organisation, the defence budgets and he sent Pug a lengthy paper on the possible solutions.[35] Montgomery even looked at some of the texts Pug had prepared for broadcasting and suggested amendments.[36] Pug's American friend General Gruenther (Chief of Staff at SHAPE since 1951) wrote him a letter with his reservations about one of Montgomery's own addresses, probably knowing that while Pug might agree he would remain loyal to Montgomery.[37] Pug always tried to avoid serious confrontation with friends and allies. During the last war he barely mentioned his occasional clashes with Brooke, he knew all about Montgomery's propensity for over confidence in himself, but he never committed to writing such sharp criticisms (despite searching his private papers for such evidence).

During these years Pug and Gruenther became good friends and in July 1953 Pug wrote to him inviting him to stay with his family at Wormington:

My dear Al, I should so much have liked to have had a yarn with you since your return from Washington, but, alas, I have had my nose to the grindstone. We leave for England on a month's leave tonight and we are going to spend nearly all of it at home…nothing would give us greater pleasure than if you and Grace could come and spend a few days with us. You could fly direct to Fairfax airfield, which is an American base for heavy bombers. It is only about 25 miles from our home, and we could have you there within an hour of touching ground…we would simply love to have you both and it really is a very easy journey. Yours ever, Pug.[38]

To which Gruenther replied:

My Dear Pug, Grace and I are in receipt of your very warm invitation to spend some time with you at Wormington Grange. You have asked us for 'only a few days' but instead of that we have decided to spend three weeks with you. So please get ready to receive us. That is the kind of a letter, Pug, that I should send you for being so free and easy with your invitations. However, I will spare you that agony. I think it is so important that the Secretary General spend this period of rest in a quiet atmosphere, that I have decided that it would be best for the safety of Western civilization that we not disturb you.[39]

The correspondence between the two men is one of warmth, with plans for Gruenther visiting Pug and Darry at their home in 1956 and as late as 1961.[40] Gruenther often signed 'Al' and frequently as 'Devotedly, Al'. In another memo he wrote to Pug that 'I value your friendship highly and it gave me a great bang to receive such a warm indorsement,' and addressed him in another letter as 'My Dear Pal, Pug'.[41] As late as 27 August 1962, Gruenther wrote from Washington looking forward to another home visit, 'please take care of the cows until I have a chance to come and check in to your supervisory methods, devotedly Al'.[42] In many ways it was men like Pug and Gruenther who maintained the Anglo-American alliance by basing it on personal friendship.

Gruenther from 11 July 1953 was made Supreme Allied Commander (he retired on 31 November 1956 and retired from the army at the end of

December) about the same time as Pug was projecting to publish a small book entitled *NATO. The First Five Years*, which was well received.

There were many issues he had to deal with, not least the question of Cyprus and the Mediterranean arena. This involved Britain and both Greece and Turkey who were making claims over the island, thereby putting Pug as a British person into a highly sensitive scenario. He managed to keep the Greek and Turkish representatives on cordial terms, but the whole situation was becoming volatile. It has been suggested that Pug's work during the Cyprus problem was 'a significant factor in keeping the Cyprus dilemmas from developing into a Mediterranean crisis'.[43] Amongst the other issues were the budgetary requirements for the various states which were always increasing. Pug developed the habit of sending his trusted colleague Coleridge ahead of him to the country he was next visiting to explain matters, so when Pug formally met the head of state he could reinforce what had been already quantified. These visits were endless, often ceremonial, could involve some interesting sight-seeing and entertainment but it was long arduous work. It has been noted that Pug's personality helped keep a sense of balance, and 'Kings, Queens, Presidents and Prime Ministers loved this gay, [written in 1970] amusing and incredibly attractive man', and Darry often kept him company.[44] They had lunches with many of Europe's monarchs and Darry often selected items and furniture for their home in Villa Saïd as they travelled.

In September 1955 Humphrey, the American Secretary to the Treasury arrived intent on reducing the financial American commitment, but according to Macmillan (who was then Foreign Secretary to Eden's administration) it was Pug who influenced Humphrey not to progress this plan. This information was first noted in a letter by Gladwyn Jebb, the British Ambassador in Paris in which he had observed 'the favourable impression made by Ismay on US Senator Humphrey who had been contemplating cuts in US expenditure on European defence'.[45]

There were also growing concerns regarding Soviet interest in the Mediterranean and the Middle East, as well as developing anxiety about events in Egypt and the Suez Canal. It was Gladwyn Jebb, mentioned above, who informed Pug that France and Britain had sent armed troops into Egypt, even the British ambassador in Cairo had first heard this information on a radio broadcast! NATO had not been informed and as is well known Britain and France were isolated and made to feel like pariah states, and as such two of the major powers found themselves divided from America, with Britain and France condemned in the United Nations. The Atlantic Council met daily, but the United Nations was now the body to make decisions. Pug was greatly upset because of Eisenhower's stance, for a time almost feeling it was a betrayal because as international as he and his post were, he was rooted in Britain, and it is tempting to feel that despite any personal views on Eden's incredible decision it was a matter of 'my country first, right or wrong'.

Pug felt he had no alternative but to resign at once because of America's attitude effecting a major part of his work while at NATO, but Darry managed to dissuade him. He continued to work and tried to reforge those links which had been twisted out of shape by the Suez fiasco. During all this upheaval Pug still found time to deliver a lecture (November 1956) to the Imperial Defence College on co-ordination of political and military views on strategy, with some reflections on the position in the First World War, the effect of an independent air force on the chiefs of staff, the operations of the famous 'war book' (record book), the defence committee and finally defining the jobs of soldier and statesman.[46]

It had long been expected that Pug would leave his NATO post in September 1957, a five-year agreed term, and now aged 70 it happened at long last. After some consideration the post went to Henri Spaak who was the Belgian Foreign Secretary, who had served the Belgian government in exile during the Second World War. It was an uneasy time for Pug as at American social gatherings he felt uncomfortable, with American friends raising the Suez business. All this was followed by state visits by Queen Elizabeth II and the Duke of Edinburgh, and from which he learnt he was to be awarded the Knight of the Garter for his services. He was offered many awards from the other nations who had noted his dedication to his tasks, but the Foreign Office could not allow Pug to accept such awards, because from the earliest of times this was a 'no-go' area except in times of war. Even the French award which by Foreign Office rules was more acceptable was banned, but there were many elaborate ceremonies and functions in Paris before Pug and Darry left. Perhaps most pleasing for Pug was that his NATO staff together purchased him a present of a Louis XV clock.

He later reflected in the conclusion of his memoirs that he was sad on departing from Paris as he felt it was like leaving his family and both he and Darry 'felt utterly miserable'. He admitted the French soldiers may have been surprised 'as I passed slowly down the ranks of the French Guard of Honour at the airport, I felt the *poilus* [French term for infantryman] must have been astonished to see a British General with tears pouring down his face'.[47] He also believed on leaving that the NATO structure was the best and only hope for peace, and unlike the fiasco in India he felt during these years that he had made a valuable contribution. Compared to his French send-off, he was not expecting the same reception in London, but he was received by those representing the Queen and the government and inspected his last guard of honour. They had a quiet dinner with Churchill, returning to Wormington for the long anticipated retirement and his Jersey cows. Perhaps it was not surprising that his last words in his memoirs related to a conversation he had with Churchill that evening who asked Pug 'Have you forgiven me for sending you to NATO? I could only reply "Sir, you were right as always."'

Chapter Four

Retirement

Before he left Paris, Pug had decided to write his memoirs possibly in the hope that it was a signal to the political community that he was retiring and that he intended to stay retired. It immediately prompted interest from newspapers and publishers. In May 1956 he was approached by the *Sunday Express* looking for the serialisation rights for his efforts, and a few days later a letter from Andre Deutsch about publishing his memoirs, and these various approaches continued from many sources, intimating that he was well-known during these years.[1]

Back in England his wife Darry was concerned for him as he was exhausted, not as robust as usual, and she was worried for his health. He attended the ceremony of his installation as a Knight of the Garter to which the Queen invited the NATO permanent representatives, and from there they drove to spend the evening with the Astor family. However, Pug was developing a temperature and was not capable of attending his much-loved horse-racing at Ascot which clearly indicated to his family that he was unwell. The doctors were concerned and thought it might be the first signs of the dreaded lung cancer, but an antibiotic cleared the lungs although it was evident that Pug was not just exhausted but unwell. He still managed to attend some horse races, but the British weather did not help. Darry's cousin Ronald Tree, who often lent his home to Churchill during the war when Chequers was considered a possible Luftwaffe target, offered Pug and Darry his holiday place in the sun in Barbados where the warmer climate helped him. It was here that he managed to finish his memoirs, noted by his friend Sir Ronald Wingate that they were written in 'his usual modesty' saying 'nothing about the part which he personally played during the last war in Allied Council'.[2] They were indeed modest, and he rarely disclosed any criticisms he may have felt of others. He returned to Barbados for health reasons and comfort, but the pneumonia attacks were becoming more serious and he had to go to hospital for further treatment.

Despite his deteriorating health he had many issues from the past which he still dealt with as important. The contentious publication of Bryant's version of Brooke's diary was for Pug highly irritating. In February 1957 he telegrammed Colin Coote, editor of *The Daily Telegraph* informing him that he would be unable to write a review of *The Turn of the Tide, 1939–1943*.[3] Had he done so he knew it would rock the boat not least because by this stage Churchill was coming under some criticism, and Pug would protect him to the end, as well as attempting to maintain his friendship with Brooke. In October 1959 Pug was asking the publishers to remove a reference to himself in the book which mentioned his resignation, which he thought might upset Churchill, but was probably unnecessary as at this stage Churchill was not reading much.[4] Pug and Brooke had often been at odds with one another at the discussion table and they were very different, one a military expert who seemingly put emotions aside, Pug deeply emotional and just as intelligent. Nevertheless, despite their differences they both wanted the war won and always remained loyal to one another and retained their friendship.

It was not the only publication causing a stir as Maurice Hankey, his old boss, wrote to him about his difficulties in obtaining official permission for the publication of his memoirs and asking Ismay to assist.[5] It was a vexatious issue and in June, Hankey wrote again seeking Pug's views on the possible consequences of publishing without official sanction.[6] Pug was often approached by many people for advice on their publications, and during the 1960s there was prolific correspondence relating to a proposed biography of his friend Sir Adrian Carton de Wiart, regarding who should be the author and the nature of the work, always seeking Pug's advice.[7] There were some fifty letters alone relating to this issue in the archives.

A month seldom passed by without correspondence seeking information about the war years, wads of papers and letters requesting information or querying some events. It was a two-way process as Pug wrote in April 1958 to Captain Stephen Roskill 'for information on the 'PQ' [Arctic] convoys to the Soviet Union', and the proportions in British and American shipping, sinkings and asking about the worst disaster of [convoy] PQ 17'.[8]

There exist in the archives endless papers discussing the precise facts and seeking opinions. As a mere example in July 1959 there was correspondence from Ismay to Sir Henry Pownall replying to a letter relating to Kesselring's parachute troops at Crete, and subsequent possibilities against Malta, and in the same month a letter from Sir Kenneth Pickthorn MP to Pug on the issue of the German invasion through Belgium being linked with uranium dumps.[9] Pug was always protecting the past whenever Churchill's name was involved, especially if the matter were personal or sensitive. There was a letter from Ismay to John Connell referring to points made in Connell's letter [6 Sep 1961] including Ismay's view that Churchill's pressure on Wavell for offensives was due to John Dill's weakness as Chief of the Imperial General Staff, and to Churchill's desire to eradicate the defensive attitude at the War Office.[10] Anything which cast a shadow over Churchill always took his immediate attention.

Occasionally it was difficult when old friends clashed as in September 1964, when Pug had to write to Mountbatten relating to some disagreements with Mountbatten's version of events, especially in his papers regarding 'Conversation with Churchill and with Beaverbrook after the Battle of Crete about the future of Hitler's campaign against USSR in 1941', and in 'Matters affecting my selection for the position in Combined Operations and South-East Asia'.[11] During his retirement Pug had become the guardian of Churchill's legacy as by this time his old friend and boss was ill and had been seriously declining for a few years.

It was not only the last war which was coming under more objective scrutiny, but perhaps with more reason, Mountbatten's role in the partitioning of India was becoming more a matter of sharp criticism rather than political adulation. Mountbatten was highly sensitive to this, as was Pug who had supported him. As early as August 1959 Ronald Wingate (his friend and author of his 1970 biography) wrote to Pug forwarding a redraft of passages regarding the transfer of power in India and mentioning the lack of national unity. It was followed by a note with a redraft of Ismay's passages on the transfer of power in India in the context of British methods of ruling India since 1858.[12] It was critical for Pug and Mountbatten that their perspective was seen in the same light as they viewed it in 1947. In November 1960 Mountbatten wrote to Pug asking him to meet a Michael Edwards who was proposing to write a book on the transfer of power in India, undoubtedly sensitive to the building criticisms relating to 1947.[13]

In March 1962 Pug was becoming concerned and he wrote to Mountbatten referring to the persistent view in the press, and in recent publications, that the rapid handover of power in India was the sole cause of the civil unrest and massacres which followed. Pug requested that an article should be published giving a full explanation of the decisions made in India and the situation faced by Mountbatten as Viceroy.[14] This was promptly followed by Mountbatten's reply regarding the recent and critical publications about himself, and the transfer of power in India, and agreeing in principle to the publication of an article giving Mountbatten's interpretation of events, as always seeking Pug's help.[15] There then followed much correspondence on Mountbatten's idea that there should be a book published on the subject, and in July 1962 he wrote to Pug taking up a suggestion of using Peter Fleming as a possible author for a proposed book on the transfer of power in India.[16] It was important for Mountbatten and Pug that amidst all the gathering criticisms their viewpoints should be heard. Looking for the right author was an ongoing issue, and a number were mentioned and usually with objections, mainly for fears of their personal views.[17]

The Indian problem caused Pug serious heartache, because he had supported Mountbatten's views, and he genuinely believed they had made the right decision, but he was becoming more and more aware of the perhaps justified criticisms that it had all happened at too great a speed. He devoted time in his memoirs trying to explain why, and although it cast some light on the situation, he, and Mountbatten, as noted above, spent time selecting the right author to explain the situation, as they perceived it essential that their points of view should be considered justified in 1947.

It was not just protecting or guarding the past which occupied Pug during these years of retirement but doing some repair work for others. Britain and France had gone to war over Poland, the Poles had fought with the British Army and their pilots serving in the RAF had proved to be courageous and willing, but now their home country was occupied by the Soviets, and understandably many had stayed rather than return. They may have found personal freedom, but many were suffering from financial hardship and Pug became deeply involved in their cause. In May 1958 he had heard of their problem from Randolph Churchill, with correspondence on this matter from Lord Alexander, and how they should be helped and forwarded the suggestions onto a Count Stefan

Zamoyski to set the ball rolling.[18] A month later others had devised a letter which they asked Pug to sign as an appeal for Polish officers in financial difficulties who were unable to return to Poland, following Pug's requests for some statistics.[19] By April 1961 a fund was in place and Pug wrote to the lawyers requesting a list of those people to whom he had sent appeal letters, and who had made donations, so that he might write personal letters of thanks, which for anyone would be a long task, let alone for Pug now in retirement and not in the best of health.[20]

In addition to all this work he broadcast an appeal on behalf of the Greater London Fund for the Royal National Institute for the Blind (1 September 1957), back to Charterhouse in 1958 giving a speech, unveiling of a panel in the memory of the Carthusians who fell in the Second World War, and a few years later was involved in fund raising for Churchill College, Cambridge.[21] This was not just a flurry of activity but these 'bits and pieces' have been selected to demonstrate that after NATO and despite ill-health Pug worked, corresponded, broadcast, and gave speeches at a simply phenomenal rate.

He stayed in constant touch with Churchill and, with Attlee, was the centre of a broadcast to celebrate Churchill's 80th birthday. Pug was the first guest and was introduced by Attlee with the words that Pug 'was the man who was at his right hand throughout the war'.[22] This summarised the war situation, and Pug had constantly admired Churchill who in turn treated Pug as a close friend. This relationship continued until death.

He was also busy meeting old friends and past acquaintances who would turn up at Wormington, some of them unexpectedly. He enjoyed his drink and these social meetings when his humour and laughter would be heard throughout the house, and as in earlier times he had regaled people with tales from Somaliland, now his main repertoire tended to revolve around amusing stories and anecdotes about Churchill. He also enjoyed a game of bridge and was a formidable player, and loved seeing his Jersey cows, but now had to be driven to their fields.

However, while he was looking at his cows, playing bridge and enjoying a glass of whisky and soda with his friends, the government had not forgotten him or his expertise. Macmillan was then Prime Minister and requested Pug's advice on various issues on the matter of the Central Organisation of Defence, and Pug and his old assistant Ian Jacob worked as a team at the various problems. It was hard work for the two of them over two months and was completed by the end of February 1963. His report was private to the prime minister and not for parliamentary or public scrutiny, but it suggested the abolition of the three forces having their own committees, instead to be co-ordinated into one responsible to the minister of defence. This was a major conclusion by the two men as an early letter to Ian Jacob from Pug mentioned the necessity of the merging of service departments into a single Defence Ministry.[23] By the end of February, Macmillan as Prime Minister wrote to Pug thanking him for the report on higher direction of defence, and mentioning its acceptance by the Cabinet.[24] His recommendations eventually happened but it was the last public service that Pug did.

In January 1965 his adored chief Churchill died and Pug was asked to be a pallbearer. He was not well himself but decided to go and for the last time follow a request. He found it exhausting but knew he had to be there. The writer of this exploration saw Pug for the only time as an undergraduate at King's College London, as one of the thousands on the streets watching. When he made his appearance at the Hyde Park Hotel where he was staying, he was greeted by many people who wanted to meet him, which by this stage he found exhausting. He attended the Garter ceremony in June, did his best to support Lady Churchill on introducing her to the House of Lords. After this he never left Wormington again, his health was deteriorating rapidly and he had to have oxygen, this decline indicating he was in his end days.

Less than a year after Churchill's death he died on 17 December 1965. His service, at which Mountbatten read the lesson, was held in St George's Chapel packed with his military friends from all three services and politicians from both sides of the House.

Chapter Five

Churchill and Pug

War Years

Churchill had countless friends, admirers, and critics, but his relationship with Pug appeared unique. On the one hand Pug virtually venerated him from the time they met when he was a desktop general, through moments of turbulence during the Second World War and thereafter a relationship of total trust, mutual respect, established on a developing affectionate relationship.

Churchill often felt that he was destined to lead his country and has been recognised as one of England's greatest leaders in times of war. The fact that Attlee replaced him as prime minister in 1945 was a clear indicator that Churchill was seen primarily as a war leader. He has remained much admired and loved by most British people because of his leadership in bringing Britain through the crisis of the Second World War. Like everyone he has had his critics, and he was frequently opposed by his military advisers. It was widely known that he could be petulant and at times behave like a dictator, but most agree he provided at the right moment a determined leadership, worked as hard as anyone could and, despite his occasional angry outbursts, was much admired and loved by those who served under him, even though he worked them, like himself, to the limit of endurance.

When after the war he wrote his lengthy six volume history of the war years (for which Pug was often called in to help) the reader only needs to check the indexes to see how close he was to Pug, and a major part of his work consists of his memos to Pug demanding answers, passing on orders, ideas to be discussed, ranging from almost irrelevant demands to major global policies. Pug is mentioned several times in the first volume concerning the build up to war, but in volumes II-VI Churchill records many of the memos Pug had to deal with, and it was simply phenomenal. Just reading them took several days hard work, let alone for Pug who had to arrange a response. Often Churchill would preface his request with 'pray let me have' which sounds like a request from someone seeking help, but it was more a demand expecting an immediate response.

In the last five volumes 'Pug memos' occur on nearly 300 pages, some short and many lengthy, and they demonstrate not only Churchill's thinking processes, but from reading just the memos it would be possible to outline the history of the war and the British policies. In volume II, memos to Pug are nearly eighty in number, and they deal with issues ranging from Churchill complaining of private secretaries addressing each other by Christian name when dealing with official matters, asking precise details about 'sticky bombs', to directions to the admiralty about the use of destroyers, notes on the arrival of Australians, and how they should be used, the situation of civilians in vulnerable port areas, ammunition supplies, questioning Beaverbrook's estimates, instructions and requests for the COS to consider. . . the list was endless.[1]

In terms of studying the war, these memos are valuable and can make interesting reading in themselves. Churchill insisted that the word aircraft should be used, not aeroplane, and airfield or airport but not aerodrome, noting 'it is a good thing to have a rule and stick to it'.[2] It would have been interesting to have had Pug's private thoughts on such memos, but his total loyalty has barred such insights. Churchill insisted on seeing code words first before they were used and challenged the light-hearted names given to operations where men could lose their lives.[3] Churchill was highly aware of the sensitivity behind names and language in general, and Pug appeared to have the same values.

The memos are endless, and Churchill often records his telephone requests for action, and had Pug not organised an outstanding administration system no single man could have coped. Churchill's questions may have taken a few lines to dictate, but the reply often meant a response taking up several pages, which Pug had to check knowing Churchill's demand for clarity and brevity. He was known as a hard worker and diligent, otherwise he would not have been kept in post for the duration. On reading Churchill's postwar history, it is apparent that Churchill worked hard and long with his well-known erratic hours, from his secretary sitting by his bed in the early mornings to the very late nights at Chequers, at times temperamental, from jovial to bad-tempered in micro-seconds. This lifestyle had to be matched by Pug whose workload at times must have been gruelling. Even the social needs of Churchill could be tiring, with one of Churchill's biographers writing that he 'sat up talking (quite unnecessarily except for his reminiscent pleasure) until 3.45 a.m. with General Ismay and Leslie Rowan', one of his private secretaries.[4]

There were occasions when Pug admitted he was Churchill's whipping boy, and there were times when Churchill was so rude to him many people would have left the room to return with their resignation. Churchill would often explode, accusing Pug of being an appeaser, saying 'all you want is to draw your pay, eat your rations and sleep' or 'very well, if you don't care about winning the war, go to sleep', but this was said in mock anger, and Ismay [somehow] knew not to take it seriously'.[5] Pug only offered his resignation once as noted in the text, and that was an attempt to stop more serious resignations and most of Churchill's closest colleagues understood his temperament. Churchill was always under tremendous strain 'which entitled him (in the view of his willing whipping-boy, General Ismay, and others) to blow off steam when he felt like it'.[6]

In his memoirs and notes Pug never complained, apart from missing his Jersey cows, and his admiration for Churchill's output developed into an adoration of his boss. The memos were also two-way, as when Pug had to report the COS questions and information to the prime minister, one of the more important being about Hitler's secret weapons of the V1 and V2 rockets.[7]

It was not just a life of memos, but Pug was constantly in Churchill's presence, even at his treasured retreat at Chequers where Churchill kept notoriously late hours, aggravating for men like Brooke more accustomed to rising early. He mentioned in his history when he took Pug, Averell Harriman and Pownall to Chequers that 'I had of course a most complete service of secretaries in the house, and also direct telephone connections with all areas'.[8] Pug enjoyed the social side, revelled in Churchill's sense of humour and use of language, but it was constant work as more often than not Churchill would be discussing policies and operations during a late evening meal. As Churchill noted later in the same volume 'General Ismay was so close to me every day' that he often called upon him for what had been said or happened.[9] When meetings were sensitive or ultra-secret it was always Pug who attended and took the necessary notes, as Churchill wrote, 'when the Defence Committee met our American friends at 10 Downing Street. This discussion seemed so important that I asked General Ismay beforehand to personally make the record.'[10] Pug was totally trusted as a man as was his professionalism by a prime minster who had exacting standards.

Post War Years

After the war the relationship of Pug and Churchill continued unabated, and with the war finished and the tensions relieved, it was abundantly clear that although Churchill continued to rely on Pug in politico-military matters and used him to assist in his memoirs, they both formed an enduring and genuine friendship. There are abundant notes from Churchill thanking Pug for birthday presents, for gifts of caviar, brandy on other occasions, and in 1958 a letter from Churchill to Ismay thanking him for his golden wedding anniversary present. They met socially on many occasions, and it included their families inter-reacting, and such is the nature of the friendly correspondence it can easily be assumed that the wartime relationship had emerged as close and personal. As early as 1949 when Churchill's wife Clementine was thinking about putting Chartwell Garden onto a commercial basis the first person she wrote to for advice was Pug.[11]

In February 1953, with Churchill's trust, Pug made a recording for the BBC relating to the prime minister's meeting with the French war leaders on 11 Jun 1940 to discuss France's inability to continue the war against Germany, and the British commitment of fighter squadrons. It was a delicate political situation by 1953 and Churchill had complete trust in Pug's ability.[12] A year later in November 1954 to celebrate Churchill's birthday there was a television programme in which it fell to Pug to introduce foreign contributors.[13]

When Churchill worked on his own history of the Second World War, he had a formidable team working for him, and he sent out frequent requests seeking information to remind him of the events. One of his main supports in this was Pug whose archives reveal simply reams of letters and memos between the two as Churchill struggled to ensure his information and memory recalls were accurate. Pug's notes to Churchill are voluminous, with suggestions politely placed such as 'Suggest this paragraph should be slightly re-arranged and amended' and checking the final works it was clear that Pug's advice was followed.[14] He also pointed out omissions such as the necessity of including a telegram from Wavell 'since the Chiefs of Staff refer to it in their telegrams of the 20th. The lead-in might be ….'[15]

Pug even travelled with Churchill to Lake Garda in Italy (August 1949) to continue this work, only relaxing when Churchill decided he wanted to paint a picture. It was an exacting task for Pug and 'every chapter was sent to him for verification and revision'.[16] The only break from helping Churchill was the nine-month interval while he was in India with Mountbatten, but it was all waiting for him on his return.

From the letters it is possible to speculate with some assurance that Churchill depended on Pug for some of the more sensitive and controversial areas of the war years. As early as 1946 he was asking him questions 'on relations with the French', the Battle of Britain and even his visits to bombed areas in the east end of London, Margate, Kent, and Bristol.[17] He knew that although he had been there, both in France and in the bombed areas of Britain he had been fully immersed in the events and emotions of the day, whereas Pug had been able to stand back and observe in an objective way which Churchill trusted. Sometimes it was pure information asking for details which explained the use of various codenames such as Operation Catapult (the attack on the French Fleet) and Code Susan (which related to the fleet not coming south of the Wash).[18]

Other correspondence between Churchill and Pug related to some delicate areas in which Churchill knew he had to tread with sensitivity. One such example was Churchill underlining that it was an erroneous impression held by some that he was opposed to Operation Overlord, which was frequently claimed by occasional frustrated American commanders, and was also the case with his views on Operation Anvil for landing in the south of France.[19] In one of his archival files was a press cutting Pug had retained from June 1944, indicating the negative view of the British contribution to the Second World War, specifically their supposed reluctance to open a second front, and he had long been aware of this attitude by many Americans.[20] Churchill, with justification, was an historian, but it was important to him that his part on the stage of events should have the right colours and shades. Pug also had to deal with contentious issues such as Mountbatten's raid on Dieppe, an abject failure, not only over what happened, but as to who gave the final orders, and the consequences, over which even the most recent studies indicated considerable uncertainty.[21] The archive materials clearly revealed there was total confusion even in 1942 over the Dieppe orders and who gave the instructions and Churchill, who was in North Africa at the time, was equally puzzled.[22] Brooke was furious with Mountbatten whose general defence was that it was so top secret hardly anyone knew what was happening. Had it not been for his popularity and royal connections Mountbatten may well have been in trouble.

By 1950 Churchill was demanding results to explain Dieppe in his history and Pug was obliged to write to 'My dear Dickie' explaining Winston's request to know why there was so much secrecy over Operation Jubilee when its predecessor Rutter had been cancelled.[23] The basic question was who gave the orders? When Mountbatten replied he was evasive, seeking information from his then naval planner and his Chief of Staff, and shifting the blame onto Churchill by claiming he was following his orders.[24] Pug, holding to his sense of loyal friendship, had already warned Mountbatten that Brooke had encouraged Churchill to delve further into the reasons why the Dieppe raid had failed and expected Mountbatten to deal with the situation.

> Back in 1995 Ziegler [Mountbatten's official biographer] refused to accept that Churchill had signed off the brief, blame-free narrative of the Dieppe raid that appears in *The Hinge of Fate*, the fourth volume of his war memoirs...it seemed unbelievable that, through 'Pug' Ismay...Mountbatten could have convinced 'the old man' to endorse a version of events which was at best highly contentious, and at worst, manifestly false.[25]

One way or another, rightly or wrongly, Pug tended to stand by friends, even though in this issue he may have been wrong or even possibly confused.

In the archive collection there remain letters from Pug to Churchill covering the conference at St Paul's School on 7 April and 15 May 1944, and the talk by Montgomery and its misreporting in Alan McCrae Moorhead's biography of Montgomery, along with such sensitive issues as Tube Alloys, the then code name for the atom bomb project.[26] There are also considerable letters of advice as Churchill's enquiring tentacles stretched across the desks of the most important people. Lindemann wrote to Pug suggesting caution in the account in Churchill's memoirs of 'the Teheran, Persia conference as regards future treatment of Germany, and regarding French General Charles de Gaulle', which at the time of writing in 1951 was a highly sensitive matter.[27] Pug also received a letter from Air Chief Marshal Sir John Slessor, Imperial Defence College, 'on the absence of an adviser on the RAF on Churchill's memoirs team'.[28] It was also Pug who received advice on the text, as when the last wartime British Ambassador to Italy, Sir Percy Loraine, who wrote to Pug on the possible correction of an error in Churchill's memoirs concerning his mission to Italy including a meeting with the Foreign Minister, Ciano.[29]

Reading much of the correspondence regarding Churchill's memoirs two thoughts emerge; the first that it may well have been the case that many of the correspondents thought it safer to write to Pug rather than directly to Churchill, and with their ongoing and trusting friendship Churchill was again heavily dependent on Pug's information and advice. Pug was once again an essential cog, but this time in Churchill's literary life. He could well have written a history as well, but he was more than happy to write his own memoirs, and when on 19 May 1958, Pug sent him the first chapters of this work in manuscript form Lord Moran noted that 'Sir Winston is fascinated. He could not put them down.'[30]

As soon as Churchill was back as prime minister he called in Pug, nominally in a role to the Commonwealth nations, but to help in the quagmire of post war defence, and it was Churchill who virtually ordered Pug to take on the senior post at NATO. When Churchill called Pug always responded and Churchill knew this would always be the case. Despite Pug's reluctance to take the NATO post they stayed close friends until their deaths in 1965, a relationship of trust and total loyalty, emerging as an affectionate friendship.

Chapter Six

Contemporaries and their Insights

Field Marshal General Alan Brooke

Brooke, the well-known Chief of the Imperial General Staff knew Pug well. They worked closely together in London, overseas at conferences and Brooke was the critical man in strategic decision making. For most of the war Brooke was the CIGS, with the nickname Shrapnel and was the top general for advising Churchill, but their views over strategy frequently differed and led to some bad-tempered interchanges during many meetings. There is no doubt that Churchill selected Brooke because of his strong personality, which indicates as much about Churchill, as it did Brooke. There seems little doubt that during the war years Pug and Brooke had friendly relationships but as mentioned in the text, when Brooke's diaries were first published under the title *The Turn of the Tide* by Arthur Bryant it disrupted their friendship.[1] Pug could do no other than support Churchill who was the subject of much vitriol in Brooke's diaries. He wrote to Churchill following Bryant's publication suggesting that Bryant 'has done Brookie an injury almost as grievous as Henry Wilson's widow did to her husband'.[2]/* Brooke was aware of the many criticisms this publication had caused and sought to mollify Churchill but not that successfully.

Later editors of Brooke's diaries published them in a better format in 2001, admitting that as Chief of Staff Pug was generally successful as 'the lubricant in the sticky relationship between Churchill and the Chiefs of Staff Committee [COS], but then cynically added that his nickname 'Pug was based on his appearance; although canine in his loyalty to his chief, his other characteristics were perhaps more feline'.[3] This comment seems somewhat unfair, although it is undoubtedly true that as far as Pug was concerned Churchill rarely made mistakes, probably at times

---

* This lady had published the diary of her husband who was the CIGS and had been killed by the IRA, but her work revealed him as somewhat foolish and disloyal.

over-justifying his beloved boss, but in his letter mentioned above it is noteworthy that Pug addresses Brooke as *Brookie* which was the more affectionate nickname used by his contemporaries.* A more generous suggestion about Ismay's nickname was given by Jock Colville, Churchill's personal civil servant, who wrote that Ismay was 'known universally as Pug, for he looked like one and when he was pleased one could almost imagine he was wagging his tail'.[4]

In these more recent and better presented diaries edited by Alex Danchev and Daniel Todman, a massive volume of over some 700 pages, a significant statistic emerges. In Brooke's diaries, Pug is mentioned about ninety times, but seventy-one of these only lists his name as one of those in attendance at meetings and only eighteen refer directly to Pug for one reason or another. It reveals that Pug attended most of the critical meetings throughout the war. At times Brooke simply refers to him as Ismay, then as the months go by, he becomes Pug Ismay, and often Pug alone. It is tempting given Brooke's forthright character that this reflects his attitude towards the general whose job it was to present Churchill's sometime unwelcome ideas.

Pug admitted in his memoirs that in his opinion Brooke was the best CIGS of all times, and Brooke's diary reveals they often ate together with their wives as company, and one time noting that he was late and had 'to rush to Pug Ismay's sherry party'.[5] When Pug was unwell, Brooke made a point of visiting him, evidently as a friend.[6] There is no question that during these fraught times they had a friendly relationship, holding one another in mutual respect. Pug wrote of Brooke that he was not a self-seeker or disloyal, but 'on the contrary, his selflessness, integrity and mastery of his profession earned him the complete confidence, not only of his political chiefs and his colleagues in Whitehall, but also of all our commanders in the field'.[7]

A reasonable conclusion would be that during the war years they worked together under trying circumstances, and when Pug had to present his chief's more unpalatable thoughts Pug became Ismay, when he was simply reporting back on other issues, he was Pug Ismay, and when not circumscribed by debate and controversy Pug became Pug. It was his duty,

---

* Ismay was probably given the nickname Pug because of his bull-dog type jaw, but it was also useful in communications for disguising his real name.

as regarded by many, to ease relationships between the military staff and Churchill. When the COS decided against sending more tanks to North Africa, they knew Churchill would be angry and General Kennedy noted that 'Ismay suggested a way of making it palatable to him,' which was his fundamental role as seen by many.[8]

Pug's role as the intermediary, or bridge, especially between Churchill and the COS, surfaces in Brooke's diaries from time to time, usually the anguished moments, as in December 1941 when Brooke noted that 'Pug Ismay produced a memo from PM to the effect that the 18th and 50th Divs were to be offered to the Russians for their Southern front!'[9] A few days later Brooke wrote that 'Pug Ismay informed us that the PM now wanted to send the 18th Div to Rangoon to attack Japs on Kra Isthmus, being now convinced that we had enough troops for the North African business!'[10] The use by Brooke of the exclamation mark indicates his feelings towards Churchill's ideas, and Pug must have been sensitive and very conscious that he was constantly the conveyor of unwelcome suggestions from Churchill. He also had to inform Brooke and the other COS members when Churchill was unhappy about them, as in Washington (21 June 1942) when Brooke was hoping for some peace and quiet and then 'Pug Ismay called up to say that PM wanted to see me and that he was very upset at the decisions we had come to with the Combined Chiefs of Staff meetings'.[11] Pug knew that like any messenger his task was not always well received, but he was generally known for staying calm and acting the traditional role of the classic messenger of doing his job and staying balanced, but others watched him in anticipation with Brooke once noting that 'when I arrived at the Chiefs of Staff meeting I found Pug Ismay in one of his excited moods!'[12] Again the exclamation mark indicating that even Pug was anxious, but this time with disturbing news from Eisenhower about the North African situation.

However, Pug was not just the messenger boy, though his role as the bridge between military and political leadership was the key to his position. He often expressed his opinions at a personal level and was part of the ongoing debates in these high-level meetings, but never mentioned his contributions in his memoirs. When Mountbatten had been appointed Chief of Combined Operations, much to Brooke's chagrin, there was a very heated debate (22 December 1942) about Mountbatten commanding naval forces for an invasion of France. Brooke noted that Pug and Portal were in support of Mountbatten, but he and Dudley Pound opposed this bitterly on the grounds that Mountbatten was an adviser not a commander.[13] Brooke and Pound won the argument, but it is mentioned here to indicate that Pug's role was more than a passive observer. These internal dissensions which inevitably involved Pug, though he rarely mentions them, continued later when the Americans argued for invading Sardinia and not Sicily, with Brooke noting in his usual style that the Americans had won Mountbatten over to their line of argument, and that Pug and Portal 'were beginning to waver'.[14]

Pug was in an invidious position with his role, and at one stage Brooke accused him of wasting 'a great deal of our time at the COS...he has been having a row with the PM in defending a document we had produced yesterday'.[15] This involved the time that Churchill wanted the Irish leader de Valera to sack the German Ambassador in Dublin, but because the COS knew his cypher could be read it was better to keep the devil they knew. It was a situation for Pug where he was 'damned if he didn't, and damned if he did', not a post to be welcomed by many but Pug was a servant to the state, as was Brooke and other service chiefs, and despite the post war friction it is clear that during the war they worked well together, and given Pug's friendly demeanour there is no doubt that this factor helped ease the way in these difficult situations.

Above all, as Brooke knew, Pug was often the soothing potion for the serious clashes between himself and Churchill, and they were frequent. In his obituary in *The Times* in 1963 Brooke was described as having 'been universally recognised as one of the greatest – intellectually and in military knowledge probably the greatest – soldiers of his generation'.[16] However, Churchill had been a soldier, studied military history and was often convinced he knew better, and whereas Pug and Churchill moved socially together, 'Churchill loved the limelight, but Brooke avoided it at all costs. Most people [especially Pug] would have enjoyed meals at Chequers and felt honoured to be invited, but Brooke detested these evenings and especially the late hours'.[17] Brooke liked Pug and Churchill, though Brooke was a very different person from Churchill and Pug, but despite Churchill's cantankerous moments, Brooke and Pug remained firm friends.

There were times when:

Brooke simply boiled over in his diary, wishing the prime minister would die before he tarnished his reputation, other times believing he had an *unbalanced mind*, but as Pug noted in his memoirs, Brooke wrote his diary last thing at night when he was simply exhausted. Churchill and Brooke were both blunt and angry with one another on many occasions, Brooke wondering at one time whether he would be dismissed, but Churchill had deliberately chosen a strong man who could challenge him.[18]

On occasion, and typically, Brooke would arrive back in the offices fuming with rage and snapping at Pug with fury over Churchill, then after being with Pug for a while 'a tired but infectious smile would touch his austere features and he would quietly say, "but what would we do without him?"'[19] The more affable Pug was often shaken by Brooke's outbursts, but he was the one man who could calm the angry CIGS. Matters became so serious on one occasion that Churchill told Pug that Brooke hated him and he would have to go, so Pug acting as the intermediary of peace saw Brooke and explained Churchill's views, and when Brooke told Pug he was angry but loved Churchill, Pug explained this to the fraught Prime Minister whose 'eyes filled with tears, and he gently murmured: *Dear Brooke!*'[20] Brooke knew that Pug at many times saved the day not only for him, but for their war administration in times of crisis because of his friendly nature, his ability to stay neutral and he was therefore an outstanding intermediary.

Perhaps the most revealing insight into the friendly but fraught relationship was best expressed in a personal letter written in green ink by Brooke to Pug as he left his post in 1946. He addressed him as 'My dear Pug' and wrote some incisive comments:

> What we should have done without your help and all your invaluable advice I hardly like to think of! I always marvel how you survived peevish remarks from the COS at our end and abuse from Winston at the other…personally I shall always feel deeply indebted to you for all your wonderful friendly help and assistance…With <u>deep</u> gratitude, Yours ever, Brookie.[21]

General Sir John Kennedy

John Kennedy was another bureaucratic officer like Pug, but his role was serving the CIGS of the day, which during the early part of the war was Dill and then Brooke for the rest of the time. As such he carried the grand title of Assistant Chief of Imperial General Staff, he was also responsible for plans and operations but answered to Brooke. In his memoirs he frequently refers to Pug, but on one occasion while writing his account of 1942 he paused and pondered his colleague, dwelling on him after they had dined together at the Carlton Grill. He wrote that:

> We were indeed fortunate to have Ismay to take so much of the initial shock of the Prime Minister's impact on the Staffs. He never claimed that he influenced Churchill to any extent, and probably did not. No man with the inclination and capacity to deal seriously with Churchill could have retained Ismay's post for very long. He was always charmingly frank in admitting that his chief function was to act as whipping boy, and as a person to whom Churchill could blow off steam at all hours of night and day, we all felt we would not have had his job for anything in the world.[22]

There is no question that at times Churchill could be volatile if not explosive if challenged, and as the messenger Pug often took the full force of the Churchillian blast as if the messenger was the message. As noted in the main text Pug even offered his resignation at one point, but most of the time he suffered his master's fury in a way most of his colleagues admired and they were happy not to have his role. Kennedy was probably correct that Pug did not influence Churchill in any major decision making, but there is no doubt that Churchill tested his ideas with him, pondered situations and people in his company, and looked to Pug's friendship and stability to help keep him steady. As Kennedy noted, Pug 'was, in his own right, one of the most remarkable men of the war', which may have been something of an overstatement, but in Churchill's invaluable sphere of influence Pug was an essential cog in that war administration.[23] The world in which Pug existed was often dark, rumoured filled with potential stabbings in the back, but there seems little doubt that everyone seemed to trust and like Pug, making him unique in such a context.

Not everyone understood 'the setting' in which he worked. Not every American general saw Pug in the same light, and the known Anglophobe General Wedemeyer described 'poor old Ismay' as 'merely a smoothie, insincere, a Mr Fix-it, a man without real convictions and incapable of reaching sound conclusions', though he had misunderstood Pug's role and later he held a more positive view of him.[24] As with the Anglophobic Mark Clark, Pug was one of the few to eventually form a warm relationship with such commanders, and in one archival letter Pug wrote to Wedemeyer to thank his wife for sending Darry peaches.[25] However, Kennedy was another desktop general who spent as much time in the same work space as Pug, and his views of Pug keeping the peace, smoothing the waters and calming contentions at critical points was perceptive, and he understood the nature of his post more than many American observers.

General Mark Clark

Turning to his American contemporaries, General Mark Clark during the early stages of the war was Eisenhower's support officer, especially during Operation Bolero and in preparation for Torch. He had travelled by submarine for a clandestine meeting with the pro-Allied French in North Africa, had set out plans for occupying Sardinia (which were later abandoned), had not been part of the invasion of Sicily, but had led the Fifth Army at Salerno and at Anzio and by disobeying orders managed to occupy Rome. Historically he has had a mixed reception, but he was well-known and whom Churchill called the 'American Eagle', but he was better known for his almost paranoid Anglophobia. Given the way some British officers arrogantly treated the Americans as newcomers to war may have aggravated his views, but it was widely known that he did not appreciate the British officer class and this resentment ran deep. It was therefore something of a surprise that when he dined with Pug, whom he described as Churchill's military adviser, he noted as they discussed Operation Torch, about which Clark and many Americans remained unsure, that even Pug was 'apprehensive'.

He was aware of Ismay's nickname Pug and wrote in his memoirs that he lived up to his name, 'he was enthusiastic, co-operative, helpful and always trying to ease our difficulties or smooth out the problems that grew out of the conflicting British and American methods of procedure'.²⁶ As is widely known and referred to in the main text, the British and Americans often held seriously divergent views on overall strategy, and Clark was utterly convinced the British were always wrong. Despite these almost paranoid feelings towards the British officer class, Clark warmed to Churchill's Chief of Staff, which never happened with other British officers, including his senior officer in the Italian campaign, Field Marshal Alexander. When Clark attended a weekend at Chequers in the company of Brooke, Eden, Mountbatten and Pug, Clark noted the whole event was taken up with British-American co-operation over Torch which Churchill enthused, Eden expressed optimism whereas as Clark wrote, 'I fidgeted and boiled inside, and I imagine Ike did too.'²⁷ Unlike Clark, Eisenhower wanted the coalition to run smoothy, and had Pug been the only company Clark would probably have felt more comfortable as Pug was polite, pleasant and not thrusting with the American allies.

Clark, like so many others was able to speak easily with Pug and call him by his nickname. Clark recorded in his memoirs when he had to make an urgent phone call to Churchill. He spoke to Pug, calling him Pug, telling him 'We've got a hot message here,' with Pug asking, 'how hot?' When he told Pug it was too hot for the telephone Churchill answered telling Clark that this phone was secret and so Eisenhower was able to speak directly.²⁸ In his memoirs Clark was less abrasive regarding senior British officers but did not conceal his feelings in his daily war diaries.²⁹ Pug was one of the few British officers whom Clark found palatable. From the earliest days (July 1943) Pug wrote letters of reassurance to Clark that he had the full support of himself and Churchill, another congratulating him on Salerno, and later more congratulations on Clark's achievements with his Fifth Army and his attending some of the various international conferences.³⁰ Pug was the one English officer whom Clark seemed able to befriend which contrasted with his often-cynical remarks about the gentlemanly Field Marshal Alexander. Their correspondence continued after the war and in November 1951 Clark wrote to Pug relating to the recent Conservative victory in the 1951 general election, congratulating him on being appointed Secretary of State for Commonwealth Relations.³¹

Eisenhower

In his memoirs in the aftermath of victory Eisenhower looked back and described Pug as:

One of the most prominent military figures in Great Britain... Ismay's position as head of the secretarial staff to the War Cabinet and the British Chiefs of Staff was, from the American point of view, a critical one because it was through him that any subject could at any moment be brought to the attention of the prime minister and his principal assistants. It was fortunate, therefore, that he was devoted to the principle of Allied unity and that his personality was such as to win the confidence and friendship of his American associates. He was one of those men whose great ability condemned him throughout the war to a staff position. Consequently, his name may be forgotten; but the contributions he made to the winning of the war were equal to those of many whose names became household names.[32]

Eisenhower never changed his mind and in 1963 wrote a personal letter to Pug stating:

I've so long believed that you were not only the greatest of modern British soldiers and at the same time the least recognised that I wanted to put my sentiments in the written record. The difficulty was that you were so valuable to Winston in the tense years of war that he would not let you go to one of the big command positions you so well deserved, and I don't blame him.[33]

There is no doubt that the Americans found men like Brooke difficult to handle, seeing him as austere, somewhat aloof, though their views moderated in time, and many of them disliked Montgomery for his sheer assertiveness. On the other hand, Pug's personality played a major part in American friendship simply because he was much more personable and amenable in conversations and at meetings. The second fact which was pinpointed by Eisenhower was that unlike some of his fellow British officers who could be somewhat condescending to the newcomers, Pug realised that American support and resources were essential, and like Eisenhower was desperate to make sure the coalition worked. Keeping the Anglo-American alliance was important to both Eisenhower and Pug, and one of Eisenhower's biographers recalled a time when it came to Eisenhower's attention that an American officer had boasted at Claridge's 'that the Americans would show the British how to fight', which sent Eisenhower 'white with rage'. He had the sort of relationship with Pug which allowed him to tell the British general that 'I'll make the son of a bitch swim back to America'; the officer was returned, but by boat.[34] Normally inhouse problems would not be shared with the partners but it was obvious that Eisenhower trusted Pug who never mentioned this conversation himself.

It took someone like Eisenhower to recognise that this inner-office bureaucrat was an important military person who played a vital part, but because he was hidden behind his desk and paperwork, he would never receive the public recognition afforded to field command officers. This was all too true of many behind the scenes, and men like Pug and Brooke and many others were virtually unknown by the public whereas Montgomery despite his military and diplomatic blunders, remains a household name to this day.

Such was the friendship between Eisenhower and Pug it lasted until Pug's death. In the archives Pug and Eisenhower's correspondence – be it telegrams, letters, memos – is simply endless, and ranges from the deeply personal to the official, as well as offering one another mutual support. Some are entirely official, but even these are phrased as between two colleagues, and many sound so personal it is as if they belonged to the same family. Even in December 1944 when the Battle of the Bulge was causing concern, Eisenhower wrote a letter to Pug claiming he enjoyed his note, and 'I fear that the other evening I got a bit loquacious in talking about my post-war plans…in any event, I would be completely helpless without the aid of you and others like you who believe the same way.'[35]

Pug was the drafter of letters when seeking to ease the coalition tensions. In May 1945 it was Pug who drafted a letter from the Chief of the Imperial General Staff 'offering trust and mutual affection', and although Eisenhower would have known it was an official communiqué the knowledge that it came from the trusted Pug would have been gratifying.[36] After the war (1946) it was Eisenhower and no one else who wrote to Pug with his hopes for the 'continuation of the mutual understanding between the USA and UK', which had been given so much personal assistance by Pug.[37] Eisenhower and Pug, unlike many of their national colleagues, had stood side-by-side to ease the coalition tensions and after the war both hoped for continued mutual support between the two countries.

Some of the correspondence clearly outlined the fact that they supported one another in a variety of ways. When Eisenhower's book *Crusade in Europe* was published it was criticised in an article in *The Sunday Times* of 21 November 1948, by the Military Correspondent. It was a nationalistic article, even stating that 'had Montgomery's plan been adopted it would have shortened the war' and given a better balance to postwar Europe, and it spent too much time on the rumoured scandal of Eisenhower's female driver Kathleen Summersby.[38]

Pug's file contained press cuttings of the various reviews and he immediately wrote to Eisenhower expressing his disapproval of such criticisms.[39] Five days later Pug immediately expressed his views in his own article in *The Daily Telegraph* and found support from Andrew Cunningham.[40] His article was forthright in its support for Eisenhower's effort, stating that Eisenhower's book was written 'with the simplicity, the sincerity and the modesty which are characteristic of the author. It has a particular lesson for us all at the present time, since it shows how strong, proud and independent peoples can be harmoniously united in the fight for freedom with irresistible effect'.[41] It was little wonder that Eisenhower treasured Pug's support.

Many followed the debate with interest and Pug's views were taken seriously and won the support of Alan Lascelles.[42] On 2 December, a few days later, the King's Secretary wrote a letter to Pug asking if Eisenhower would send the King a copy, and adding the lines that 'at the same time, you could say that there is nobody in this house who did not think *The Sunday Times* article damnable'.[43]

Eisenhower had been disappointed at some of the negative responses to his effort, but promptly wrote to Pug thanking him for his 'public defence' of his literary historical effort.[44] Even Brooke who had been highly critical of Eisenhower in his own diaries, wrote and thanked Pug for helping him draft his own letter of support to *The Daily Telegraph*; there was no doubt that Pug was recognised for his English communication skills, which also helped him with Churchill who was highly critical over the precise use of the English language.[45] There was a deep mutual trust between Eisenhower and Pug, and when Eisenhower asked for Churchill's reasons for wanting the Greek islands during the war, Pug admitted that

Churchill, whom he all but venerated, had a good knowledge of the broad strategy of war, but 'a weakness on practicalities'.[46] This admission by Pug of his adored chief underlined the way Pug trusted his American friend. When Eisenhower decided that his military assistant during the war, Brigadier James Gault, should have had an award he knew he could bring Pug to assist, who using his friendship with Churchill and his private secretary Jock Colville meant it became a rapid reality.[47]

Other letters emphasise the friendly relationship between two ex-comrades in arms who had become close friends. As early as 20 May 1945 Eisenhower wrote to Pug about events in Europe but concluded on the note of their special friendship.[48] This correspondence continued up to Pug's death and each year Eisenhower always remembered to send Pug birthday greetings.[49] Such was their genuine friendship that in 1951 Eisenhower wrote to Pug offering the use of his Scottish estate for a holiday.[50] They followed one another's career moves with care, sending congratulations on going to new postings, and regrets at leaving old ones, perhaps the most significant being Pug's letter to Eisenhower on becoming the US President Elect.[51]

When the BBC did a recording on Eisenhower, Pug was one of the contributors and paid tribute to his character and his role in the Allied victory during the war, as well as the way he had improved Anglo-American relationships.[52] Despite the fracture caused by Eden creating the Suez crisis, when Pug was ill during his closing years Eisenhower would write to him, asking questions about the political situation in the UK and developments of NATO in defending Europe against the USSR.[53] It remained a deeply personal friendship, and on 8 January 1957, Eisenhower had read a letter Pug had written to his wife about his retirement, writing to Pug: 'Dear Pug, I read, with envy in my heart, your letter to Mamie. As you know we have never had a home of our own. Now that we have built one near the little town of Gettysburg'…and went on to explain he hoped to 'raise pure bred Aberdeen Angus cattle'.[54] It was clear that despite the Suez crisis rift, Eisenhower had no intention of losing his friendship with Pug. The correspondence was continuous and a year later (25 January 1958), Pug received a letter from the White House regarding Pug's explanation of Brooke's recently published diary and accepted Pug's explanation that 'as you suggest, mental and physical fatigue [on Brooke's part] so I simply ignore the book and on to something else'.[55]

One of Eisenhower's main critics in the British camp had been Brooke, but he admitted that when he heard Eisenhower speak at the end of the war, he had underrated him and admitted he was a man of outstanding ability. Pug was a very different person, avoided direct criticism, keeping it privy to himself, and offered prompt and immediate friendship. This personality, recognised by many, formed the basis of a lifelong friendship with the overall commanders of Allied troops in Europe and one who would one day be the American President.

Harold Macmillan

A future prime minister who was involved with Churchill during the war years was Harold Macmillan who wrote many extensive books on his personal experiences. He met most of the important people of the day at a national and international level, his experiences were more diplomatic, reaching agreements, advising, though not military, but naturally he was acquainted with the military leaders and most of the field commanders. In his war diaries which are nearly 700 pages long, he refers to Pug only eight times, half of which are only mentioning that he was present at this or that gathering. He did not rate Pug's position as important, referring to him in one meeting of senior commanders as a 'junior' along with 'Wrens, Waafs, typists, telegraph officers'.[56] Later in his diaries he lists as was his habit all the people at a meeting he was attending, adding 'in addition, all the well-known figures in the minor ranks – Pug Ismay, Admiral Leahy (President's aide), etc., etc'.[57] Another time he had added that Pug and his assistant were in attendance, but later he did suggest to General (Jumbo) Wilson that it would be a good idea to organise a proper secretariat copying Pug Ismay's administration.[58]

There is no indication that these were 'cutting remarks', and Pug would probably have agreed, and as this is not a hagiography Macmillan's viewpoint must be explored. For Macmillan and many others Pug was a mere administrator and in many senses this was true. He did not organise or initiate any major operations or strategic policies, he merely presented them to Churchill, or back to the COS, and sometimes gave talks on the decisions to other allied bodies to explain British thinking. It was because of his personal ability and charm that these difficult decisions could often be agreed and with the pugnacious Churchill and stalwart members of COS, Pug often helped avoid the possible deadlocks. When Colville wrote after the war about Lindemann he penned, 'he became the great interpreter, a man who did more to ease the load and illumine the dark corners than anybody other than General Ismay'.[59] Despite his important roles during the war, Macmillan was not part of the central war machinery operating out of No. 10 Downing Street, and apart from possible rumours he did not know how Pug acted as the so-called 'oil-can' which lubricated the major cogs of Britain's war administration, which without his help may have ground to a halt. Macmillan was a politician and Pug was for him a junior military man, very much like another future prime minster, who in a major volume of memoirs never mentions Pug.[60]

During the Great War there had been serious contentions between politicians and military, the former known as 'frocks' and the latter called the 'brass hats'. Much of this had been eliminated by Churchill, who because of his war experience, unlike Lloyd George, had managed to meld the two into a workable arrangement. However, despite his early war experience and later study of military matters Churchill was a politician and was frequently at odds with his Chiefs of Staff, which as noted above could have led to disasters and had 'it not been for the tact, patience and skill in promoting compromise shown by one man…that man was General Sir Hastings Ismay, to whom Churchill owed more, and admitted that he owed more than to anybody else, military or civilian, in the whole of the war'.[61] It took the men at the very top of the political tree such as Churchill, Attlee, and Roosevelt to understand the nature and value of Pug's work, which for many politicians was hidden by the military veil, but it was worthy of note that as late as 1963 when Macmillan was Prime Minister he sought Pug's advice on defence policies.

Lord Moran

Lord Moran has written much about his time with Churchill, as he was Churchill's main doctor and a keen observer of events and people. He was one of the few who had a less impressive image of Pug, commenting on him at times in an almost derisory fashion implying that he lacked substance. Although Moran was often in the presence of Churchill and others, he was not central to the great strategic debates, and his social comments on Pug tended to arise from the gatherings he attended and hanging around in corridors. He described in one of his books a time he met Pug on one of these occasions when as 'he stopped to speak to me I felt his eye roaming around the hall, seeking some profitable anchorage'.[62] This is an irritating experience felt by many, but while not trying to present a hagiography of Pug, it may well have been, given Pug's propensity for work, he was looking for someone he needed to speak with on more professional matters. Moran continued in the same vein claiming one could not call Pug a serious soldier, but 'a gifted if rather inexperienced politician perhaps, but a born courtier without any doubt', then somewhat acidly explained his nickname as looking like the pugdog, 'and this smile works pretty hard when the P.M. is in his lighter mode; sometimes his amusement seems a little out of proportion to his wit'.[63]

Moran does not mention Colville by name, but it is clear from his own diaries that Colville heard Moran's views on this occasion. However, despite his caustic views Moran described to his readers that Pug was a 'kind of filter between the Prime Minister and his Chiefs of Staff, only letting through what is helpful and unprovocative', which although meant in a cynical fashion underlined the importance of his work and undoubtedly avoided many potentially bitter rows during these difficult days, but Moran expanded further by stating that Churchill never took Pug seriously, unlike when he listened to Brooke, whereas Pug 'has to depend on seizing the right moment and on the way he says his own piece'.[64] Almost grudgingly he concludes this social attack on Pug by admitting he has a remarkable knowledge of human nature, and his influence is increasing, as the drip of water in time makes its mark on stone'.[65]

When attending Churchill during his time of illness in Marrakesh, Moran described how Churchill was intent on planning the landing at Anzio in Italy when the COS were not available, but he had 'plenty of lesser fry to work out the details…Hollis [General Sir Leslie Hollis, Pug's assistant] and there is Pug'.[66] Later, on 13 February 1945, he recalled Pug grumbling about Churchill being late to address a ship's crew, saying that 'it's very naughty of the P.M., it's unbridled power. The heating throughout the ship has all been cut off because his room seemed too warm for a moment'.[67] Had Moran said this to Pug, it was unlikely he would have repeated it in his memoirs, an annoyance to historians as Pug's gentlemanly approach probably conceals many of his opinions of others.

However, Moran's reference did indicate that although Pug admired Churchill, he was still capable of standing back and seeing his foibles and shortcomings. There is a distinct impression that Moran was one of the very few who, although realising that the COS were more significant, saw little of value in Pug's contribution and dwelt on his character which Moran did not appreciate as much as others.

Moran never changed his views on Pug and on 23 August while in Quebec he described Pug as a 'perfect oil-can' serving as a filter between Churchill and the COS, and only letting through, as far as he can what is helpful and unprovocative. In the short passage between the two parties, he is said to forget everything that could only ruffle and anger his masters.[68] He did, however, add that it was a 'useful role beyond question' and Pug was 'the necessary man'.

Sir John Colville

Colville, commonly known as Jock, was a senior civil servant who worked closely with Churchill and, although technically illegal, kept a diary of his time at 10 Downing Street. He was not only aware of Churchill's thinking and attitudes, but equally aware of the various people who surrounded Churchill allowing him to offer observations and insights which were often revealing.

At the end of his diary, he made notes on the various personalities he met, writing of Pug that 'nobody did more to oil the wheels on the sometimes bumpy road between the service chiefs and the politicians… his ability and dedication to hard work was matched by his personal charm'.[69] He noted that Pug was always diplomatic in his memoirs, probably not wanting to meet the criticisms levelled against Brooke, but he held forthright opinions on some subjects, especially the French military and their politicians in 1940. All this only came to light in Pug's evidently frank conversations with Colville, which have from the historian and biographer's point of view provided many insights into Pug's thinking. He also provides many personal perceptions into Pug's personality, Coleville describing in September 1940 how he had gone to the Central War Office to have a whisky with three friends, one of whom was Pug who 'was giving his usual description of the French collapse and the helplessness of the statesmen and generals', obviously an event which had a major impact on Pug.[70]

Like many others Pug had many personal and political views which he avoids in his memoirs, one time discussing the Munich meeting, with Pug pointing out that it was not the government finding waiting time to prepare for war, as was the point being made, but 'to avert war, not to postpone it, was the sole object'.[71] Although, as mentioned in the text, Pug was averse to making judgments on commanders to Churchill, on the grounds of not alienating the COS as a biased bridge, he nevertheless held opinions about others, Colville recording talking to Pug 'about the megalomania of Sir Roger Keyes who had had the effrontery to suggest that the P.M. should appoint him his deputy to preside over the Chiefs of Staff'.[72]

Colville observed Pug not only from the official meeting level, but at the social occasions, dining at Downing Street and more often at Chequers, noting his love of Churchill, even quoting from his published histories as they strolled together, noting that 'his admiration for the P.M., as a man who has himself experienced the warfare which he now directs, knows no bounds'.[73] Colville's diary records that Pug was a very social person who enjoyed company and his presence was welcomed. At the end of 1940 when the New Year was being celebrated, he described how in the war rooms 'General Ismay plied Tommy Thompson and me with brandy and regaled us with stories of the field of battle, and then proceeded upstairs to drink to the New Year in champagne.'[74] The year 1940 had been a dismal one for Britain, but Pug never lost his *joie de vivre* despite being down at heel on hearing the news about the collapse of France. It was his pleasant personality and sociability which made him friends, and when Colville heard Lord Moran criticise Eden and Pug he wrote 'I cannot quite make up my mind whether he is right about Eden, He is certainly wrong about Pug.'[75] Colville was astute enough to identify that it was Pug's pleasant personality which made him not only popular but trustworthy and reliable.

Sir Alan Lascelles

Lascelles was King George VI's private secretary throughout the war years and spent much social time in the company of Pug as well as many professional moments. Like others he realised that Pug was an essential component in his work for Churchill, noting that Churchill would often not exchange any words with members of his entourage for many days, 'communicating with them, including Mrs Churchill, by chits; rather like Queen Victoria and Sir Henry Ponsonby', and in a footnote underlining that Pug was the main channel of communication 'between the P.M. and the Chiefs of Staff'. The senior military staff were constantly aware of Pug's role, so were some politicians and the royal household, and it was apparent that Pug was deeply trusted even by the sensitive organisation surrounding the monarch.

Pug shared many of his thoughts with Lascelles, his opinions and insights which rarely occur in his own memoirs. In 1943 he explained, for example, why Churchill suddenly became almost obsessed with the Japanese campaign despite opposition from the COS, revealing that the 'P.M. had become convinced that Germany couldn't last out the winter, and he wanted to be in a position to exert maximum pressure on the Japs in the early spring'.[76] Pug had described Churchill as a 'Western Front' man intimating that this was unusual, but carefully not stating, as Pug well knew, that Churchill was concerned about British global influence and the empire. He also shared with Lascelles his opinion that Britain should have gone to war in 1938 because the Germans were not so well prepared, but with Lascelles, probably rightly, pointing out that had this happened the support of many of the Dominions may not have happened at that point in time as they needed the next few years to realise the danger of the Nazi threat.

Lascelles recognised that Pug was a hard worker and had much to shoulder with his responsibilities, and in January 1944 he was pleased Pug came to dinner 'which was good of him, as he is up to his eyes in work, under a trilateral bombardment from Winston in Morocco, the Chiefs of Staff in Whitehall, and the American ditto in Washington'.[77] Lascelles had not seen him since his trip to Moscow with Eden and the strenuous Sextant Conference 'with Winston which nearly killed him'.

Despite all this gruelling hard work Lascelles observed that Pug had recovered and was amusing and excellent company, Lascelles thereby underlining that Pug was good socially and known for his sense of humour. This sociability and sense of fun was undoubtedly one of the features which ensured he worked for Churchill for the duration of the war and well beyond, as at times Churchill when relaxed had the same disposition. Churchill used to enjoy relating one of Pug's apocryphal and humorous stories of a Royal Marine being shown around Moscow by a guide, who pointed out that 'this is the Eden Hotel, formerly Ribbentrop Hotel. Here is Churchill Street, formerly Hitler Street. Here is Beaverbrook railway station, formerly Göring railway station. Will you have a cigarette, comrade? The marine replied thank you, comrade, formerly bastard.'[78]

Pug was an invaluable link with the palace, not least when Churchill decided that he wanted to cross with the Overlord troops to Normandy. Lascelles wrote that 'Winston knows perfectly well that he oughtn't to do this, but when he gets these puckish notions, he is just like a naughty child.'[79] Pug had been watching this development from the side-lines, and went to the palace to see Lascelles and pointed out the professional point of view that it was 'wrong for the Prime Minister and Minister of Defence to be inaccessible (if not dead) on a day when vital decisions might have to be taken in a hurry'.[80] As noted in the biographical text Churchill had cunningly tried to keep Pug onside by offering to take him for company, at first exciting Pug until he realised the ramifications. Every form of argument was used and rebutted by Churchill. When Lascelles argued no minister of the crown should leave the country without the king's permission, Churchill countered by saying he would be 'in one of His Majesty's ships' – but out of territorial waters, Lascelles persisted.[81] None of this worked, and it was proving almost impossible to dislodge Churchill but Pug, by conveying the seriousness of the project and its dangers to the royal household, helped in the end to save Churchill from his predisposition for personal recklessness as Churchill felt obliged to obey his king.

At times there is an impression that Pug was not only Churchill's personal carer in terms of his conduct, but also trying to manage him in maintaining the Anglo-American coalition, as when Lascelles went to see Pug on other business and 'found him busy trying to tone down a decidedly petulant telegram which the PM wishes to send to F.D.R. [Roosevelt]'.[82] There were many times and reasons that Churchill and Roosevelt did not agree. Despite the happy photographs and a seemingly genuine friendship there were moments when these two major democratic leaders clashed, with Roosevelt often suspicious of Churchill's empire plans, and Churchill thinking that Stalin was not correctly understood in his true lights by Roosevelt. It was a difficult and delicate task for Pug to calm down the irrepressible Churchill. Pug knew there were tensions with the Americans at command level with Eisenhower being criticised by Brooke, Montgomery, and others, but according to Lascelles, Pug was not overly worried about this on the grounds that:

> The Americans have won their spurs and the days are past when we could treat them as green and untried soldiers; in fact he went so far as to say we might have something to learn from them and that we may have been a bit too 'staff collegey' in our conduct of the war.[83]

It was evident from this conversation recorded by Lascelles that Pug had a balanced view of the overall dilemmas in the Anglo-American alliance.

According to Lascelles he heard from Pug that he thought the Potsdam conference had gone well, that 'he is convinced that they are feverishly anxious to keep well in with us…and they know nothing at all about the atomic bomb'. Pug was wrong on both accounts as he later came to realise, and his Achilles's heel tended to be the occasional sweeping statements he made when mixing socially, but in his memoirs he often admitted he made errors of judgment. Lascelles as a friend of Pug gave many insights into Pug's thinking at the time of events. Sadly Lascelles lost his son Tommy in 1951, but not before Tommy had served as Pug's personal assistant when the latter was seconded to Mountbatten in India for the independence and partition.

Chapter Seven

Final Words on Pug Ismay

In writing any form of account of a person's life it is easier to admire more than denigrate the subject, and many of the earlier biographies of important national figures can be hagiographical. This writer wrote the biography of Field Marshal Kesselring and nearly fell into this trap, until after further research in the various archives new material started to change the picture, which demanded not one but two rewrites to produce a balanced and truthful portrait of the subject, and it necessitated the removal of the projected halo from Kesselring's head. The same problem emerged in exploring Pug, not helped by his clinically clean memoirs; only one of his contemporaries expressed a mild criticism, whereas the rest were either full of praise or mainly affection.

Research amongst the Ismay Papers held at King's College London did not produce a murky side as other archives had revealed about Kesselring. For those observers who regarded Pug as 'Churchill's whipping-boy', his role was still regarded as highly significant, indeed essential. His only other biographer (1970), who as noted was a friend, concluded his study by writing that 'Ismay's place in the history of our country is assured as Churchill's faithful and wise counsellor in war. Without him Churchill might not have brought us to final victory.'[1] On first reading these lines it struck this writer as an exaggeration since Pug was a bureaucrat, a desktop general, at least on reading general histories. It is true that the war was won by the men and women who fought it under the guidance of famous field commanders, who in turn relied on the strategy conveyed from the top by the Chiefs of Staff. Being a democratic society, even in war, the COS needed political agreement and it is at this juncture that Pug emerges as a critical element not only in Britain but in the essential relationship between Britain and America.

The sometimes derisory term that Pug was 'an oil can' who smoothed the way is far from a cynical exaggeration. When, as mentioned in the biographical part of the text, on the way to Quebec for the Octagon

Conference when Churchill was not that well and a major heated debate had developed between him and the COS, there was talk of mass resignations, which Pug appeared by many accounts to have avoided by offering his own resignation as the sacrificial lamb. In terms of progress being made towards victory as well as the safety of British democracy it was simply unthinkable for a total breakdown between the senior military and the prime minister. As such, Wingate's final statement in his book of Pug saving the day may feel hagiographical, but it contains an element of undeniable truth.

Nevertheless, no man is perfect, a statement not just based on the Christian theology of original sin but on human experience, for even venerated saints had flaws in their life. Some of these emerge in this chapter, raising questions that Pug tended to look back with rose-coloured glasses, that as an emotional man he was prone to snap decisions, that perhaps he over-defended his hero Churchill, that he made some serious judgemental errors in supporting Mountbatten in India and when he was Secretary-General of NATO a touch of unadulterated nationalism emerged, blemishing his reputation as a neutral man and a mere patriot. To balance this picture it is necessary to mention his strengths, his abilities, and notably that despite his background as he descended from the back of a camel to stand next to the thrones of human power, his sense of discretion, his optimism, loyalty, honesty, duty and even humility. Most of his strengths emanate from his personality, which created a genuine sense of affection for him, which not every saint can claim; he was from this perspective unusual.

Background Influence

Churchill and Brooke and many others came from various levels of an aristocratic background or held estates and land. Pug had none of these advantages as his father had gone to India to restart his life and finances because of failed gambling. His family was deep in India, money was not so easy to find and the family had no influence in Britain, but his education at Charterhouse and determination won him a place at Sandhurst. India attracted him because of financial problems and it was easier to survive on that sub-continent on a soldier's pay. He had no money or politics to back him, just his love of the British Army. It was probably here as a young soldier that he was imbued with those elements which characterised the rest of his life. He had a strong feeling of camaraderie with those with whom he worked, accepted the traditional army call for loyalty, and always needed that sense of working as a team. The subject of nationalism will rise again in this chapter, but he was a patriotic person rather than a nationalist. He tended to put his country first, believed in Britain but not at the expense of other countries which is often a characteristic of a nationalist. Occasionally the nationalistic streak might emerge, but from the overall image of his life he emerges as the traditional patriot.

His youthful experience on the northwest frontier and in the Somaliland Camel Corps gave him some experience of fighting, but these were minor commands, and he never held any major posts in the field of combat. Many of his Sandhurst colleagues took part in the Great War, many never returned, and it always concerned him that he had not taken part. His post in the War Office was insignificant and he had hoped for a command in India for which he had already purchased a new uniform but he was propelled, probably by a political move by others, which returned him to India in virtually a ceremonial role with the new Viceroy Willingdon. There was evidently an ability in Pug which had been identified by others, not least Hankey who regarded him as a potential talent, and by the late 1930s his stature in the eyes of others was developing in the corridors of administrative power. There is no evidence of their views, but it is easy to speculate that he was intelligent, hardworking, could express himself well on paper, and they may well have looked for those critical elements of trustworthiness, loyalty, and discretion. He was already noted as a likeable person.

Discretion

Anyone working in Whitehall and especially in the military sectors had to be totally trusted, and not known to gossip or brag about the nature of their work, or publicly express opinions on others, whether they were civil servants, politicians, or military. Auchinleck who knew him well said he was totally trustworthy, humorous, never boring, and informed, stating 'What you told him went no further.' It was this last statement, which was important to those who worked with Pug, namely that he may have enjoyed a social chat, but he was not prepared to pass on gossip about others or important information. Even his memoirs can be described as clinically clean, he rarely condemned or even criticised anyone and never raised sensitive subjects. It is known that he held strong opinions on some events and people only because others reported their conversations with him, but such information rarely came from Pug himself. His private letters to Darry reveal some of his inner thinking, and Colville heard from him that he found little encouragement from the French politicians or their army in 1940, and later that Pug and Colville had not appreciated Roger Keyes.

Pug shared with Lascelles and Colville that in his opinion Britain should have declared war earlier, but little of any substance regarding Pug's private views on people and critical events can be found in anything he put on paper (with a few exceptions to Darry), which was why he was so upset when Brooke 'spilt the beans' by allowing Bryant to publish his diaries. In his earlier life, in Somaliland and his start in the Intelligence corridors of Whitehall may have underlined his sense of discretion, and it may be speculated that from his early youth he had always enjoyed company and fun, but it was in his nature to be discreet. It also accounts for why so many people in later life approached him about publishing their literary efforts, even his old boss Hankey wanted his advice on his own memoirs.

Rose-coloured glasses

Discretion for Pug was important, but he had the tendency to look back with rose-coloured glasses, seeking the best or kindest explanations of past events. In his memoirs he noted that England had not rearmed as fast as others, calling England's previous stance a form of 'unilateral disarmament', which had been well-intentioned in trying to lead the world towards a general disarmament. He did not point to other possible reasons, the economic after-effects of the Great War which witnessed the decline of the army in particular, a preoccupation with communism and not the rise of fascism, the victor's psychology that all was done and dusted, and it could not happen again with the popular feeling that such a war could not be repeated. Instead, his beloved England was showing the world the way forward in a moral way which was all too true of Pug's view of life. He accepted he often made mistakes in his analysis of situations, revealing his known propensity of accepting he could make errors of judgement showing a degree of natural humility.

On looking back Pug admitted that Chamberlain's statement that *Hitler had missed the bus* seemed right, he had agreed, and like many others he had hoped the impending storm would blow over. In his memoirs he admitted he had been mistaken to be so optimistic. When on one of Churchill's many visits to France Pug met Weygand and believed he was just the right man to turn the Germans back, but his colleague General Kennedy described Weygand as a 'romantic and remarkable figure… but he looked old, and yellow and unhappy', which by other accounts was more accurate, illustrating Pug's over optimism and belief in other people.[2] When in his traditional almost addictive support of Churchill in later years, he pointed out that sending British troops to help the Greeks against Mussolini, which was uniformly criticised at the time and since, Pug suggested it took the Nazi eyes off Russia for a time. A more cynical historian would note that the sooner the Germans attacked the Russians the more beneficial for Britain, because as alien as the Soviet system may have been, they were essential as the major collaborator in the war against Nazi Germany. Pug was both military and political, but above all he was a constant admirer of Churchill and wrote that a 'military failure may be excused, but failure to keep a promise to help a friend in trouble is not easily forgiven or forgotten', thereby supporting many of Churchill's actions.[3]

Over-justification of Churchill

This last point naturally leads on to the reasonable observation that Pug admired Churchill so much he became and remained his main apologist, the guardian of Churchill's legacy. When some, including members of COS, accused Churchill of 'pestering' or 'bombarding' commanders in the field with various demands, Pug accused such critics as failing 'to understand Churchill's motives'. He argued that apart from other reasons, Churchill 'wanted them to feel that they were always in his thoughts, that he was sharing their problems and their difficulties, their hopes and their fears, their failures as well as their successes'.[4] This was evidently far from the case because it was generally understood, rightly or wrongly that Churchill was always hammering away at commanders and demanding results.

Pug always looked for the best side of Churchill whatever the circumstances. He observed that when Stalin was obnoxious over his various demands, he noted that Churchill always turned the other cheek which Pug described as the 'Christian spirit'. Only Pug could make such an observation, as everyone then and now knew Churchill never trusted Stalin, and he knew the best way forward with the allied tyrant was to let him grumble and ignore him. Much of the defence of Churchill probably stemmed from the war days when he had to act as the bridge between the Service Chiefs and Churchill. It is known from Brooke's diaries that the professional military leaders often found Churchill's ideas too risky, and the ensuing heated arguments, often accompanied with the threats of resignation, had to be calmed by Pug, making his defence of Churchill part of his lifestyle. Pug often acknowledged he was the 'whipping boy' and Churchill would be angry with him in bringing the COS ideas or changes to his plans to his desk. The defence of Churchill's character and motives appear as his raison d'être, but he was privately to admit to Eisenhower in later days that Churchill had a good knowledge of the broad strategy of war, but 'a weakness on practicalities'.[5] There would have been times when Pug would know that the COS were correct and Churchill was on the verge of a blunder, but not once did he even infer such a thought in his written work. He later acknowledged to Brooke that Churchill was not the easiest of taskmasters, but Pug's main defence was based on Churchill's determination that Britain should survive the Nazi onslaught and Hitler should be totally defeated, and few would disagree with this viewpoint.

Snap Decisions

His friend and first biographer Ronald Wingate wrote that Pug was a deeply emotional man, and as such was prone to make snap decisions, which may be true of people who are emotional, and since he knew Pug, he must have been correct in this assumption. The one time that Pug appeared to make a snap decision with serious ramifications was his support and agreement with Mountbatten over the question of the partitioning of India and Pakistan. In his memoirs and by his careful evaluation of the situation as he perceived it, and his professional report on the matter, Pug tried to convince the reader that the situation was an impossible task leading in his words to offering a Hobson's choice. His outline of the possibility of a major revolt in the sub-continent or a deeply religious civil war appears clear enough, though there is a sense that his usual natural optimism was this time misplaced.

Over the decades since the 1947 independence on the sub-continent the role played by Mountbatten and his team has come under intense scrutiny, and it is generally highly critical in terms of the haste, the decisions, and Mountbatten himself is attacked for his style and mismanagement in many such studies. Pug continued to stand by Mountbatten in the following years as an act of friendship on the one hand, and on the other he had supported him, even when, as he wrote to Darry, he questioned Mountbatten's efficiency in not reading the various reports well. Their efforts in India and Pakistan produced horrific massacres and a lasting hostility which bothered Pug for the rest of his life. He managed to establish his sense of neutrality between Muslim and Hindu which both sides of the rift recognised, the same sense of neutrality he maintained in home politics, seeing Attlee as a friend, and sitting on the cross benches in the House of Lords. At the personal level he did his best and in his compound in India he kept many Muslims in safety.

NATO

It was because of his natural friendly style and ability to mediate, as he had done in the last war, that Pug was seen by most as the suitable candidate for the role of Secretary General of NATO. He was known as a deeply patriotic Englishman but not regarded as a nationalist, and as such was able to visit all the NATO countries and be welcomed. Even the French who were not overly happy with Britain at this time welcomed him, both in his role and him as a person. He played his part, according to many sources well, and as he had proved to be the 'smoothing oil-can' in the cantankerous COS meetings in the last war, so in NATO he was the man behind the scenes in encouraging West Germany to be treated as an ally. The only hiccup for him in these years was when he felt Eisenhower had betrayed the British by condemning the Anglo-French attack on Egypt over the Suez crisis. Most observers believe Eden made a gross mistake in resorting to war and Eisenhower was right to object. Not even Pug had been warned about Suez, and perhaps it is possible at this stage to see his normal patriotism descend to that of a nationalist as he considered resignation, but Darry managed to persuade him otherwise, which said much about the nature of his supporting and wise wife.

His Personality

Pug had started life as a fighting soldier and finished as a desktop general who loved his country, and because of his amicable and mainly neutral approach he, more than most others, managed to resolve the age-old problem of the clash between brass hats and frocks (military and politicians). In a fascist country the leader is the military as well as the political power, and it was the same with Stalin's form of communism. The danger for any democracy is when these two elements of political and military fail to work together, and since 1945 there have been too many countries where there has been a military take-over leading to disaster, the latest being Myanmar (formerly Burma). Pug somehow managed to make this adjoining of political and military powers work despite the tensions. It was well known that he could write well, present able reports, and reduce major written articles into a more presentable form. He was more than capable of organising the necessary teams and committees to help a country at war, he was a hard worker, diligent, a man of duty and known for his loyalty while retaining a political neutrality.

It was his character/personality which attracted others to him. He was always humble telling other commanders he was having an easy war compared to them, which with Churchill he was not, as Brooke's description of some COS meetings demonstrates. Everyone recognised Pug's patience, and many Americans believed a grand strategy would have been impossible without him because he would help everyone agree. He even managed to make Anglophobes into friends, maintained life-lasting relationships by letters and inviting friends to his home. He was more than an oil-can, he often contributed in debate, and although he was never an executive making policy, he ensured the details and all decisions and plans were understood and presented clearly.

He had a kind personality, even when he felt betrayed by Eisenhower over Suez, he did not allow it to interfere with their close relationship.

This also arose with his clash over Brooke's diaries being published, he wrote and suggested to Brooke that he would have been better served not to have permitted direct quotes but adding 'you yourself were bearing an almost intolerable load of responsibility and working long hours. Consequently, many of the entries must have been made when you were "all-in", physically, and mentally, and some of them when you were in ill health, or full of justified ill humour as well'.[6] He had been angry at the publication and was honest enough to say so directly to the formidable Brooke, but he did so, and even gently suggested reasons why this may have happened. He was quintessentially a kind, pleasant person and this never appeared to change.

Pug enjoyed social gatherings, meeting new people and putting them at their ease, and even won over a few notable American Anglophobes such as Generals Wedemeyer and Clark. He enjoyed his drink, food, and was ready for banter, known for his jokes and sense of humour, his roar of laughter was easily recognised, and he had an easy smile, all of which endeared him to most people. He was fortunate with his wife Darry as he spent months away from her from the moment they married, yet she remained his total supporter as did his daughters. This background man, the behind-the-scenes desktop bureaucrat accomplished more than most people realised, and he managed it because he was a decent lovable person who offered affection and friendship, best summarised by Churchill's wife Clementine who often addressed him as 'my dear sweet Pug', a view shared by most, and unusual when it came to generals.[7]

Notes

Introduction
1. See Davies, Norman, *No Simple Victory* (New York: Viking, 2006), Liddell Hart, B. H., *History of the Second World War* (London: Book Club Associates, 1973), Hastings, Max, *All Hell Let Loose* (London: Harper Press, 2011), Shirer, William L., *The Rise and Fall of the Third Reich* (London: Mandarin, 1997), and Corrigan, Gordon, *The Second World War* (London: Atlantic Books, 2012).
2. See Gilbert, Martin, *Second World War* (London: Phoenix Books, 1997) and Roberts, Andrew, *The Storm of War* (London: Allen Lane, 2009).
3. See Michel, Henri, *The Second World War* (London: Andre Deutsch,1975) p.149, and Weinberg, L. Gerhard, *A World at Arms* (Cambridge, CUP, 1994) p.660.
4. Beevor, Antony, *The Second World War* (London: Weidenfeld & Nicolson, 2012), p.98.
5. Hastings, Max, *Armageddon* (London: Macmillan, 2004) p.113.
6. Burleigh, Michael, *Moral Combat* (London: Harper Press, 2010).
7. LHC, KCL, Ismay: 2/3/293.
8. See Colville, John, *The Churchillians* (London: Weidenfeld & Nicolson, 1981) p.192.
9. Knight, Nigel, *Churchill, The Greatest Briton Unmasked* (Cincinnati: D & C, 2009) p.217.
10. See Ziegler, Philip, *Mountbatten, The Official Biography* (London: Collins, 1985) p.195.
11. See Roberts, Andrew, *Masters and Commanders* (London: Penguin Books, 2009) p.77.
12. See Ibid., p.530.

Part I: India to the War Office

Chapter 1
1. Ismay, General the Lord, *The Memoirs of Lord Ismay* (London: Heinemann, 1960) p.4.
2. LHC, KCL, Ismay: 1/1/2–5.
3. Ibid., Ismay: 1/14/30.
4. Ibid., Ismay: 1/17.
5. Ismay, *Memoirs*, p.5.
6. Ibid., p.13.

Chapter 2
1. LHC, KCL, Ismay: 1/18.
2. Ibid., Ismay: 1/1/10–11.

3. Ibid., Ismay: 1/1/14, and 1/1/15, and 1/1/16.
4. Ibid., Ismay: 3/1/15.
5. Ibid., Ismay: 3/1/20.
6. Ismay, *Memoirs*, p.28.
7. LHC, KCL, Ismay: 3/1/19a.
8. Ibid., Ismay: 3/1/23.
9. Ibid., Ismay: 3/1/27, and 3/1/32.
10. Ismay, *Memoirs*, p.30.
11. LHC, KCL, Ismay: 3/1/78.
12. Jardine, Douglas, *The Mad Mullah of Somaliland* (London: Herbert Jenkins, 1922).
13. LHC, KCL, Ismay: 3/1/85.
14. Ibid., Ismay: 3/1/87.
15. Boyle, Andrew, *Trenchard* (London: Collins, 1962).
16. LHC, KCL, Ismay: 3/1/85.
17. In Wingate, Sir Ronald, *Lord Ismay* (London: Hutchinson, 1970) p.10.
18. LHC, KCL, Ismay: 3/1/83.
19. Ibid., Ismay: 1/2/19.
20. Ibid., Ismay: 1/2/13a.
21. Ibid., Ismay: 1/2/1, 1/2/3, 1/2/8, 1/2/9, and 1/2/10.
22. Ibid., Ismay: 1/7/35.

Chapter 3
1. Ismay, *Memoirs*, p.38.
2. LHC, KCL, Ismay: 3/2/00001, and 3/2/1.
3. Ibid., Ismay: 3/2/00001.
4. Ibid., Ismay: 3/2/14, 3/2/18, and 3/2/26.
5. Ibid., Ismay: 3/2/40.
6. Ibid., Ismay: 3/2/110.
7. Quoted in Wingate, *Lord Ismay*, pp.16–17.
8. Ismay, *Memoirs*, p.41.

Chapter 4
1. Ibid., p.43.
2. See LHC, KCL, Ismay: 3/3/1–5, 6–8 *et al.*
3. Ismay, *Memoirs*, p.58,
4. Ibid., p.63.
5. LHC, KCL, Ismay: 4/16/3, and 4/16/5.
6. Ibid., Ismay: 4/16/6.

Chapter 5
1. Ismay, *Memoirs*, p.64.
2. LHC, KCL, Ismay: 1/1/18.
3. Sangster, Andrew, *Secret Service, 1918–1939: Their Development in Britain, Germany, and Russia* (Newcastle, Cambridge Scholars, 2020) p.111.
4. Wingate, *Lord Ismay*, p.30.
5. LHC, KCL, Ismay: 1/1/29.
6. Ismay, *Memoirs*, p.70.
7. LHC, KCL, Ismay: 3/4/3, and 3/4/8.

Chapter 6
1. Ismay, *Memoirs*, p.76.
2. Jeffery, Keith, *MI6 The History of the Secret Intelligence Service, 1909–1949* (London: Bloomsbury, 2010) p.304.
3. Ibid., p.322.
4. Ismay, *Memoirs*, pp74–5.
5. Ibid., p.80.
6. Douhet, Giulio, *The Command of the Air* (New York: Arno Press, 1972).
7. See Wingate, *Lord Ismay*, p.32.
8. Ismay, *Memoirs*, p.51.
9. Ibid., p.95.
10. Ibid., p.98.
11. Wingate, *Lord Ismay*, p.39.

Part II: Second World War

Chapter 1
1. Colville, John, *The Fringes of Power* (London: Hodder and Stoughton, 1985) p.80.
2. Ibid., p.80.
3. Ismay, *Memoirs*, p.104.
4. Colville, *The Churchillians*, p.127.
5. Ismay, *Memoirs*, p.111.
6. Ibid., p.112.
7. Fraser, David, *Alanbrooke* (London: Collins,1982) p.208.
8. Jenkins, Roy, *Churchill* (London: Pan Books, 2001) p.576.
9. Quoted in Churchill, Winston S., *The Second World War*, Volume 1 (London: Cassell & Co, 1948) p.506.
10. Ibid., p.507.
11. Churchill Papers, 4/143, 30 May 1946.
12. See Gilbert, Martin, *Finest Hour, Winston S., Churchill, 1939–41* (London; Heinemann, 1983) p.323.
13. Roberts, *Masters*, p.110.
14. Brendon, Piers, *Winston Churchill, A Brief Life* (London: Pimlico, 2001) p.148.
15. Hansard, Vol 38, No 67 (Columns 1–204).
16. Wingate, *Lord Ismay*, p.45.
17. Churchill, *The Second*, Volume I, p.499.
18. Churchill, Winston S, *The Second World War*, Volume II (London: Cassell & Co, 1949) p.17.
19. Burleigh, *Moral*, p.335.
20. Sangster, Andrew, *The Diarists of 1940: An Annus Mirabilis* (Newcastle: Cambridge Scholars, 2020) p.118.
21. Colville, *The Fringes*, p.98.

Chapter 2
1. Ibid., p.131.
2. Churchill, *The Second*, Volume II, p.45.
3. See Colville, *The Fringes*, p.133.
4. Kennedy, General Sir John (Ed by Fergusson Bernard) *The Business of War* (London: Hutchinson,1957) p.43.

5. See Colville, *The Fringes*, pp138–9.
6. Ismay, *Memoirs*, p.142.
7. See Colville, *The Fringes*, p.175.
8. See Burleigh, *Moral*, p.162.
9. Ismay, *Memoirs*, p.138
10. Ibid., p.141.
11. Ibid., p.143.
12. Jeffery, *MI6*, p.349.
13. Ismay, *Memoirs*, p.153.
14. Ibid., p.159.
15. LHC, KCL, Ismay: 4/19/2.
16. Smith, Adrian, *Montgomery: Apprentice War Lord* (London: I. B. Tauris, 2010) pp.173–4.
17. LHC, KCL, Ismay: 4/19/5.
18. Ibid., Ismay: 4/19/14.
19. Ibid., Ismay: 4/19/15.
20. Hansard, *Parliamentary debates, House of Commons, 25 Nov 1941* (HMSO, London, 1941).
21. LHC, KCL, Ismay: 4/19/22.
22. Ismay, *Memoirs*, p.168.
23. Colville, *The Fringes*, p.213.
24. Gilbert, *Second*, p.118.
25. See Ismay, *Memoirs*, p.167.
26. Gilbert, *Second*, p.173.
27. Burleigh, *Moral*, p.165.
28. Colville, *The Fringes*, p.287.
29. Ismay, *Memoirs*, p.209.
30. LHC, KCL, Ismay 3/4/9/9.
31. Wingate, *Lord Ismay*, p.60.
32. See Ismay, *Memoirs*, p.167.
33. Ismay, *Memoirs*, p.208.
34. See Wingate, *Lord Ismay*, p.54.
35. LHC, KCL, Ismay: 4/9/23.
36. Ismay, *Memoirs*, pp.213–4.
37. See Wingate, *Lord Ismay*, p.68.
38. Churchill, *The Second*, Volume III, p,380.
39. Ismay, *Memoirs*, p.224.
40. Quoted in Wingate, *Lord Ismay*, p.68.
41. Ismay, *Memoirs*, p.228.
42. See Ismay, *Memoirs*, p.230.
43. Kennedy, *The Business*, p.231.
44. LHC, KCL, Ismay 3/4/11a.
45. Alanbrooke, *Diaries*, p.124.

Chapter 3
1. Ziegler, *Mountbatten*, p.182.
2. Cray, Ed, *General of the Army, George C Marshall, Soldier and Statesman* (New York, Cooper Square Press, 2000) pp.309 & 311.

3. LHC, KCL, Ismay: 4/22/3, 4/22/5 and 4/22/13.
4. Quoted in Wingate, *Lord Ismay*, p.80.
5. Cray, *General,* p.324.
6. Ibid., p.545.
7. See Churchill, Winston S., *The Second World War*, Volume IV (London: Cassell & Co, 1951) p.343.
8. Ismay, *Memoirs*, p.255.
9. Ibid., p.257.
10. Churchill, *The Second*, Volume IV, p.347.
11. Ismay, *Memoirs*, p.291.
12. Ibid., p.260.
13. Bradley Omar, *A General's Life* (London: Sidgwick & Jackson, 1983) p.159.
14. Ismay, *Memoirs*, p.264.
15. Ibid., p.289.
16. See Wingate, *Lord Ismay*, p.82.
17. Quoted in Ibid., p.61.
18. Quoted in Gilbert, *Finest,* p.1151.
19. Ismay, *Memoirs*, p.270.
20. LHC, KCL, Ismay: 4/9/34.
21. Ismay, *Memoirs*, p.277.
22. Ibid., p.282.
23. See Churchill, *The Second*, Volume IV, pp.419–20.
24. Colville, *The Churchillians*, p.140.
25. Ismay, *Memoirs*, p.241.

Chapter 4

1. Lascelles, Alan, *King's Counsellor* (London: Weidenfeld & Nicolson, 2006) p.147.
2. See Churchill, *The Second*, Volume IV, p.615.
3. Ismay, *Memoirs*, p.300.
4. LHC, KCL, Ismay: 4/30/2.
5. See Wingate, *Lord Ismay*, p.94
6. Ziegler, *Mountbatten,* p.217.
7. Ibid., p.223.
8. See Wingate, *Lord Ismay*, p.95.
9. Ismay, *Memoirs*, p.313.
10. Ziegler, *Mountbatten,* p.176.
11. LHC, KCL, Ismay: 4/20/2.
12. Churchill, *The Second*, Volume III, pp.414–15.
13. Ibid., pp.465–6.
14. Ismay, *Memoirs*, p.328.
15. Ibid., p.329.
16. Lascelles, *King's,* p.178.
17. LHC, KCL, Ismay: 11/3/4.
18. See Churchill, Winston S., *The Second World War*, Volume V (London: Cassell & Co, 1952) p.288.
19. Ismay, *Memoirs*, p.336.
20. See Sudoplatov Pavel et al., *Special Tasks, The Memoirs of an Unwanted Witness* (London: Little, Brown and Company, 1994) p.130.

21. Gellately, Robert, *Stalin's Curse, Battling for Communism in War and Cold War* (Oxford: OUP, 2013) p.80.

Chapter 5
1. LHC, KCL, Ismay: IV/2/4 and quoted in Weinberg, *A World*, p.660.
2. Ismay, *Memoirs*, p.347.
3. Ibid., p.350.
4. Jenkins, *Churchill*, p.744.
5. Churchill, *The Second*, Volume V, pp.552–3.
6. Ziegler, *Mountbatten*, p.215.
7. Ismay, *Memoirs*, p.362.
8. Colville, *The Fringes*, p.509.
9. Quoted in Wingate, *Lord Ismay*, p.112.
10. Kennedy, *The Business*, p.336.
11. See Fraser, *Alanbrooke*, p.416.
12. Alanbrooke, *Diaries*, p.592.
13. Quoted in Wingate, *Lord Ismay*, p.113.
14. Alanbrooke, *Diaries*, p.593.
15. Quoted in Wingate, *Lord Ismay*, p114.
16. See Wingate, *Lord Ismay*, p.117.
17. Ismay, *Memoirs*, p.382.

Chapter 6
1. See Lascelles, *King's*, p.315.
2. LHC, KCL, Ismay: 4/29/FO.
3. Ibid., Ismay: 4/29/36.
4. Lascelles *King's*, p.297.
5. LHC, KCL, Ismay: 4/24/23a.
6. Ismay, *Memoirs*, p.387.
7. Ibid., p.392.
8. See Ismay, *Memoirs*, p.399.
9. Ibid., p.401.
10. Cray, *General*, p.545.
11. Lascelles, *King's*, p.339.
12. LHC, KCL, Ismay 4/3/6.
13. Lascelles, *King's*, p.366.
14. Ismay, *Memoirs*, p.406.
15. See Lascelles, *King's*, p.381.
16. LHC, KCL, Ismay: 4/2/7.
17. Ibid., Ismay: 3/4/9.

Part III: India, Nato, and Other Posts

Chapter 1
1. Ibid., Ismay: 1/5/3a.
2. Ibid.
3. Ibid., Ismay: 1/5/4.
4. See Ismay, *Memoirs*, p.409.

5. Montgomery, Bernard Law, *The Memoirs*, (New York: The World Publishing Company,1958) p.437.
6. LHC, KCL, Ismay: 4/1/3.
7. Ibid., Ismay: 4/1/4.
8. Ibid., Ismay: 1/5/10.
9. See Ibid., Ismay: 1/1/42.
10. Ibid, Ismay: 3/16/4.
11. Ismay, *Memoirs*, p.414.
12. Wingate, *Lord Ismay*, p.130.
13. See Lownie Andrew, *The Mountbattens* (London: Blink Publishing, 2019) p.198.
14. Quoted in Wingate, *Lord Ismay*, pp.137–8.
15. Ismay, *Memoirs*, pp.409–10.
16. LHC, KCL, Ismay: 4/9/17.
17. Ibid., Ismay: 4/9/18.
18. Ibid., Ismay: 4/6/3.
19. Ibid., Ismay: 4/6/9.
20. Ibid., Ismay: 4/9/10a.
21. Ibid., Ismay: 111.8/13A.
22. Lownie, *The Mountbattens*, p.365.
23. Ismay, *Memoirs*, p.417.
24. Ibid., p.419.
25. LHC, KCL, Ismay: 3/8/1.
26. Ibid., Ismay: 3/8/4.
27. Ismay, *Memoirs*, p.420.
28. Lownie, *The Mountbattens*, p.211.
29. LHC, KCL, Ismay: 3/8/7.
30. Ibid., Ismay: 3/8/5.
31. Quoted in Arnold, Matthew, *Hollow Heroes* (Oxford: Casemate, 2015) p.260.
32. Ismay, *Memoirs*, p.421.
33. Ibid., p.422.
34. Ibid, p.430.
35. LHC, KCL, Ismay: 3/8/13.
36. Wingate, *Lord Ismay*, p.163.
37. Ismay, *Memoirs*, p.425.
38. Ibid., p.428.
39. Wingate, *Lord Ismay*, p.164.
40. Ismay, *Memoirs*, p.431.
41. See LHC, KCL, Ismay: 3/8/28.
42. Ismay, *Memoirs*, p.434.
43. LHC, KCL, Ismay: 3/8/18.
44. Ibid., Ismay: 3/8/20.
45. Ismay, *Memoirs*, p.435.
46. Picknett, L. et al., *War of the Windsors* (London: Mainstream Publishing, 2002) p.212.
47. LHC, KCL, Ismay: 3/8/22.
48. See Ibid., Ismay: 3/8/20.
49. Quoted in Arnold Matthew, *Hollow Heroes* (Oxford: Casemate, 2015) pp.275–6.
50. Picknett, *War of the Windsors*, p.212

51. LHC, KCL, Ismay: 111/8/20.
52. Arnold, *Hollow*, p.261.
53. LHC, KCL, Ismay: 3/7/47.

Chapter 2
1. Wingate, *Lord Ismay*, p.178.
2. LHC, KCL, Ismay: 1/8/3.
3. *Daily Telegraph*, 16 August 1951.
4. *Hansard*, Lords, Vol 170, No 34, Cols. 521–523.
5. Ismay, *Memoirs*, p.448.
6. Ibid., p.448.
7. Ibid, p.449.
8. Ibid., p.451.
9. LHC, KCL, Ismay: 4/24/23a.
10. Ibid., Ismay: 1/6/1.
11. Ibid., Ismay: 1/6/2.
12. Brendon, *Winston*, p.210.
13. Knight, Nigel, *Churchill*, p.341.
14. Ismay, *Memoirs*, p.453.
15. Colville, *The Fringes*, p.633.
16. Ibid., p.633.
17. Wingate, *Lord Ismay*, p.188.
18. Ismay, *Memoirs*, p.453.
19. LHC, KCL, Ismay: 2/2/24.
20. Colville, *The Fringes*, p.637.
21. Moran, *Churchill at War*, p.351.
22. Moran, Lord, *Winston Churchill, The Struggle for Survival* (London: Constable, 1966) p.378.
23. Ismay *Memoirs*, p.454.
24. Ibid., p.456.
25. Ibid., p.458.

Chapter 3
1. Ibid., p.462.
2. Wingate, *Lord Ismay*, p.190.
3. Ismay, *Memoirs*, p.460.
4. LHC, KCL, Ismay: 3/11/1–2 and 3/11/5.
5. Ibid., Ismay: 3/11/22.
6. Colville, *The Fringes*, p.752.
7. Ibid., p.645.
8. Lascelles, *King's*, p.406.
9. Foreign Relations of the United States, 1952–1954, Western European Security, Volume V, Part 1, 740.5/3–1052.
10. Ibid.,
11. LHC, KCL, Ismay 4/15/1.
12. Ibid., Ismay: 4/12/90.
13. Ibid., Ismay: 3/13/17.
14. Ibid., Ismay: 3/13/20.

15. Ibid., Ismay: 3/14/23.
16. Ibid., Ismay: 3/13/34.
17. Ibid., Ismay: 3/13/16a
18. Quoted in Wingate, *Lord Ismay*, p.197.
19. LHC, KCL, Ismay: 3/14/18.
20. Ibid., Ismay: 3/14/19 and 3/14/22.
21. Ibid., Ismay: 3/16/1.
22. Ibid., Ismay: 3/16/13.
23. Ibid., Ismay: 3/16/17.
24. Ibid., Ismay: 3/20/14.
25. Ibid, Ismay: 3/17/14.
26. Foreign Relations of the United States, 1952–1954, Western European Security, Volume V, Part 1, 740.5/3–1253.
27. Ibid.
28. Ibid., Part 2, 396.1/12–753.
29. Moran, *Churchill at War*, p.510.
30. LHC, KCL, Ismay: 3/12/27.
31. Ibid., Ismay: 3/15/16.
32. Moran, *Churchill at War*, p.617.
33. LHC, KCL, Ismay: 4/24/47.
34. See Wingate, *Lord Ismay*, p.203.
35. LHC, KCL, Ismay: 3/12/5.
36. Ibid., Ismay: 3/12/9.
37. Ibid., Ismay: 4/15/43.
38. Ibid., Ismay: 4/15/3.
39. Ibid., Ismay: 4/15/4.
40. Ibid., Ismay: 4/15/72 and 4/15/85.
41. Ibid., Ismay: 4/15/58 and 2/15/78a.
42. Ibid., Ismay: 4/15/go
43. Wingate, *Lord Ismay*, p.205.
44. Ibid., p.206.
45. LHC, KCL, Ismay: 3/12/30.
46. Ibid., Ismay: 3/4/15.
47. Ismay, *Memoirs,* p.464.

Chapter 4
1. LHC, KCL, Ismay: 1/10/1 and 1/10/3.
2. Wingate, *Lord Ismay*, p.214.
3. LHC, KCL, Ismay: 4/1/10.
4. See Ibid., Ismay: 4/1/26, and 4/1/27.
5. Ibid., Ismay: 4/16/13.
6. Ibid., Ismay: 4/16/15.
7. For example, see Ibid., Ismay: 4/5/52.
8. LHC, KCL, Ismay: 1/14/125.
9. Ibid., Ismay: 1/14/104, and 1/14/115.
10. Ibid., Ismay: 4/9/39.
11. Ibid., Ismay: 4/24/126.
12. Ibid., Ismay: 1/14/130.

13. Ibid., Ismay: 1/24/50.
14. Ibid., Ismay: 4/24/51.
15. Ibid., Ismay: 4/24/52.
16. Ibid., Ismay: 4/24/71.
17. See, for example, Ibid., Ismay: 4/24/93, and 4/24/101.
18. LHC, KCL, Ismay: 3/10/1.
19. Ibid., Ismay: 3/10/6.
20. Ibid., Ismay: 3/10/26.
21. Ibid., Ismay: 1/7/29, 1/7/40 and 2/1/49.
22. Wingate, *Lord Ismay*, p.215.
23. LHC, KCL, Ismay: 3/4/76.
24. Ibid., Ismay: 3/4/95.

Chapter 5
1. Churchill, *The Second*, Volume II, pp. 610, 149, 207, 217, 237, 287, and 321.
2. Churchill, *The Second*, Volume V, p.566.
3. Ibid., p.580, and p.583.
4. Jenkins, *Churchill*, p.716.
5. Roberts, *Masters*, p.111.
6. Brendon, *Winston*, p.150.
7. Churchill, *The Second*, Volume V, p.201.
8. Churchill, *The Second*, Volume III, pp.272–273.
9. Ibid., p.308.
10. Churchill, *The Second*, Volume IV, p.283.
11. LHC, KCL, Ismay: 2/2/9.
12. Ibid., Ismay: 2/2/25.
13. Ibid., Ismay: 2/2/26.
14. Ibid., Ismay: 2/3/195.
15. Ibid.
16. Wingate, *Lord Ismay*, p.178.
17. See LHC, KCL, Ismay: 2/3/3 and 2/2/21.
18. Ibid., Ismay: 2/3/33.
19. Ibid., Ismay: 2/3/162 and 2/3/288.
20. LHC, KCL, Ismay: 4/8/1.
21. See Ibid., Ismay: 2/3/250.
22. See following files: Ibid., Ismay: 2/3/243a, 2/3/244a, and 2/3/245
23. Ibid., Ismay: 2/3/254a.
24. Ibid., Ismay: 2/3/256, and 2/3/260.
25. See Smith, *Montgomery*, pp.254–5.
26. See LHC, KCL, Ismay: 2/3/238 and 2/3/199.
27. Ibid., Ismay: 2/3/267.
28. Ibid., Ismay: 2/3/105.
29. Ibid., Ismay: 2/3/150.
30. Moran, *Churchill at War*, p.741.

Chapter 6
1. Bryant, Arthur, *Turn of the Tide* (London: Collins, 1957).

2. Quoted in Alanbrooke, Field Marshal Lord, *War Diaries 1939–45* (London: Weidenfeld & Nicolson, 2001) p.xxii.
3. Alanbrooke, *Diaries*, p.xliv.
4. Colville, *The Fringes*, p.752.
5. Alanbrooke, *Diaries*, p.432.
6. Ibid., p.492.
7. Fraser, *Alanbrooke*, p.196.
8. Kennedy, *The Business*, p.100.
9. Alanbrooke, *Diaries*, p.206.
10. Ibid., p.210.
11. Ibid., p.268.
12. Ibid., p.330.
13. Ibid., p.350.
14. Ibid., p.366.
15. Ibid., p.518.
16. *The Times*, 18 June 1963 *Obituary*.
17. Sangster, Andrew, *Alan Brooke: Churchill's Right-Hand Critic* (Oxford: Casemate, 2021) p.xxi.
18. Ibid., p.xxii.
19. Fraser, *Alanbrooke*, p.211.
20. Ibid., p.295.
21. LHC, KCL, Ismay: 4/1/3.
22. Kennedy, *The Business*, p.239
23. Ibid., p.239.
24. Roberts, *Masters*, p.148.
25. LHC, KCL, Ismay: 4/32/4.
26. Clark, General Mark W., *Calculated Risk* (New York: Enigma Books, 2007) p.40.
27. Ibid., p.44.
28. Ibid., p.58.
29. See Clark, General Mark, *Papers*, The Citadel Archives and Museum, Charleston.
30. LHC, KCL, Ismay: 4/7/1, 4/7/3, and 4/7/7.
31. Ibid., Ismay: 4/7/7.
32. Eisenhower, Dwight D., *Crusade in Europe* (London: William Heinemann, 1948) p.487.
33. Wingate, *Lord Ismay*, p. 121.
34. Ambrose, Stephen E., *Eisenhower, Soldier and President* (London: Pocket Books, 2003) p.66.
35. LHC, KCL, Ismay: 4/12/12.
36. Ibid., Ismay: 4/12/14.
37. Ibid., Ismay: 4/12/22.
38. *The Sunday Times*, 21 November 1948
39. LHC, KCL, Ismay: 4/12/29.
40. Ibid., Ismay: 4/12/32.
41. *Daily Telegraph*, 26 November 1948.
42. LHC, KCL, Ismay: 4/12/33.
43. Ibid., Ismay: 4/12/39
44. Ibid., Ismay: 4/12/34.
45. Ibid., Ismay: 4/12/49.

46. Ibid., Ismay: 4/12/84.
47. Ibid., Ismay: 4/12/99, and for his letter see 4/12/95.
48. Ibid., Ismay: 4/12/23.
49. See Ibid., Ismay: 4/12/27, 4/12/67, 4/12/72 4/12/79, 4/12/104.
50. Ibid., Ismay: 4/12/81.
51. Ibid., Ismay: 4/12/106.
52. Ibid., Ismay: 4/12/122.
53. Ibid., Ismay: 4/12/140.
54. Ibid., Ismay: 4/12/124.
55. Ibid., Ismay: 4/12/129.
56. Macmillan, Harold, *War Diaries* (London: Macmillan, 1984) p.8.
57. Macmillan, *War Diaries*, p.304.
58. See Ibid., p.385 & P.472.
59. Colville, *The Churchillians*, pp.35–6.
60. Eden, Anthony, *The Eden Memoirs* (London: Cassell, 1962)
61. Colville, *The Churchillians*, p.124.
62. Moran, Lord, *Churchill at War 1940–45* (London: Robinson, 2002) p.137.
63. Ibid., p.137.
64. Ibid., p.137.
65. Ibid., p.137.
66. Ibid., p.193.
67. Ibid., p.287.
68. Ibid., p.114.
69. Colville, *The Fringes*, p.752.
70. Ibid., p.242.
71. Ibid., p.273.
72. Ibid., p.283.
73. Ibid., p.237.
74. Ibid., p.325.
75. Ibid., p.515.
76. Lascelles, *King's, p*.166.
77. Ibid., p.193.
78. See Churchill, *The Second*, Volume III, p.416.
79. Lascelles, *King's*, p.226.
80. Ibid., p.227.
81. Churchill, *The Second*, Volume V, p.549.
82. Lascelles, *King's*, p.241.
83. Ibid., p.250.

Chapter 7
1. Wingate, *Lord Ismay*, p.277.
2. Kennedy, *The Business*, p.43.
3. Ismay, *Memoirs*, p.209.
4. Ibid., p.208.
5. LHC, KCL, Ismay: 4/12/84.
6. Ibid., Ismay: 4/1/19/1.
7. Wingate, *Lord Ismay*, p.225.

Bibliography

Primary Sources
Churchill Papers, 4/143, 30 May 1946.
Clark, General Mark *Papers*, The Citadel Archives and Museum, Charleston.
Foreign Relations of the United States, 1952–1954, Western European Security, Volume V, Parts 1 and Part 2.
Hansard, *Parliamentary Debates, House of Commons*, (London; HMSO)
Liddell Hart Centre, King's College London, hereafter LHC, KCL, Ismay
Newspapers: *Daily Telegraph*, 16 August 1951. *The Times*, 18 June 1963, Obituary *The Sunday Times* 21 November 1948, Article on Eisenhower's book. *Daily Telegraph, 26 November 1948,* Article on Pug's support of Eisenhower. *Gloucester Echo, Western Daily Press, Birmingham Post.*

Diaries and Memoirs
Alanbrooke Field Marshal Lord, *War Diaries 1939–45* (London: Weidenfeld & Nicolson, 2001)
Bradley, Omar, *A General's Life* (London: Sidgwick & Jackson, 1983)
Clark, General Mark W., *Calculated Risk* (New York: Enigma Books, 2007)
Colville, John, *The Fringes of Power* (London: Hodder and Stoughton, 1985)
Eden, Anthony, *The Eden Memoirs* (London: Cassell, 1962)
Ismay, General the Lord, *The Memoirs of Lord Ismay* (London: Heinemann, 1960)
Kennedy, General Sir John (Ed by Fergusson Bernard) *The Business of War* (London: Hutchinson,1957)
Lascelles, Alan, *King's Counsellor* (London: Weidenfeld & Nicolson, 2006)
Macmillan, Harold, *War Diaries* (London: Macmillan, 1984)
Montgomery, Bernard Law, *The Memoirs*, (New York: The World Publishing Company,1958)
Moran, Lord, *Churchill at War 1940–45* (London: Robinson, 2002)
Sudoplatov, Pavel et al., *Special Tasks, The Memoirs of an Unwanted Witness* (London: Little, Brown and Company, 1994)

Other Publications
Allan, James, *No Citation* (London: Panther Books, 1956)
Ambrose, Stephen E., *Eisenhower, Soldier and President* (London: Pocket Books, 2003)
Arnold, Matthew, *Hollow Heroes* (Oxford: Casemate, 2015)
Beevor, Antony, *The Second World War* (London: Weidenfeld & Nicolson, 2012)
Boyle, Andrew, *Trenchard* (London: Collins, 1962)
Brendon, Piers, *Winston Churchill, A Brief Life* (London: Pimlico, 2001)
Bryant, Arthur, *Turn of the Tide* (London: Collins, 1957)
Burleigh, Michael, *Moral Combat* (London: Harper Press, 2010)

Churchill, Winston S, *The Second World War*, Volume 1 (London: Cassell & Co, 1948)
Churchill, Winston S, *The Second World War*, Volume II (London: Cassell & Co, 1949)
Churchill, Winston S, *The Second World War*, Volume III (London: Cassell & Co, 1950)
Churchill, Winston S, *The Second World War*, Volume IV (London: Cassell & Co, 1951)
Churchill, Winston S, *The Second World War*, Volume V (London: Cassell & Co, 1952)
Colville, John, *The Churchillians* (London: Weidenfeld & Nicolson, 1981)
Connell, John, *Auchinleck: a critical biography* (London: Cassell, 1959)
Corrigan, Gordon, *The Second World War* (London: Atlantic Books, 2012)
Cray, Ed, *General of the Army, George C Marshall, Soldier and Statesman* (New York, Cooper Square Press, 2000)
Davies, Norman, *No Simple Victory* (New York: Viking, 2006)
Douhet, Giulio, *The Command of the Air* (New York: Arno Press, 1972)
Eisenhower, Dwight D., *Crusade in Europe* (London: William Heinemann, 1948)
Fraser, David, *Alanbrooke* (London: Collins,1982)
Gellately, Robert, *Stalin's Curse, Battling for Communism in War and Cold War* (Oxford: OUP, 2013)
Gilbert, Martin, *Finest Hour, Winston S, Churchill, 1939–41* (London; Heinemann, 1983)
Gilbert, Martin, *Second World War* (London: Phoenix Books, 1997)
Hastings, Max, *Armageddon* (London: Macmillan, 2004)
Hastings, Max, *All Hell Let Loose* (London: Harper Press, 2011)
Jardine, Douglas, *The Mad Mullah of Somaliland* (London: Herbert Jenkins, 1922)
Jeffery, Keith, *MI6 The History of the Secret Intelligence Service, 1909–1949* (London: Bloomsbury, 2010)
Jenkins, Roy, *Churchill* (London: Pan Books, 2001)
Knight, Nigel, *Churchill, The Greatest Briton Unmasked* (Cincinnati; D & C, 2009)
Liddell Hart, B. H., *History of the Second World War* (London: Book Club Associates, 1973)
Lownie, Andrew, *The Mountbattens* (London: Blink Publishing, 2019)
Michel Henri, *The Second World War* (London: Andre Deutsch,1975)
Moorhead, Alan McCrae, *Montgomery, A Biography* (Hamish Hamilton, London, 1946)
Moran, Lord, *Winston Churchill, The Struggle for Survival* (London: Constable, 1966)
Picknett L., et al., *War of the Windsors* (London: Mainstream Publishing, 2002)
Roberts, Andrew, *The Storm of War* (London: Allen Lane, 2009)
Roberts, Andrew, *Masters and Commanders* (London: Penguin Books, 2009)
Sangster, Andrew, *Secret Service, 1918–1939: Their Development in Britain, Germany, and Russia* (Newcastle, Cambridge Scholars, 2020)
Sangster, Andrew, *The Diarists of 1940: An Annus Mirabilis* (Newcastle: Cambridge Scholars, 2020)
Sangster, Andrew, *Alan Brooke: Churchill's Right-Hand Critic* (Oxford: Casemate, 2021)
Shirer, William L., *The Rise and Fall of the Third Reich* (London: Mandarin, 1997)
Smith, Adrian, *Montgomery Apprentice War Lord* (London: I. B. Tauris, 2010)
Weinberg, L. Gerhard, *A World at Arms* (Cambridge, CUP, 1994)
Wingate, Sir Ronald, *Lord Ismay* (London: Hutchinson, 1970)
Ziegler, Philip, *Mountbatten, The Official Biography* (London: Collins, 1985)

Abbreviations

ADC	Aide-de-camp
BEF	British Expeditionary Force
CID	Committee of Imperial Defence
CIGS	Chief of Imperial General Staff
COSSAC	Chief of Staff to Supreme Allied Command
COS	Chiefs of Staff
CCOS	Combined Chiefs of Staff (Anglo-American)
EDC	European Defence Community
NATO	North Atlantic Treaty Organization
NWFP	North-West Frontier Province
RFC	Royal Flying Corps
SEAC	South-East Asia Command
SIS	Secret Intelligence Service (sometimes referred to as MI6)
SHAPE	Supreme Headquarters Allied Powers Europe

Index

Abell, George 124–5
Adenauer, Chancellor Konrad 151
Alexander, Field Marshal 19, 62, 66–7, 69, 75, 78, 83, 91, 95, 97, 100, 110, 139–40, 151, 160, 177
Anglo-American tensions xiii, xvii, 29, 88, 101, 178, 181, 188–9
Arnold, General 61, 73, 108
Attlee, Clement viii, xiv, 29, 38, 110–11, 117–21, 125–6, 128, 135, 137–8, 147, 161, 163, 183, 196
Auchinleck, Field Marshal 14, 63, 67–70, 80, 119–20, 122, 127–8, 132, 192

Baldwin, Stanley 24–5
Barratt, Air Marshal 32–3
Battle of Britain 29, 47–8, 167
Beaverbrook, Max 41, 48, 57–9, 159, 164, 188
Bedell Smith, General Walter 94, 103
Beria, Lavrenty vii, 87–8
Beria, Sergo 87
Bermuda Conference 150–1
Bevin, Ernest 94, 109
Bór-Komorowski, General 96
Bradley, General Omar 66
Bridges, Edward, Cabinet Secretary ix, 27, 34, 36, 107, 143
Brooke, General 32, 36–7, 41–2, 48–9, 52, 54, 60–2, 64, 66, 68, 77, 80, 82, 93, 98, 100–101, 108, 114, 171–4

Cairo and Teheran Conferences 85–9
Camel Corps ix, xiii–xiv, 1, 8–10, 50, 192
Casablanca Conference 72–5
Casey, Richard Gardiner 119
Chamberlain, Neville ix, 27–9, 32–4, 36, 38, 51, 194
Charterhouse School 3–4, 113, 161, 191
Chatfield, Lord 24, 33
Chiang Kai-Shek 75, 81, 85–6
Chiang Kai-Shek, Madame 86
Churchill
  And Communism 96–7, 105, 107, 141

Clashes with the Military xvi, 37, 41, 51–4, 67–8, 73, 81, 97, 108, 163, 172–3, 183
In Moscow 100–101
Personality 17, 35, 40, 44, 47–9, 52, 58, 61, 68, 76, 85, 87, 91, 93, 95, 98, 119, 138, 140, 142–3, 147, 156, 163–5, 167, 188
CID, Explanation thereof 16
Clark, General Mark xi, 62, 64, 78, 95, 176–7, 198
Clegg, Darry's parents' name 12, 15, 19, 20–1
Coleridge, Richard 145, 154
Colville, John (Jock) xi, xiv, 27, 32, 37, 39–40, 45, 51, 71, 139–40, 143, 152, 171, 181, 183–6, 193
  On Pug 185–6
Cripps, Stafford 117–18
Cunningham, Admiral Andrew 82, 180
Curzon, Lord, Viceroy 115

Daladier, Édouard, French PM 31, 39
Damaskinos, Greek Archbishop 97
Danzig Corridor 23, 27
Darlan, Admiral 40, 56
Darry (Laura Kathleen) x, xv, 12–15, 18–19, 21, 27, 57, 114, 118–22, 124–7, 129–31, 133, 137, 144, 153–7, 176, 193, 196–8
Delhi-Lahore Conspiracy 115
Dervishes vii, viii, 7–9
Dick, Admiral 145
Dieppe Raid xvi, 167–8
Dill, General John xvii, 32, 39, 41–2, 51, 59–62, 73, 99, 159, 175
Douhet, Giulio 25–6
Dowding Hugh 41–2, 47

EDC, European Defence Community 145, 150–2
Eden, Anthony 47, 50–1, 82–5, 97–100, 142–3, 154–5, 177, 181, 186–8, 196
Edinburgh, Duke of 145, 155

Eisenhower, Dwight 61, 64–6, 70, 74–5,
  77–8, 80–1, 91–5, 102–103, 107, 141,
  145, 149, 151, 155, 176–8, 189, 197
  On Pug 177–81
El Alamein, Battle of 48, 70, 110
Esher, Lord 18

Festival of Britain 138
First Quebec Conference 78, 80, 82
Franco, Spanish Dictator vii, 106
Freyberg, General 53

Game, Air Vice-Marshal Philip 15
Gamelin, General Maurice 26, 31, 39–40,
  136
Gandhi 13, 20, 116–17, 125, 128, 132, 134
Gaulle, General de 41–3, 66, 94, 101, 145,
  169
General Elections 1950–51 138
General Strike, 1926 17
Ghadar Mutiny 116
Gibson, Wing Commander Guy 79
Gort, Field Marshal 4, 32, 85
Gott, General 70
Graziani, Marshal 50
Greenwood, Arthur 38
Gruenther, General Alfred 142, 151–3
  On Pug 144

Halifax, Lord xvii, 38, 110
Halifax, Viceroy 117
Halsey, Admiral 108
Hankey, Sir Maurice 1, 15–22, 26–7, 158,
  192–3
Hardinge, Lord, Viceroy 115
Harriman, Averill 56, 58, 100, 165
Harris, Air Marshal Arthur 71, 92
Herbert, General 81
Hitler, Adolf 23, 25–7, 32, 37, 50–2, 57, 74,
  90, 95, 102, 106, 159, 165, 188, 194, 195
Hobart, General 91
Hollis, General Joe xvi, 56, 184
Hopkins, Harry 55–7, 60, 99
Humphrey, US Senator 154

India, Background to 1947 problems 115
Indian Army structure 5
Inskip, Sir Thomas 24
Interservice Friction 32–3, 71
Ismay, Pug
  And Brooke xi, xv, 53, 82, 158, 170–1,
    173
  And Churchill x, xvi, 17, 25, 36, 44, 48,
    51, 68, 91, 98, 114, 135, 139, 142, 156,
    159, 163, 165–6, 169, 175, 186–7

And Eisenhower xi, 64, 81, 107, 179–81
And General Mark Clark xi
And George Marshall xi, 61
And Hankey 19
And Historians xi–xii
And Montgomery 70, 93, 101, 152
And Mountbatten xvi, 61, 79, 95, 118,
  121, 125, 127, 132, 140, 159, 168, 195
And Stalin 88, 91, 107
Assisting Anglo-American Alliance
  176–9, 189–90, 197
At Quartermaster General's Branch 14
CID 22, 25
CID, becomes Secretary to 27
Early days in War Office 16–18, 21
Family background and Childhood 3–4
His pastimes 5, 13, 19–20, 146, 148,
  157, 161
His personality 40, 45, 48, 58–9, 61, 63,
  65, 67, 69, 84, 92–3, 109, 120, 175,
  182, 185, 191
His personal views 24–8, 31–2, 39–40,
  42, 53, 70, 74, 79, 86, 88, 90, 97, 100,
  102, 106, 108, 110, 122, 124, 128,
  133, 135, 186
His Strengths and Weaknesses 190–7
His wife and daughters 13, 18, 21, 120,
  129, 141
His youth 4–5
India Independence 1947 x
India with Mountbatten 121–32, 134
In India with Viceroy 19–20
In Somaliland 7–11
Nature of his work ix, xiii, xv, 35, 37, 41,
  46–7, 51, 57, 63, 67–8, 70, 74, 80–1,
  83, 85, 90, 98, 103, 106, 123, 127,
  146, 164, 172, 182, 187
North-West Frontier 4–6, 13
Regarding nickname vii, 170–1, 176, 184
Secretary Commonwealth Relations
  139–41
Secretary General to NATO 142,
  144–6, 148–52, 154–6
Staff College 13–14
Supports Polish Officers 160
Ismay, Stanley 3
Ismay, Thomas Henry 3

Jacob, General Ian xvi, 56, 114, 161–2
Jebb, Gladwyn 154
Jefferies, Major 45
Jenkins, Sir Evan 128
Jinnah, Muhammad Ali 117, 123, 125,
  127–32
Juin, General 101

Index

Kennedy, General John xi, 40, 59, 98, 172, 175–6, 194
Kesselring, Field Marshal 159, 190
Keyes, Admiral Sir Roger 44–5, 186, 193
King, Admiral xi, 61, 73, 99
King Edward VIII, Abdication 23
King George VI ix, xi, xiv, 18, 73, 93, 95, 107, 138–9, 141, 186
Koenig, General 101

Lahore Resolution 117
Lascelles, Alan xi, xiv, 27, 73, 82, 84, 94, 102–103, 108–109, 140, 143, 180, 186–9, 193
On Pug 187–9
Leahy, Admiral xii, 182
Leathers, Lord 72
Leeper, British Ambassador, Greece 97
Lindemann, Professor 35, 45, 169, 183
Linlithgow, Viceroy 117
Litvinov, Maxin 83
Lloyd George, David 26, 41, 183
Lyttelton, Oliver 35

MacArthur, General 81, 108, 149
Macmillan, Harold xi, 100, 111, 154, 161–2, 182–3
Mad Mullah 6, 8–9
Maharaja Hari Singh 131
Marshall-Cornwall, General 41
Marshall, General George xi, xvii, 41, 60–3, 73, 78, 80, 102–103, 108, 169
Menon, Vappala Pangunni 126
Menzies, Head of SIS 43
Miéville, Sir Eric 120
Molotov, Vyacheslav 83–4
Molotov-Ribbentrop Pact 28
Montagu Declaration 1917 116
Montgomery, Field Marshal 66–70, 81, 91–3, 101–102, 106–107, 110, 114, 151–2, 168, 178–9, 189
Moran, Lord xi, xiv, 112, 140, 151–2, 169, 183–6
On Pug 184–5
Morrison, Herbert 137–8
Morton, Desmond 35
Mountbatten, Edwina 121, 123, 133, 152
Mountbatten, Lord xvi, 61, 75, 79–81, 86, 95, 135, 140, 152, 159–60, 162, 167, 172–3, 177, 189, 191, 195–6
India 118–34
Mullaly, Lady. Pug's Aunty 3, 12
Muslim League 115, 117–18, 121, 123
Muslim Redshirt Congress 121
Mussolini, Benito 9, 23, 50–1, 106, 194

NATO vii–viii, x, xiii, xiv, 97, 111, 136, 141–7, 149–50, 152, 154–6, 161, 181, 191, 196
Nehru, Jawaharial 122–7, 130–2, 135

Octagon Conference 97–9
Operation Overlord – from Ismay's perspective 90–5

Parsons, Geoffrey 146
Patton, General George 64, 66–7, 92, 101
Pearl Harbor 50, 60, 71
Phillips, Admiral Sir Thomas 71
Portal, Air Chief Marshal 61, 82, 172–3
Potsdam Conference 108–109
Pound, Admiral 75, 81–2, 173
Putna, General 56

Queen Elizabeth II 140, 142, 147, 155–7

Radcliffe, Sir Cyril 123, 128
RAF/RFC in Somaliland 9
Ramsay, Admiral 93
Reynaud, Paul 39, 42
Ritchie, General 69
Rommel 52, 54, 68–9
Roosevelt xii, 55–7, 60, 62–3, 65–6, 72–6, 78, 82, 85, 87–9, 92, 96–7, 99–100, 102–103, 106, 109, 116–17, 139, 183, 188
Roskill, Captain Stephen 158
Rundstedt, General von 94, 101

Sandhurst ix, 1, 4, 122, 191–2
Sayyid Mohammed Abdullah Hassan
The Mad Mullah 8
Scobie, General 97
Sinclair, Archibald 41
Sinclair, Hugh (SIS) 23–4
SIS (MI6) 21, 23, 43
Slim, Field Marshal 14, 108
Soames, Christopher and Mary 140
Somerville, Admiral Sir James 79
Spaak, Henri, succeeded Pug in NATO 155
Spaatz, General 92
Stalin, Joseph xii–xiii, 29, 52, 56–60, 62, 69, 71–2, 82–4, 86–8, 94, 96, 97, 100, 102, 104–107, 109, 139, 189, 195, 197
Stilwell, General Joseph 64
Sudoplatov, Russian agent 87
Suez Canal crisis 154
Swinton, Lord 67

Tree, Ronald, MP 52, 157
Trident Conference 75–7
Truman, President 107, 109

Unconditional Surrender Policy 74, 99

Vandenberg Resolution 141
Vichy France 40, 43, 53, 56, 66–7
Voroshilov, Marshal 88

Warsaw Pact 151
Wavell, Field Marshal Archibald xii, 50, 53–5, 80, 90, 118–20, 124, 126, 159
Wedemeyer, General Albert 64, 176, 198

Weygand, General 40, 194
Wiart, Carton de 81, 158
Willingdon, Lord, Viceroy India ix, 1, 19, 117, 119–20, 192
Wilson, General 51, 100, 170, 182
Wingate, Orde 79

Yalta Conference 102, 104–106

Zhukov, Marshal 107